The 25-Year War

The 25-Year War

America's Military Role in Vietnam

GENERAL BRUCE PALMER, Jr.

THE UNIVERSITY PRESS OF KENTUCKY

Scholarly publisher for the Commonwealth,
serving Bellarmine College, Berea College, Centre
College of Kentucky, Eastern Kentucky University,
The Filson Club, Georgetown College, Kentucky
Historical Society, Kentucky State University,
Morehead State University, Murray State University,
Northern Kentucky University, Transylvania University,
University of Kentucky, University of Louisville,
and Western Kentucky University.

Editorial and Sales Offices: Lexington, Kentucky 40506-0024

Library of Congress Cataloging in Publication Data

Palmer, Bruce, 1913–
    The 25-year war.

    Bibliography: p.
    Includes index.
    1. Vietnamese Conflict, 1961–1975—United States.
I. Title. II. Title: Twenty-five-year war.
DS558.P337   1984   959.704'3   84-5091
ISBN 0-8131-1513-2

Contents

Illustrations follow page 118.

To my wife, Kay Sibert,
and our children, Robin Helen,
Maurene Elizabeth, and Bruce III,
who knew full well the life
of a military family—

And to the men and women
who served in Indochina
on the side of the Free World

Preface

Exactly twenty-five years from 1 May 1950—the day President Truman authorized the first U.S. military assistance to Indochina—Saigon and the South Vietnamese government fell to the communist regime of North Vietnam, on 30 April 1975. Thus ended the longest conflict in American history.

After every prolonged conflict in its experience, the United States has plunged into a period of assessment, trying to sift out the meaning of the memorable events of the recent past while searching for the key to a conflict-free future. This happened in the 1870s after our Civil War, in the 1920s after World War I, and for a relatively brief period in the late 1940s after World War II. But with the advent of the Cold War in 1947, followed by the Korean War in 1950—our first experience with limited war—we lived through over a quarter of a century during which the United States was continuously involved in some sort of emergency, contingency, or actual hostilities somewhere in the world. And so, after our agonizing experience in Vietnam, the first clear failure in our history, it is not surprising to find the United States of the 1970s and 1980s brooding over its frustrations and reevaluating its role in the world.

Vietnam, Laos, and Cambodia (the whole peninsula of Indochina) present a puzzling picture, enigmatic to most foreigners and especially so to Americans. The very name Vietnam evokes deep emotions and bitter memories in our countrymen. But the tendency to blame Vietnam for all our domestic ills has no foundation in fact. The problems of urban decay, racial disharmony, drug abuse, and all the rest were bound to plague us, whether or not we became involved in Vietnam. Indeed, one can argue that in the 1950s, well before we became heavily committed in Vietnam, a sense of national direction and purpose appeared to be lacking in the United States.

This book looks at the Vietnam War from the perspective of a senior military professional who held important positions of responsibility during the conflict. Among other things, I will seek to bring out the lessons we have learned or should have learned from the war, and their implications for the future. The severe impact of the war on our armed forces and its almost disastrous effect on the U.S. Army will receive special treatment.

The focus of this book is not on the fighting—bloody, uncompromising, and frustrating—nor is it on the dauntless American men and women who served in the operational areas. It is rather on the higher levels of the conflict, including the strategic crossroads of the political and the military. It will also show how the war was conducted in the theater of operations and will bring out the cumulative effects of our military policies on our defense establishment.

Critical remarks in this book may reflect on the top leaders, civilian and military, who made the key decisions affecting the direction and conduct of the war, as well as on commanders in the field, *but not on the fighting men who carried out their orders.* No nation was ever blessed with more stouthearted men than the Americans who fought and died in southeast Asia. What is even more extraordinary is that the overwhelming majority remained loyal and continued to fight for months and even years after it was clear that our leaders and people at home were deeply divided.

We could beg many questions by simply concluding that the United States should not have intervened in Indochina in any manner whatever. But of course we did intervene, and the president, other civilian leaders, and military leaders at the time of those earlier, fateful decisions generally agreed that it was the right thing for the United States to do. Our government, itself lacking a clear understanding of what it means and what it takes to commit a nation to war, failed to persuade the public that it was necessary for us to fight in Vietnam. This was a fatal weakness, and as a result of it the American people did not lend their wholehearted support to the war effort. This might have been obtained had the Congress been deeply involved in the decision to commit our forces to battle and been persuaded that a declaration of war was in the national interest. But this was not the case. Rather, the president unilaterally committed the nation to war without real congressional backing. A confused American people could not even dimly grasp the reasons why we were fighting in a little-known region halfway around the world. Nevertheless, our motives and objectives as a government were straightforward and devoid of territorial ambitions or self-aggrandizement.

True, we made mistakes in Vietnam, but by and large they were honest mistakes, and many were mistakes only in hindsight. Calling something a mistake is, of course, an exercise of personal opinion and can set off controversy. Significant mistakes, nevertheless, will be pointed out, but with no intent to place the blame for them on any particular individuals.

After a prologue addressing the early years of U.S. involvement in Vietnam, 1950–63, this book covers generally the period from President Diem's assassination in Vietnam in November 1963 to the fall of Saigon in April 1975. Part I examines various stages and major aspects of the war during this period, while Part II assesses the performance of our troops and our conduct of the war, concluding with a discussion of the larger lessons to be learned from the war.

Since I have thought about this book and worked on it for over ten years, I cannot list all of the many people who have helped me with it in one way or another. Rather I will mention only a few who have been particularly influential or helpful, and express my gratitude and appreciation for their unflagging support:

Ambassadors Ellsworth Bunker, the late Samuel Berger, and William Leonhart; former Secretaries of the Army Stanley R. Resor and Robert F. Froehlke; the late General Harold K. Johnson; retired generals Arthur S. Collins, Jr., Eugene P. Forrester, Donn R. Pepke, John T. Carley, Jr., Chester V. Clifton, and James L. Collins, Jr.; the late Major General (and author) Frank Davis; retired Colonels E. P. Lasché, A. C. Smith, Jr., and John Sitterson; Generals William E. Klein and Lincoln Jones, III; and Colonels George W. Sibert and James R. Rowe (prisoner of war of the Vietnamese for five years), all active duty, U.S. Army; respected U.S. intelligence officers Richard Lehman, George Allen, Paul Walsh, Paul Corscadden, Nate Nielsen, and Dwain Gatterdam; L. James Binder, editor in chief of *Army* magazine; and Benjamin F. Schemmer, editor and publisher of *Armed Forces Journal*.

Particularly valuable for their advice and assistance were Douglas Kinnard, chief of Military History, U.S. Army, and Professor Vincent Davis, director of the Patterson School of Diplomacy and International Commerce, University of Kentucky. I am likewise indebted to Anne T. Burke, Linda Bradbury, Thelma C. Brown, Judith S. Betts, Barbara Wingfield, and Mary Mitiguy for their patient and professional work in refining many draft manuscripts, as well as to Steve Hardyman, who created the maps and charts.

Finally I must acknowledge the wise counsel of my brother, Harding Palmer, and the constant support of my wife, Kay, a critic of sound judgment and much good humor.

Prologue: 1950-1963

My first encounter with the Vietnam question occurred in August 1951, when I joined 145 career officers of the U.S. Army plus a handful of Air Force, Navy, and Marine officers assembled at Carlisle Barracks, Pennsylvania, home of the newly reinstituted Army War College, to attend the first full-fledged course in over a decade. Classes had been suspended during the 1940–50 period, and the National War College had been established soon after World War II at the site of the original Army War College at Fort Lesley J. McNair in Washington, D.C. In 1950, a rump preliminary session of the reincarnated Army War College had been held at the Command and General Staff College at Fort Leavenworth, Kansas.

Our War College class, composed almost entirely of full colonels, most in their early forties, was a fairly senior group of veterans of World War II and the old prewar Army. More than a third of our class were later to become general officers. Almost a fifth were fresh from Korea, where many of them had commanded infantry regiments in battle.

In this period of international uncertainty, particularly coming so close on the heels of World War II, most of us could see that we had better make the most of even a short opportunity to live a more normal life with our families. And so the great majority of the families came with the men, despite the dearth of housing at the barracks and in the town of Carlisle. Consequently we were scattered all over the rural Pennsylvania landscape, some living as far away as Gettysburg and Harrisburg. This and a severe winter failed to dampen our class spirit, however, and we enjoyed a lively, very full, and rewarding ten months.

The Korean War, which had broken out in June 1950, was only a little over one year old at the start of our War College course. In late November 1950 the massive Chinese intervention had driven the U.S. 8th Army back deep into South Korean territory, until General Matthew B. Ridgway took command of the Army and turned it around. President Truman then relieved General MacArthur in April 1951, Ridgway replacing him as the supreme commander of United Nations forces in Korea.

By mid-1951 the maneuver phase of the war had largely ended and negotiations for a cease-fire between UN and communist forces had begun. By the time our class graduated in June 1952 the war had settled down to a basically static one, and the main battle line between the opposing forces changed very little during the remainder of the fighting.

Although our War College class was intensely interested in the Korean War, we were also watching with great personal interest the buildup of U.S. forces in Germany committed to the North Atlantic Treaty Organization. But there was also a third region of special interest to the class, Southeast Asia, specifically Indochina. We had seen what had happened in Korea and quite naturally were concerned about the implications of American involvement on the other mainland flank of China bordering on the western Pacific.

The faculty was likewise concerned, and early in the fall of 1951 assigned about a fifth of the class to a study of U.S. policy in Southeast Asia. It was an unfamiliar area for virtually all of the class, and those of us (myself included) assigned to study it devoured a great amount of official reports and other literature about the region. Other groups in the class were assigned similar policy studies pertaining to other important areas—Europe, the Middle East, Northeast Asia, and the Indian subcontinent.

In October 1951 the student conclusions to their study of U.S. policy in Southeast Asia were presented to the college.[1] Although opinions were somewhat divided, a large majority opposed any major U.S. involvement. The conclusions of the majority could be summarized as follows:

(1) The United States had probably made a serious mistake in agreeing with its allies to allow French power to be restored in Indochina. As a colonial power, France had done little to develop indigenous civilian and military leaders and civil servants in preparation for the countries' eventual independence.

(2) Indochina was of only secondary strategic importance to the United States. The economic and military value of Vietnam, the most important state in the region, was not impressive. Politically and socially Vietnam was obviously entering an unstable period with uncertain consequences. In any event, it did not warrant the commitment of U.S. forces to its defense.

(3) General war planning by the U.S. Joint Chiefs of Staff (JCS) envisioned a strategic defense in the Pacific, drawing the U.S. forward defense line to include Japan, South Korea, and the offshore island chain (Okinawa-Taiwan-the Philippines). But in Southeast Asia the line was drawn through the Isthmus of Kra on the mainland, excluding all of Indochina and most of Thailand. Thus the Strait of Malacca and populous,

richly endowed Indonesia were considered to be the prime strategic targets of the region.

(4) Militarily the region in general and Vietnam in particular would be an extremely difficult operational area, especially for U.S. forces. Unlike the relatively narrow Korean peninsula, Vietnam presented very long land and coastal borders that would be almost impossible to seal against infiltration and difficult to defend against overt military aggression. Much of the region was covered with dense jungle and much was mountainous. Weather, terrain, and geographic conformation combined to present formidable obstacles for military operations and logistic support.

(5) Politically and psychologically the United States, if it were to become involved, would have to operate under severe disadvantages, for it would inherit the taint of European colonialism. The United States should not become involved in the area beyond providing materiel military aid.

When our academic year was completed in June of 1952, our War College class scattered to the four corners of the globe, most of us being ordered to Korea or Japan. Having served in the Pacific during World War II with combat experience in New Guinea and the Philippines as well as postwar experience in Korea, I fully (and logically) expected to be ordered to Korea or Japan. Instead I was sent to Germany where, after a tour on the general staff of Headquarters, U.S. Army Europe, I ended up commanding a regiment of the 1st Infantry Division. Almost a decade was to pass before I saw duty again in the Far East.

While I was in Germany I voted by absentee ballot for General Eisenhower in the presidential elections of November 1952. As soon as he was elected, Eisenhower set out to fulfill his campaign promise to end the war in Korea. But it was to take months of fighting and marathon negotiations before the armistice was signed on 17 July 1953.

But let us turn to the roots of the Vietnam problem for the United States—to the closing months of World War II when the allies began to devote increasing attention to postwar matters, such as the future of their colonial territories. Postwar prospects did not look promising for France and its overseas interests, particularly in Asia. President Roosevelt had firmly opposed the French return to power in Indochina, and proposed instead an internationally supervised trusteeship. But the idea did not survive Roosevelt's death. The allies solved the immediate problem of accepting the surrender of the occupying Japanese forces at the Potsdam conference in the summer of 1945. Here it was agreed that Chinese Nationalist troops under Chiang Kai Shek's China Command, an allied headquarters in South China, would occupy Vietnam north of the 16th parallel. British Indian troops under another allied command, Lord Mountbatten's Southeast Asia Command, were to take control of Vietnam south of the parallel. Territorial division at the 16th parallel was intended to be a temporary administrative convenience until the Allies could work out a more permanent arrangement. (French Indochina included Vietnam with three more or less autonomous regions—Tonkin in the north, with its capital at Hanoi; Annam in the center, capital Hue; and Cochin China in the south, capital Saigon—plus Laos and Cambodia.)

The United States at the time also supported Ho Chi Minh, who had led a relatively small nationalist movement for Vietnamese independence for many years and had been waging a campaign against the Japanese since 1941. Ho's movement, known as the Viet Minh, consisted of quite diverse Vietnamese groups, but was dominated by Ho and his fellow Communists. By the time Chinese Nationalist troops arrived to receive the Japanese surrender, Ho Chi Minh had gained control of much of northern and central Vietnam, and the Chinese tacitly allowed the Viet Minh to remain in control, there being no French troops in the region to dispute the issue. South of the 16th parallel, however, it was a different story. By September 1945, British Indian Army and Free French troops established firm control of the Saigon area, the Viet Minh being relatively weak in the south. The British, sympathetic to the French position, persuaded the allies to turn over responsibility in the south to the Free French in October 1945. Meanwhile, the Viet Minh on 16 August 1945 proclaimed all of Vietnam as the Democratic Republic of Vietnam (DRV) under the leadership of Ho Chi Minh.

Then in March 1946 the French and the Viet Minh agreed to French recognition of the DRV as an independent state within the French Union (along with the associated states of Laos and Cambodia), and the entry of a limited number of French troops into Tonkin and Annam to replace Chinese Nationalist troops who returned home by the end of that month. By the end of 1946, however, the French agreement with Ho had collapsed, Ho and his followers had retired to their rural and mountain strongholds, and the first Indochina war began. Thereafter, the French exercised little real power in the north, and Vietnam in effect was divided along the 16th parallel.

Only a few years later, in 1948–49, the Communist Chinese armies defeated Nationalist Chinese forces. The People's Republic of China was proclaimed in Peking under Mao Tse-tung in September 1949, while the Nationalist government fled to Taiwan in December of that year. In 1950 the Soviet Union and Communist China signed a thirty-year treaty of friendship, repudiating the 1945 treaty between the Soviet Union and Nationalist China sanctioned by the Yalta Agreement.

Looking back from the vantage of thirty years, it is difficult to appreciate how these truly momentous events were viewed in the United States at the time. Americans tended to view the worldwide communist threat as homogeneous and monolithic in nature, and initially to assess the Sino-Soviet accord as a strong, durable one despite the deep-seated, centuries-old enmity existing between the two countries. Many years were to pass before U.S. policymakers gained a clearer understanding of Sino-Soviet relations as well as a realization that Ho Chi Minh and his successors were not easily manipulated as anyone's puppets, not even by the Soviet Union or China.

The Korean War, which began with the invasion of South Korea by North Korea in June 1950, also had a prolonged and significant influence on the United States. American involvement in a major conflict so soon after the allied victory in World War II and its inconclusive ending were difficult for the American people to understand. The massive Chinese intervention in the Korean War, moreover, conditioned early U.S. thinking with respect to Indochina as the United States looked beyond the Vietnamese insurgency in the north and perceived China as the ultimate communist threat to be contained in Southeast Asia. This perception persisted for almost the duration of the Vietnam War.

President Truman's decision on 1 May 1950 to provide aid to Indochina, just before the outbreak of the Korean War, was strongly influenced by the military stalemate that had evolved in Vietnam, where the French held the main population centers and lines of communications in the north while the Viet Minh controlled the surrounding rural areas and mountainous regions. A small U.S. military assistance and advisory group (MAAG) was established in Saigon in September 1950. The French, however, retained the military training and operational role, the U.S. role being logistical only.

In retrospect it seems clear that the Truman administration's decision to begin military aid for Indochina was taken in more or less instinctive support of the U.S. umbrella policy of containment everywhere in the world without much regard for the merits of each case and, in this instance, with little knowledge of the Indochina situation.

Meanwhile, Peking's recognition of Ho Chi Minh in February 1950, and the start of substantial Chinese military aid to the Viet Minh at about the same time, badly hurt French prospects. Especially damaging was the loss of French outposts along the Chinese border, coming at about the same time as the Chinese intervention in Korea in November 1950. These French border defeats were at the hands of Viet Minh "main force" regiments organized, trained, and equipped with the help of Chinese military aid. By far the most significant impact of this development was that it opened the major overland routes linking China to the vast mountainous region of northeastern Vietnam, thus assuring a free flow of Chinese aid and the ready establishment of Viet Minh bases. It brought a fundamental change in the nature of the war—henceforth, any expansion of Western forces in Vietnam or Laos could be readily offset by Viet Minh force escalation.[2]

In the following years, French efforts against the insurgency in Vietnam went from bad to worse. Successive military defeats eroded the French will to carry on the war, even though by 1954 the United States was bearing about three-fourths of the war's financial cost. In the spring of 1954, Viet Minh forces under General Vo Nguyen Giap finally succeeded in investing the French stronghold, Dien Bien Phu, located in the remote jungle mountains of northwestern Vietnam. Unwilling to pay the price of relieving Dien Bien Phu on their own, the French asked for direct U.S. military support as a matter of urgency. The JCS were split on the question of providing U.S. combat support to the French garrison. General Ridgway, now the Army's chief of staff, strongly opposed any direct U.S. involvement in the war, pointing out that large U.S. ground forces would be required, in addition to U.S. air and naval support, to make any significant difference in the war. Admiral Radford, chairman of the JCS, on the other hand, pushed hard for employing U.S. airpower to support the French. After determining that the British wanted no part in an Indochina war, President Eisenhower wisely decided against armed intervention, and Dien Bien Phu fell early in May 1954.

The ongoing international conference on Indochina, which had already begun in Geneva in April, concluded in July 1954. It resulted in the partition of Vietnam at the 17th parallel, a division intended to be temporary pending elections two years later that were never held. France and North Vietnam were the two signatories of the Geneva agreements. The United States did not sign the accords, but in a separate declaration agreed to support them.

Although the JCS (strongly influenced by Ridgway) opposed deeper involvement in Vietnam, declaring it "hopeless" to expand U.S. military aid when an effective government capable of raising and maintaining armed forces was lacking, the Eisenhower administration in December 1954 nevertheless concluded a formal agreement with France and South Vietnam to provide direct U.S. military assistance. The initial objective of the U.S. MAAG was to create a conventional South Vietnamese army whose primary mission was to defend the country from external attack.[3] And so the die was cast that directly involved the United States in a war over the control of Indochina.

Meanwhile, Ngo Dinh Diem, an autocratic Catholic mandarin who had impressed some prominent Americans, was appointed premier of South Vietnam. Immediately setting out to centralize control of the country, Diem ran into opposition from the French. Wishing to break away from French influence, Diem was quietly assisted by a U.S. Air Force colonel, Edward G. Lansdale, working under the CIA station chief in Saigon, who covertly assisted Diem's secret services. (Lansdale had a flair for dealing with emerging colonial nations and for countering guerrilla warfare. In the Philippines he had worked successfully with President Magsaysay in coping with the Huk rebellion.) Diem moved swiftly, subduing the private armies, river pirates, and religious sects that held sway in many areas in the South. His initial success earned him the firm support of the Eisenhower administration.[4]

It was now abundantly clear that American and French objectives in Vietnam were incompatible. The French wanted to preserve their special relationship with Vietnam, as well as with Laos and Cambodia, while the United States sought an independent, noncommunist Vietnam oriented toward the West. This basic contradiction led to the displacement of France in the region by the United States in 1955–56, a result which the French bitterly resented. Indeed, American insistence on the rapid liquidation of European colonies in the Middle East, Africa, and Asia, while at the same time supplanting the French in Vietnam, seemed hypocritical to our European friends, who consequently remained unwilling to support the United States in Vietnam throughout the war.

In July 1955 the South Vietnamese government, with the acquiescence of the United States, declined to prepare for reunification elections scheduled for 1956 on the grounds that free elections would be impossible in North Vietnam. The South Vietnamese were also well aware of the demographic arithmetic—the North with over fifteen million people, compared to the South's fewer than twelve million. And Saigon also knew of the swift and bloody consolidation of control of North Vietnam under a single-party police state. Then in the fall of 1955, Diem completed the initial stage of his consolidation of power in the South by deposing Bao Dai as chief of state through the vehicle of a national referendum, and on 26 October 1955 proclaimed Vietnam to be a Republic under his own presidency.

By this time the French recognized the futility of their position in Vietnam, and in April 1956 the last French troops and army advisers left the country. (French air and naval advisers remained for one more year.) The French withdrawal left an enormous military, political, and psychological vacuum in South Vietnam, the significance of which seems to have escaped U.S. policymakers at the time. The Vietnamese Army, most of whose officers had been French and whose noncommissioned officers had been mostly French colonials, was in a sorry state. Not entirely trusting the Vietnamese, the French had been unwilling to develop professional officers and NCOs in any significant number, and the Vietnamese as a result were ill-prepared to assume the responsibility of leading their Army, especially at higher command and staff levels, and in technical areas such as logistics. On the nonmilitary side, the French departure was likewise a severe loss. French officials held influential positions not only at the bureau level in Saigon but also at province and even district levels. And again the French had failed to develop Vietnamese abilities to govern themselves, ruthlessly suppressing the emergence of Vietnamese leadership. Overall, the situation in Vietnam inherited by the United States from

France in 1956 was disadvantageous, if not hopeless.[5] In retrospect, it is difficult to escape the conclusion that the United States, in deliberately pushing the French out of the way and replacing them in Vietnam, acted rashly, to say the least.

At this point a brief description of the political-military doctrine used by the Viet Minh in the North would be helpful in understanding the nature of the war. In the South this same doctrine was adopted by the insurgents aided and controlled by Hanoi, who by 1957 were commonly known as the Viet Cong (a pejorative term meaning literally Vietnamese Communists). This was essentially the doctrine of a "People's War" which called for the gradual development of conventional capabilities and concurrently a parallel emphasis on the development of guerrilla warfare capabilities. Theoretically the orchestrated employment of a wide variety of unconventional and conventional capabilities would ultimately wear down opposing government forces to the point where a climactic "general counter offensive" could be launched that would overwhelm remaining opposition.

Under this doctrine, the Viet Minh's major conventional capabilities were vested in their "main force" units, organized into battalions, regiments, and up to divisions in size whose role was to draw government forces into combat under conditions where their superiority in firepower, mobility, and air support could be neutralized. The other elements of the Viet Minh's three-tiered military capabilities consisted of those forces designed primarily for guerrilla operations—the guerrilla-militia forces and the regional forces.

At the bottom or "people's" level—the hamlet—local citizens were formed into partially armed militia units, usually platoons of 30 to 50 people each, which also provided a manpower pool for the other categories of military forces. The next step up from the hamlet militia was the village guerrillas, who were somewhat better armed and performed broader duties. Next came the regional forces, also called "local force" units, usually a company (about 100 soldiers) at district level and a battalion (200–300 soldiers) at province level. District and provincial soldiers were essentially full-time in contrast to the mostly part-time guerrilla forces. The main objectives of local force units (regional) and guerrilla-militia forces were to pin down government forces, cause them to disperse in order to protect vulnerable targets, and constantly wear them down, thus limiting their ability to take the offensive against Viet Minh bases and forces.

In the South the development by the Viet Cong of this organized, tiered structure, which operated from the "people's" level to large regular unit echelons, created the necessity to develop and maintain South Vietnamese security forces that could effectively counter the threat at each level at any time. The underground nature of the political-military command and control apparatus, and the existence of a "shadow" government in the countryside also required the development of a clandestine special police organization that could identify and root out the so-called political infrastructure. Only in this way could the South Vietnamese government protect the population wherever threatened.

The Viet Cong force structure and tactics described above were not universally understood by the Americans or South Vietnamese, especially in the earlier years of the conflict. Failing to grasp the nature of the total threat, U.S. leaders initially perceived the major threat to be an overt, across-the-border invasion by North Vietnamese or Chinese forces, and were slow in recognizing the serious threat posed by subversion, infiltration, and guerrilla warfare. But even after the need for paramilitary forces to counter internal subversion and insurgency was recognized in the 1959–60 period, U.S. assistance for such forces was not provided in adequate amounts until 1964. So-called popular forces at hamlet and village level (originally called the Self-Defense Corps) and regional forces at district and province level (originally called the Civil Guard), although authorized in 1956, did not achieve significant size and capabilities until the early 1960s. To illustrate their ultimately recognized importance, the peak strength of these territorial forces was 532,000 (248,000 popular forces and 284,000 regional forces) reached in 1972, somewhat larger than the 1972 peak strength of the regular forces, 516,000. Thus these paramilitary forces eventually achieved at least a kind of parity with the regular forces.[6]

Although South Vietnam under Diem appeared to be making progress in the 1955–58 period, the seeming quiet was only the lull before the storm. Hanoi was simply lying low until its 10,000 hard-core, paramilitary communist agents in the South were ready to go into action. In late 1958 and 1959 armed terrorist activities steadily increased, the pattern indicating that the Viet Cong was carving out secure base areas in the countryside in the traditional manner. In January 1960, when a battalion-size Viet Cong force overran a South Vietnamese army regimental headquarters in Tay Ninh Province, less than a hundred miles from Saigon, it seemed evident that a second People's War was well under development.[7] President Diem responded in 1959 with countermeasures and the conversion of some regular infantry units to rangers for counterinsurgency duty, but the situation continued to deteriorate. In early 1960 Diem declared the country to be in a state of war against the Viet Cong, and asked for increased U.S. military assistance in both materiel and training.

Concurrently with the stepped-up pace of insurgency in Vietnam, internal conflict was reaching crisis proportions in neighboring Laos, which was supposed to remain neutral as a result of the 1954 Geneva agreements. Rivalry between the Hanoi-controlled communist Pathet Lao in the extreme northern part of Laos and right-wing and neutralist factions brought on increasing armed conflict in the late 1950s with the entry of North Vietnamese troops and Soviet arms. This marked the beginning of American participation in the so-called "secret war" in Laos. Again taking over from the French, the United States provided U.S. Army special forces training and CIA logistic support for the Meo tribes conducting guerrilla warfare against communist troops in the region.[8]

Although the Eisenhower administration did agree to increasing support to Vietnam in its fight against insurgency, it was only a half-hearted holding action that left the Southeast Asia problem for the next administration to handle. Indicative of this attitude was the indifferent treatment accorded numerous U.S. Army officers returning from duty in Vietnam who had gained valuable experience and knowledge about the Vietnam situation. Lieutenant General Samuel T. Williams, who served almost five years (1955–60) as chief of U.S. MAAG, Saigon, cooled his heels in the Pentagon for three weeks upon his return in September 1960 without being consulted about the Vietnamese problem. There were numerous others who were similarly ignored upon their return to the United States. A contributing factor was the traditional reluctance of Washington-level staff officers (military and civilian bureaucrats) to accept the judgments of the officials in the field trying to fathom the constantly shifting intricacies of the Vietnamese scene.[9]

Not long after John F. Kennedy was inaugurated as president on 20 January 1961, he reviewed the situation in Southeast Asia and reaffirmed the U.S. objectives of preventing Communist domination of South Vietnam and developing a viable, democratic, independent country.[10] He was much impressed by a January 1961 report about the insurgency in South Vietnam by the much-traveled Edward G. Lansdale, now a general of the U.S. Air Force, who since 1959 had been serving on his second assignment in Vietnam with the CIA.[11] In his report, Lansdale, deeply concerned about the growing strength of the Viet Cong, assessed President Diem's strengths and weaknesses as well as the substantial opposition to Diem existing in the country, but urged nevertheless that the United States continue to support him.

Kennedy was also impressed by General Maxwell D. Taylor, the Army chief of staff during the previous administration and now a presidential special assistant. (Taylor had become disenchanted with the Eisenhower administration's reliance on nuclear weapons and advocated a balanced military posture resting on both nuclear and conventional military strength.) As a result of Taylor's thoughtful, reasoned recommendations, the president directed a major expansion of the American military advisory effort, which saw the number increase from about 900 in January 1961 to almost 17,000 by the end of 1963, and authorized the commitment of U.S. Army helicopters in support of the Army of the Republic of Vietnam (ARVN).[12]

The first airmobile assault against the Viet Cong by ARVN soldiers taken into battle by U.S. helicopters took place in December 1961 in an area about fifteen miles west of Saigon. More and greatly improved troop-carrying helicopters and armed helicopters soon followed. By June 1963 many ARVN troops had become accustomed to working with American helicopters, in particular the UH-1B, dubbed the "Huey," later to become the universally recognized silhouette in Southeast Asia.

One rather immediate result of the presidential interest in insurgency warfare was a boom in U.S. armed forces with respect to special forces and special operations, the objective being to develop a more sophisticated understanding of unconventional warfare. The effect on the U.S. Army was dramatic. The Army's Special Warfare Center at Fort Bragg, North Carolina, was renamed the John F. Kennedy Center for Special Warfare, and Army special forces were rapidly expanded in size. Training in counterinsurgency was emphasized in many Army units, while practically all Army service schools developed and taught counterinsurgency doctrine appropriate to their specialty. To cap it all, the president personally approved the wearing of green berets by Army special forces personnel. In a remarkably short time this became their sobriquet, and the American green berets became well known worldwide.

Kennedy also approved a broad new U.S. program in support of Vietnam that involved primarily the State and Defense departments, the CIA, and the Agency for International Aid. In February 1962 a new command was created, the U.S. Military Assistance Command, Vietnam (MACV), under a four-star Army general, Paul D. Harkins, a protegé of General Taylor. The tall, handsome, polished Harkins was an imposing figure, though he was not regarded within the Army as an intellectual giant. But he got along well with the U.S. ambassador in Saigon, Frederick E. Nolting, and both men were firm supporters of President Diem. In Washington, however, the debate over Diem's capacity to govern South Vietnam effectively was mounting. Diem's brother, Ngo Dinh Nhu, and his wife were becoming increasingly unpopular with the Vietnamese, and Diem, while surviving several coup attempts, became more introverted and suspicious of both Vietnamese and American advisers.

To deal with the urgent problem of Laos, President Kennedy decided to use the diplomatic route and to neutralize Laos, trying to separate it from the larger conflict in Vietnam. To this end the three Laotian factions—the Pathet Lao, the neutralists, and the right wing—were persuaded to form a coalition, with neutralist Prince Souvanna Phouma as premier. A fourteen-nation conference in Geneva then signed accords in July 1962 guaranteeing the neutrality and independence of Laos. As a result, the CIA ceased support of the Meos, and the U.S. Army's training teams were withdrawn from Laos. Unfortunately, however, approximately 7,000 North Vietnamese troops in northern Laos never left the country but continued to assist the communist Pathet Lao in undermining the coalition government. By 1964 the Pathet Lao had withdrawn from the coalition and with the aid of North Vietnamese troops resumed operations against the government. Some time later the United States reinstated its support of the Meo effort, and the "secret war" in Laos escalated. (By 1972 North Vietnamese forces in Laos numbered over 70,000 and the CIA-supported Meos roughly half that number.) Regrettably, the U.S. government failed to take effective early actions to preserve the guarantees of the 1962 accords. I share the view of some like William Colby (a former Director of Central Intelligence) that this was a tragic mistake.[13]

In Vietnam during 1962, Diem's strategic hamlet program appeared to be progressing and his armed forces seemed to be performing better, but it was only illusory. The simmering Buddhist revolt boiled over in Hue in May 1963 and then worsened; and Diem, relying more and more on his brother Nhu and Madame Nhu, responded harshly, declaring Saigon under martial law. Then in August 1963 Nolting was replaced in Saigon by the well-known Massachusetts Republican and Boston Brahmin, Henry Cabot Lodge, who promptly joined the anti-Diem faction led by the under secretary of state, Averell Harriman. Lodge, aloof and aristocratic in manner, played a lone wolf game and quickly succeeded in alienating other key U.S. officials in Saigon, especially Harkins. With the official U.S. community in both Saigon and Washington divided over the question of Diem, the Kennedy administration soon became committed to the overthrow of Diem without having thought through the likely consequences.[14] It was not a good performance.

Very late in the hour, in late September 1963, the president sent his secretary of defense, Robert S. McNamara, and Taylor (chairman of the JCS since October 1962) on a quick trip to Saigon to size up the situation. Misled by the unsubstantiated assertions of progress on the military front made by Harkins, McNamara and Taylor upon their return to Washington gave a monumental misreading of the Vietnamese situation to the National Security Council on 2 October 1963. Among other things, they stated that the major military tasks requiring a significant U.S. military presence could be completed by the end of 1965, and recommended that the number of American military personnel in Vietnam be reduced by one thousand by the end of the current year.[15] In hindsight their report was so unrealistic as to be almost ludicrous. One month later, on 2 November 1963, Diem and Nhu were assassinated in Saigon, and Vietnam plunged into a prolonged state of disarray.

In sum, it seems clear in retrospect that the U.S. government, during the first stages of American involvement in the mid-1950s and early 1960s, was slow in recognizing the nature of the conflict in Southeast Asia and in realistically evaluating the situation in Vietnam. Although a few of our early American advisers had a good grasp of the situation, most lacked familiarity with the Vietnamese language and culture, and consequently did not understand or were misled by their Vietnamese counterparts.[16] During this same period the Hanoi-controlled Viet Cong and the National Liberation Front, successors to the Viet Minh in the South, sank deeper roots, including a political organization and military base system, in South Vietnam as well as in the border areas of Cambodia and Laos. Influenced by unreliable, overly optimistic assessments of progress and by the desire to look successful in the public eye, successive U.S. administrations seriously underestimated the situation in those crucial early years.

PART I

American Involvement in Vietnam

1

1963-1967:
The JCS and Vietnam

The period 1963–65 was one of the most tumultuous times for the United States in all its history, for these years saw American military power committed to a war in Indochina which was to divide Americans to a degree unprecedented since the Civil War a hundred years before. Two presidents served during these years—John F. Kennedy and Lyndon B. Johnson.

In examining this critical period, this chapter will focus on the role of the U.S. Joint Chiefs of Staff. To place their role in the proper context it is important to understand the nature and organization of the JCS and the unified command system, as well as the parameters of the statutory duties of the JCS. Obviously the personalities and styles of top civilian and military leaders in Washington and abroad had significant influence on how the chiefs carried out their responsibilities.

The JCS as a corporate entity was not formally organized until after World War II, although an informal U.S. organization did exist, and a combined mechanism for the overall coordination of U.S. and British military activities, known as the Combined Chiefs of Staff, came into being during the war. After a long national debate, the National Security Act of 1947 created a Department of Defense under a secretary of defense, to include the JCS with a separate staff called the Joint Staff. The act created a loose confederation of the military services, each continuing to be organized and administered under its own secretary, and an overall secretary of defense with his own secretariat. (Only the secretary of defense, however, was made a member of the cabinet, and the service secretaries were downgraded.) Thus the services were not integrated but were unified only in the sense that they were placed under a single overall head.

This fact remains pertinent to date. Among other things, it means that only the service staffs possess the technical expertise in all matters affecting their respective services—force structure, logistic support, detailed knowledge of their ships, aircraft, and weapons systems, and so forth. This means that the Joint Staff cannot possibly duplicate the know-how existing in each service staff. This is why it is essential that the service staffs participate in the joint process functioning under the JCS.

Since 1947 more and more authority has been centralized under the secretary of defense, whose staff has been expanded and strengthened. Likewise the central role of the chairman of the JCS (CJCS) has been clarified and formalized, while the Joint Staff has been expanded in size. These changes were articulated in amendments to the original act, the last of which (1958) also made a significant change in the chain of command extending from the president as commander-in-chief. Before 1958 the chain of command extended from the president to the secretary of defense and then to the unified commands through the JCS and the executive agent system. At that time the JCS designated a service chief to act as their executive agent for each of the unified commands. The chief of staff, U.S. Army, performed that function during the Korean War and provided the link between the JCS and the unified commander whose area included the Korean theater of war. This commander was known then as the commander-in-chief, Far Eastern Command—CINCFE. The Korean War was the last one fought under the executive agent system.

The Defense Reorganization Act of 1958 abolished the executive agent arrangement and in effect took the JCS out of the chain of command, charging the chiefs instead with assisting the secretary of defense in directing the unified commanders. The chiefs, however, were expected to supervise the unified commanders, if not to command them. Orders to the unified commanders from the JCS are issued under the authority and in the name of the secretary of defense. Vietnam was the first war conducted under the provisions of this statute. The soundness of the present command arrangements and recent proposals to reform the JCS organization will be examined later in this book.

As the principal military advisers to the president, the secretary of defense, and the National Security Council, the JCS have specific statutory responsibilities, including strategic planning and the strategic direction of the armed forces, joint logistic planning, and reviewing the major materiel and personnel requirements of the armed forces. The chiefs also establish unified commands in various strategic areas of the world to control the operations of assigned U.S. forces from the Army, Navy, Air Force, and Marine Corps.

The Kennedy national security team that came to power in January 1961 was a strong one. The constant and courageous Dean Rusk was secretary of state, and the cool, unflappable Robert Strange McNamara was secretary of defense. Recognizing the increasing scope and pace of U.S. involvement in world events and the interlocking complexity of foreign, defense, and economic policy, the president at the outset had decided to build a strong National Security Council staff in the White House under the presidential assistant for NSC affairs, the brilliant and able McGeorge Bundy. Assisted initially by another bright star from the academic world, W.W. Rostow, until he left in December 1961 to head the State Department's policy planning staff, Bundy served under both Presidents Kennedy and Johnson. He was succeeded on 1 April 1966 by Rostow, who served for the rest of Johnson's term.

Although neither the director of Central Intelligence nor the chairman of the Joint Chiefs of Staff is a statutory member of the National Security Council, they are nevertheless statutory advisers to the NSC and are essential players in that organization. Allen W. Dulles overlapped with the incoming Kennedy administration until he was succeeded by John A. McCone as director of Central Intelligence in November 1961. General Lyman L. Lemnitzer, U.S. Army, then chairman of the JCS, likewise continued to serve under the new administration until Kennedy replaced him on 1 October 1962 with General Maxwell D. Taylor, another former Army chief of staff. Taylor initially had served as a special assistant to the president, but this had proved to be a little awkward because it gave the president two equally senior military advisers.

President Kennedy expected his secretaries of state and defense, as well as his other cabinet members, to run their own departments as they saw fit, but he wanted independent advice from his NSC staff, analyzing the various factors and views involved and laying out the options for presidential consideration. This became Bundy's major role (and later Rostow's), and each performed it well, in the process setting the precedent and tradition of a strong and influential presidential assistant in the national security arena. Fortunately both Rusk and McNamara possessed more than average self-discipline and got along together extremely well. McNamara, moreover, readily recognized the primacy of State in shaping international policy, although in the Pentagon, McNamara reigned supreme.

My personal involvement in Vietnam matters began in September 1963 when I joined then Lieutenant General Harold K. Johnson, deputy chief of staff for operations (DCSOPS), Army, as his number two man. During the next twenty months I had a ringside seat at the deliberations of the Joint Chiefs of Staff and gained new insights into civil-military relations at the seat of government. During my apprenticeship in JCS affairs the chairman was General Taylor and the service chief lineup was General Earle G. Wheeler, Army; Admiral David L. McDonald, Navy; General Curtis E. LeMay, Air Force; and General Wallace M. Greene, Marine Corps.

In the late 1950s, when Taylor was the army chief during the Eisenhower administration, I served in his office as the deputy secretary of the General Staff and made several official trips overseas with him. (The secretary of the General Staff at the time, then Major General William C. Westmoreland, coordinated the activities of the army staff and in effect was chief of staff to the Army Chief.) General Taylor was an impressive figure, known as an intellectual, a soldier statesman, and a talented linguist. But it was an unhappy period for Taylor, who did not see eye-to-eye with the commander-in-chief or the other military chiefs as to the proper role of the Army. After he left the Army, Taylor laid out his deep misgivings about the national military establishment in a highly critical book, *The Uncertain Trumpet*,[1] which caught the attention of many prominent people, including John F. Kennedy. Particularly intense and somewhat aloof during this period, Taylor appeared to those who did not know him as cold, humorless, and unbending. But he had another side—he could be friendly, a genial host, and a witty conversationalist with a well developed sense of humor. For many people, however, these more endearing qualities were not revealed until after he retired from public life at the end of Johnson's presidency.

In any event, Kennedy's military chiefs were a lively group, each chief having strong views of his own and not bashful about voicing them. The handsome, steely-eyed Taylor, a Kansan, was incisive and forceful and made a formidable chairman. Wheeler, a personable and suave Washingtonian (D.C.), was unusually articulate and especially effective in finding middle ground when the chiefs seemed to be deadlocked over an issue. The quiet, gentlemanly McDonald, from Nebraska, grizzled from many years of sea duty, was a thoughtful, serious man who spoke sparingly but with authority. LeMay, a big, cigar-chewing midwesterner from Ohio, was often arrogant and rude in manner, talking loudly (partly no doubt because of hearing difficulties) with an abrasive voice that could whine like a turbine engine. The courteous, poker-faced Greene was sometimes quite professorial in his approach, which had earned him the nickname of "Schoolboy Greene."

Taylor, however, was clearly the dominant figure within the JCS. Having just served in the White House as a close personal adviser to the president, he had become in effect the number one military adviser to the Kennedy administration. Thus when Kennedy brought him out of retirement to be the chairman, Taylor possessed far more clout than the average CJCS. At the same time, having become closely associated with the inner political-military thinking of the administration, Taylor's objectivity and independence of mind had to be somewhat compromised, which may explain why he sometimes appeared, at least to me, to be ambivalent on the basic issues of Vietnam.

The JCS conference room, the "Gold Room," is commonly called the "Tank," probably in reference to its lack of windows. Maps of various regions of the world are displayed on two walls, a screen for projecting slides and a large board showing the expected location of each chief for months ahead take up the third wall, and a clock adorns the fourth wall. Two podiums are available for briefers, as well as chairs for staff action officers whom the chiefs might want to call on for additional details. But the dominant feature is a large, highly polished, rectangular mahogany table which takes up most of the space.

The JCS seating arrangement has the chairman in the center of the long axis of the table with his back to the clock. The Air Force chief sits to the right of the chairman, and the director of the Joint Staff is on the chairman's left. Across the table the Army chief sits facing the director, and the chief of Naval Operations faces the Air Force chief. The commandant of the Marine Corps sits at one of the short ends of the table between the Air Force and Navy chiefs, while the secretary of the Joint Staff (the note-taker and drafter of conference minutes) holds down the other end. Each operations deputy (deputy chief of staff for operations) sits alongside his chief, while the assistant to the chairman sits behind his principal.

This traditional seating arrangement resulted in a special problem for this particular group of chiefs. Both Taylor and LeMay were somewhat hard of hearing in one ear, and as fate would decree, their weak ears were side by side. According to his aides Taylor was quite adept at reading lips, but LeMay lacked this talent and the consequences were unpredictable. Since both men were quick-tempered and short on patience, the discussions could be lively, and there was rarely a dull JCS meeting.

The normal attendance at a JCS meeting consists of the chairman, the service chiefs with their respective operations deputies, and the director of the Joint Staff, a three-star position normally rotated every three years among the services. Each chief is expected to handle the subject at hand with no assistance other than from his operations deputy. As the principal assistant to the service chief of staff in carrying out his statutory duties as a member of the JCS, the service operations deputy is the focal point of the service staff for all joint matters (that is, subjects involving more than one service) and must be knowledgeable about whatever questions are addressed by the JCS.

In addition to attending the regular three-times-a-week JCS meetings with their four-star bosses, the director of the Joint Staff and the service operations deputies meet as a group several times a week. Known as the "Operations Deputies," this group of five three-star officers, chaired by the director, handle less critical or noncontroversial matters that do not require the attention of the chiefs. In effect, the group functions as a sort of junior JCS.

In October 1963, only a few weeks after I joined the Army staff in the Pentagon, a disturbing episode occurred which gave an inkling of the quicksands that lay ahead for the United States in Vietnam. An Army friend of mine, Lieutenant Colonel John Paul Vann, called on me in my office. About ten years earlier he had served under me in Germany, and I knew him to be tough, mentally and physically, but with a short-fused temper that was hard to handle. Vann shocked me when he said that he was about to resign. He had returned in June from a tour in the upper Mekong Delta of South Vietnam as adviser to the commander of the 7th ARVN Division and had been engaged in a running fight with his superiors as to the true situation in this southernmost region of the country. General Paul D. Harkins, the U.S. military commander in South Vietnam, who had assumed command of the brand new Military Assistance Command, Vietnam (MACV) in February 1962, had reprimanded Vann for conduct bordering on insubordination and had recommended that he not be debriefed, that is, consulted about his experiences and views, after he left Vietnam. On his own, Vann had persisted in talking to anyone who would listen and by July 1963 had impressed enough people in the upper civilian and military circles (including Lieutenant General H.K. Johnson) of the Department of Defense to get himself on the agenda of a JCS meeting, only to be cancelled at the last minute at the direction of General Taylor.

Discouraged and frustrated, Vann resigned from the Army shortly thereafter and vowed to return to Vietnam in a civilian capacity to continue the fight against the Viet Cong for as long as it would take. But it was over a year before he was permitted to return, in early 1965 to work for the Agency for International Development, because senior American officials in Vietnam opposed the fiery Vann's presence. When Vann did return he was assigned to the province of Hau Nghia just west of Saigon and contiguous to the Cambodian border, an area demanding priority attention because it was infested with Viet Cong, yet close enough so that the U.S. mission in Saigon could keep an eye on him. Vann soon became a legendary figure, admired and respected throughout Vietnam, although he was very hard on people and was not universally liked. The country was his consuming passion until his death in a helicopter crash near Kontum in June 1972. His death came as no surprise to those who knew him well, for he was fearless, defying the enemy day and night, and the Viet Cong had a price on his head. Vann understood the political nature of the conflict and probably knew Vietnam better than any other American of his day.

The thrust of Vann's allegations in the summer of 1963 was that the 7th ARVN Division was conducting operations against areas believed to be free of Viet Cong. This tactic inflated Vietnamese and MACV statistics on offensive operations conducted by ARVN troops and held down friendly casualties. Vann was convinced that Harkins was being duped

Vietnamese statistics on strategic hamlets and villages reported as being under government control had been greatly exaggerated.[6] (John Vann's views on the situation in the Delta were thus vindicated.)

One of the worst aspects of Diem's death was the loss in continuity of the South Vietnamese government and in any momentum achieved in critical government programs supported by the United States. Five major coups and changes in government in rapid succession had a highly debilitating effect. This was due in no small part to a fundamental characteristic of Vietnamese society that sanctioned the buying and selling of even small favors and simple services. A change in government meant a purge from the Saigon bureau level down to the province and district chiefs and their staffs. A corps commander had about a dozen province chief jobs to sell; in turn, each province chief had about a half dozen district chief positions to peddle. Influence and affluence were gained quickly and concurrently, and fortunes were made as each change occurred. The wholesale shifts worked havoc on programs under way in the field, and years passed before the system stabilized. Indeed, it took four years for Nguyen Van Thieu to emerge finally and, after national elections, to be inaugurated as president of the Republic of Vietnam on 31 October 1967.

Three weeks after Diem's death, John F. Kennedy was assassinated. When the news was first flashed over the TV and radio in the early afternoon, I was with General Johnson in his office. Stunned and disbelieving, we were brooding about the implications when our chief of staff, General Wheeler, joined us. There was little of a factual nature known about the tragic episode, and Wheeler told us that as a precaution, in the event there was a domestic or foreign conspiracy afoot, the JCS had quietly dispatched a warning to the U.S. unified commanders and the services to be on the alert. It was a miserable moment and all of us felt both anger and sorrow as the horror of the despicable act began to sink in.

Since that day I have often asked myself what would have happened with respect to South Vietnam if President Kennedy had lived. It is a fascinating question on which to speculate. My own view is that he would not have committed major U.S. combat forces and that quite a different story would have unfolded, although the ultimate fate of South Vietnam might well have been the same. Some students of the Vietnam War argue that Kennedy in fact put Americans into combat situations in 1961 and that he would have been compelled by the same course of events as President Johnson was to commit U.S. forces to an air war in the North and a land war in the South. Others feel that had Kennedy early emphasized the development of Vietnamese special forces and paramilitary forces to combat counterinsurgency, rather than development of Vietnamese conventional military forces, the outcome might have been different. Still others argue that the most difficult problems of later years might have by the South Vietnamese.[2] Taylor and McNamara, however, not only supported Harkins's rosy view of the situation, but in October 1963 predicted success against the Viet Cong by the end of 1965 if the political controversy surrounding President Ngo Dinh Diem and his brother, Ngo Dinh Nhu, could be resolved.[3] It is almost impossible to resist the conclusion that Taylor and McNamara were playing U.S. presidential politics—the 1964 elections were only a year away. Obviously the Kennedy team had decided how it wanted to handle Southeast Asia, was confident at the time that its plans and actions would be successful, and did not want mavericks like Vann rocking the boat. Nevertheless, I thought that it was a mistake to deny the JCS a sharply different view of Vietnam. Indeed, the incident left me deeply disappointed with Messieurs McNamara, Taylor, and Harkins.

A few weeks after Vann's trip to Washington, on 1 November 1963, President Ngo Dinh Diem and his brother, Nhu, were assassinated in Saigon. In the United States there was much speculation, some in the press, as to what had transpired behind the scenes. But it was clear that the U.S. administration had actively supported the coup, not necessarily wanting or expecting Diem to be murdered, but wanting him out of power. Later I learned that the State Department, led by the Under Secretary, had been the core of the anti-Diem faction in the U.S. policymaking community that in the end prevailed despite the fact that the secretary of state, secretary of defense, the JCS, and the MACV commander supported Diem, for whom there was no viable successor in sight. In Saigon, Ambassador Henry Cabot Lodge (in place only a few weeks before the coup), using CIA officers to contact Vietnamese officials in an attempt to conceal the U.S. hand, played a lone game, taking counsel only with himself.[4]

Although the coup was executed successfully, it turned out to be a disaster of the first magnitude. According to Taylor, President Kennedy was stunned by the news and bitterly regretted President Diem's death. Certainly the coup was an important cause of the costly prolongation of the war into the 1970s. It also presented perhaps the last opportunity for the United States to assess the situation coldbloodedly and to opt gracefully out of its commitments in Vietnam. But that was not to be.

Diem's downfall was a great morale boost to North Vietnam and th Viet Cong, who took the offensive, politically and militarily, to explo the removal of their mortal enemy. In South Vietnam the Diem-Ngu p litical organization, including the secret security and intelligence service disintegrated, and it did not take the Viet Cong long to dismantle Diem vaunted strategic hamlet program. After the coup it was discovered th the security situation in South Vietnam was far worse than thought. the Delta the Viet Cong was *not* being compressed into smaller base are but was lying low and in reality gaining strength. A large proportion government attacks had been launched against non-targets, and U.

The concept, fathered by the brilliantly creative General H.H. Howze, U.S. Army, was tested during 1964 using a provisional organization called the 11th Air Assault Division, and was generally supported by the Army but opposed at every turn by the Air Force. After joint tests in which a standard Army division was supported by standard tactical air elements of the Air Force, an attempt was made to compare the two concepts, but with predictable results—they were simply not comparable. As General Johnson said, "it was like trying to compare a gazelle with an elephant."

Early in 1965, the secretary of defense resolved the Army-Air Force dispute in favor of the Army and the inexorable advance of technology. And so a new and different type of division, officially called an airmobile division, was added to the Army's roster. The test division, now permanently organized and given the designation of the famous 1st Cavalry Division by General Johnson, was deployed to Vietnam in the late summer of 1965. By late October the division was fighting a decisive campaign in the Central Highlands, where it thwarted the offensive plans of a North Vietnamese Army division to overrun this rugged jungle region. Airmobility had come of age for the Army, and the chopper was here to stay.

Two subissues raged during this interservice wrangle, both involving ongoing operations in South Vietnam. One involved the armed helicopter, used primarily to escort airmobile formations (helicopters carrying assault infantry troops) and to support them while the actual assault was placing infantrymen on their landing zone. The other involved the arming of the Mohawk, a small, two-engine, fixed-wing aircraft used by the Army for reconnaissance and surveillance missions. Eventually the decision was reached to accept the armed chopper as an essential part of the air mobility concept but not to allow the Army to use the Mohawk as an attack aircraft, confining it to the reconnaissance role. Both were wise decisions.

But prior to these decisions there were some hot and emotional sessions of the JCS. One concerned the armed Huey, which was then being used successfully in Vietnam to support ARVN operations, but which was considered by the Air Force as illegal poaching on their roles and missions. This was in the midsummer of 1964. General LeMay suddenly took his cigar out of his mouth and, gesticulating wildly, challenged General Johnson to an aerial duel. He screamed, "Johnson, you fly one of these damned Huey's and I'll fly an F-105, and we'll see who survives. I'll shoot you down and scatter your peashooter all over the goddam ground." I was eager to defend my chief, both verbally and physically (LeMay would have made two Johnsons in body weight, if not in mental poundage), but Johnson motioned me to keep quiet and responded quietly: "I'm not a flier, but I will be happy to get qualified and take you on—we can agree on a time and place later. But let's not waste the valuable time of our colleagues on such a trivial matter." This served only to enrage LeMay

further and his bellows became louder, while his operations deputy tried
to calm him down. Finally, the chairman stepped in and, after stating that
the discussion had gone far enough, asked the belligerents to cool off and
retract their duelish statements. This was accomplished amicably and the
chiefs switched to a less contentious subject. It had been a difficult time,
but Wheeler was adept at spreading oil on stormy waters.

As the Vietnam crisis deepened, the JCS and the services debated
and discussed at great length the question of the U.S. commitment. General Johnson, perhaps the most knowledgeable and understanding of any
American leader on Vietnam, often remarked that if the United States
was not willing to "go all the way," that is, to include direct confrontation
with the Soviet Union and China, who supplied Hanoi with the means to
attack the South, then we had best not go in at all. But the problem was
to delineate just where our interests lay in Southeast Asia and to define
U.S. objectives—specifically, what we were trying to do in South Vietnam.

A brief reconstruction of what at that time appeared to be our interests
and objectives may be appropriate at this point. National security was a
legitimate interest, but South Vietnam was not vital to the United States.
Peace in the area and a South Vietnam reasonably compatible with our
ideas of democracy were clearly U.S. interests throughout our whole involvement. Once we were deeply committed in 1965, our credibility
worldwide also became an important U.S. interest.

As to U.S. objectives, the one goal that held steady throughout was
to develop a viable nation that could withstand subversion and block communist expansion. (With the example of Yugoslavia, however, the United
States should have realized that the so-called "Communist Bloc" was neither monolithic nor unbreakable. The reality of the Sino-Soviet split should
have been recognized by the U.S. government much sooner than it was.
Moreover, our government should have realized that Hanoi was determined to go its own way regardless of the views of China or the Soviet
union.) Beginning in the early 1960s, this containment objective was reinforced with a new objective of defeating the communist concept of revolutionary war in order to discourage the Soviet Union and China from
further adventures elsewhere. Still another objective in the 1969–73 period was to withdraw U.S. power and achieve "peace with honor," an
essential ingredient of which was to free our prisoners of war and gain
information on our men missing in action.

On the South Vietnamese side, their unchanging interests were survival and independence, their objectives being to eliminate the Viet Cong,
drive out the North Vietnamese Army, and build a strong nation that
could survive. In direct opposition, Hanoi's interests lay in expanding its
own power and enhancing its economic well-being, while pursuing the
objectives of controlling and communizing all of Vietnam, and in the

process eliminating any U.S. influence. As the United States became more deeply committed, this latter objective went far beyond mere elimination to become one of humiliating the United States in the eyes of the world. Of paramount significance was the fact that the survival of the Hanoi regime was never at stake, our topmost leaders having made it perfectly clear through both official statements and U.S. actions that the United States had no intention of invading North Vietnam—a major mistake on our part.

During this period when our civilian and military leaders in Washington were debating and hammering out specific U.S. policies and actions, one of the techniques used was a series of politico-military war games in which senior officials, civilian and military, played specific roles within opposing red and blue teams in various situations. It was during one of these games that General LeMay made the famous proposal to bomb North Vietnam "back to the Stone Age." It was hoped that the games would lend valuable insights into the imponderables of Vietnam, but one serious shortcoming was the almost complete absence of experts on Asia among the players. The reactions of the red teams, representing the Hanoi regime, tended to be rational in terms of American and European occidental philosophy, but hardly representative of dedicated Asian communists.

The overall U.S. command structure for the war in Southeast Asia evolved during 1964 in a pattern which did not change appreciably for the entire war. The Military Assistance Command (MACV) remained a subunified command, that is, a lesser unified command with limited authority and subordinate to a full-fledged unified commander, in this instance the commander-in-chief, Pacific (CINCPAC), whose area of responsibility covered the entire Pacific Ocean from the Aleutian chain through the Strait of Malacca and most of the Indian Ocean, a vast area, indeed. CINCPAC had come into being after the Korean War when the Far Eastern Command was disestablished. The commander-in-chief of this earlier unified command, known as CINCFE, initially General MacArthur, with headquarters in Tokyo, was responsible for the northeast Asia area and directed the Korean War, while CINCPAC, with headquarters at Pearl Harbor and assigned only naval and marine forces, was responsible for the sea lines of communication in the Pacific Ocean area, and supported CINCFE.

The Army had adamantly resisted this change, but lost the interservice battle when the Air Force sided with the Navy and Marines. The Army's objections, which made much sense, were that the area was far too large for one commander, whose headquarters was many thousands of miles from the land areas bordering the western Pacific (the United States was almost as far away); that the CINCPAC solution made sense only in the event of a general nuclear war; and that any limited war (that is, hostilities other than general nuclear war) involving land areas in the western Pacific should be conducted by a unified commander much closer to the scene than Honolulu. Thus, when the United States became involved in ground fighting in Vietnam, albeit vastly different from the fighting in Korea, the Army's very logical argument was that MACV should be a unified commander reporting directly to the secretary of defense and the JCS in Washington, with CINCPAC in a supporting role. There was much support for this view at the time, and our subsequent experience clearly demonstrated that this would have been a greatly improved command structure for conducting the war. But it was not to be.

As it was, the commander of the U.S. Military Assistance Command, Vietnam, (COMUSMACV) directed all U.S. military operations in South Vietnam, including air operations in the "extended battle zone" in the area of the demilitarized zone along the 17th parallel dividing the two Vietnams, but was still subordinate to CINCPAC. Air operations against North Vietnam and in the panhandle of Laos were generally conducted by CINCPAC through the commander of the Pacific Air Forces and the commander of the Pacific Fleet.[8] As a result, undivided responsibility and unified direction of the war were conspicuously absent.

The political side was even more fragmented, with the U.S. ambassadors in Saigon, Vientiane, Phnom Penh, and Bangkok each reporting directly to the secretary of state. The secretary of defense, however, realized that only COMUSMACV had first-hand knowledge of the military situation in South Vietnam, and directed that all MACV communications be sent direct and undiluted to Washington, although CINCPAC normally commented in each instance.

But even within South Vietnam itself, unity of effort was not fully achieved, intelligence being an important area where responsibility was divided. A major reason for this was a U.S. jurisdictional one. In peacetime the CIA station chief in a foreign country normally functions as the senior intelligence adviser to the U.S. ambassador, while in wartime the senior military commander becomes preeminent and CIA assets are turned over to the military. But Vietnam was unique. Legally the United States was not at war, and military assumption of control was never invoked. Although the MACV J-2 and the CIA station chief generally cooperated with each other, duplication of effort and undue competition did occur, with less than optimum results. The lack of an effective combined U.S.-South Vietnamese approach to intelligence also hurt the overall war effort. Nevertheless, on the military side, American and South Vietnamese forces did achieve a measure of coordinated intelligence effort at corps (military region), province, and district levels.

In May 1964 an almost unnoticed but very significant change took place within the U.S. military structure in Vietnam when the Military Assistance and Advisory Group, Vietnam (MAAG-V) was abolished and its functions integrated with HQ MACV. The stated purpose of the action was to achieve unified direction of U.S. military activities by putting all operational and support activities, as well as advisory efforts, directly under MACV. In effect, the operational and advisory channels were merged into a single one, resulting in centralized control of all activities under MACV, but fragmenting the old MAAG-V advisory functions among the numerous staff sections of HQ MACV. The plan came to the attention of the JCS in the spring of 1964, and some doubts were raised as to its wisdom, recalling our experience with the famous KMAG, the U.S. Army Assistance and Advisory Group in Korea, not to mention the Air Force, Navy, and Marine Corps advisory counterparts in that country. Commanded by a senior U.S. Army officer and dedicated purely to building up the South Korea Army, KMAG was kept separate and intact from Headquarters U.S. Eighth Army, which directed all operations. The results, in terms of the development and performance of the Korean Army, speak for themselves.

Despite some misgivings the JCS approved the MACV plan on the grounds that a senior commander, in this instance a subunified commander, but in reality a theater commander, should be allowed wide latitude in organizing his command. The soundness of this move is debatable because it meant that the advisory effort, crucial to the development of the ARVN, would more and more take a back seat as U.S. operational activities expanded in Vietnam.

During this same 1964 period, the major outlines of the overall U.S. military organization in South Vietnam were fixed and no significant changes were made for the rest of MACV's existence. COMUSMACV, a joint commander, also assumed command of all Army forces in Vietnam under a separate hat, designated the commanding general, U.S. Army, Vietnam (USARV). In this way General Westmoreland and his MACV staff directly controlled all U.S. operations; directly commanded all Army elements; directly managed the U.S. assistance and advisory effort; directly performed the politico-military functions of an allied theater commander, overseeing the activities of the numerous allied units and agencies in Vietnam; and directly advised and supported the U.S. ambassador to South Vietnam. The ambassador advised the South Vietnamese government on political, economic, and social matters, and at this time was responsible for the U.S. side of pacification efforts to root out the Viet Cong organization in the country.

As American forces continued to expand in strength and in the scope of their operations, a sounder organization would have kept MACV purely as a joint theater headquarters handling the myriad politico-military matters that arose daily, and working in a close relationship involving daily contact with the U.S. mission in Saigon, while discharging its military responsibilities through subordinate service headquarters—Army, Navy,

Chart 1: U.S. Command Structure
in Southeast Asia, 1967

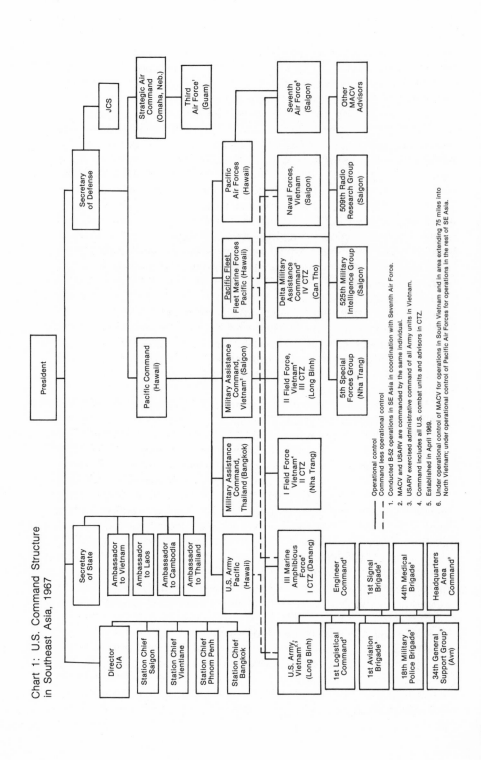

Operational control
Command less operational control

1. Conducted B-52 operations in SE Asia in coordination with Seventh Air Force.
2. MACV and USARV are commanded by the same individual.
3. USARV exercised administrative command of all Army units in Vietnam.
4. Command includes all U.S. combat units and advisors in CTZ.
5. Established in April 1969.
6. Under operational control of MACV for operations in South Vietnam and in area extending 75 miles into North Vietnam; under operational control of Pacific Air Forces for operations in the rest of SE Asia.

Air Force, and Marine Corps. Under such an arrangement, a separate field army type of headquarters would have controlled ground operations, at least U.S. army operations in Vietnam, and a separate army military assistance and advisory group (MAAG) would have handled the advisory mission to the ARVN, the South Vietnamese army.

The primary argument for double-hatting COMUSMACV as both a joint and an Army commander was to parallel the South Vietnamese organization, where the Joint General Staff of the Vietnamese armed forces was both a joint and an Army staff, so that there was no Vietnamese counterpart to USARV HQ. This is a cogent, logical reason, but centralizing all these vital functions under one man, COMUSMACV, seriously overloaded the top U.S. commander and his staff, and precluded continuous priority attention on the part of senior personnel to each major responsibility. The Army chief of staff, General Johnson, strongly favored the establishment of a separate army component commander under COMUSMACV, but was unable to persuade his JCS colleagues to insist on such a command arrangement.

Early in 1964, while American leaders in Saigon focused on stabilizing the situation in South Vietnam and were lukewarm about the United States taking direct action against North Vietnam, American officials in Washington discussed in increasingly serious tones the necessity of not only an intensified counterinsurgency campaign in South Vietnam, to include even U.S. ground combat forces, but also air and naval attacks against North Vietnam. The JCS, feeling that the situation was urgent, proposed drastic measures against North Vietnam. Although no such actions were approved by President Johnson at the time, he did direct that plans be prepared for retaliatory air strikes on short notice. He also told the secretary of defense to develop longer-term, more deliberate plans for full-scale air attacks. By June 1964 the JCS had received CINCPAC's recommendations and had developed a comprehensive target list for air operations against North Vietnam which became the basis for JCS planning for an air war. But it was not until the controversial incidents in the Tonkin Gulf in early August that the president authorized the first attack, a small naval air strike against a few selected military targets in the North. It was a major juncture in our involvement.

The role of air power was one of the most debated subjects within the JCS arena during this period. In terms of opposing North Vietnamese air forces, there never was any question that the United States could establish air superiority, nor was there ever any real enemy air threat to our position in South Vietnam. In terms of defense, however, with the aid of massive support, principally from the Soviet Union, Hanoi eventually developed the most formidable air defenses our forces had ever encountered. Thus the price of admission for our attacking forces ultimately became very high, almost prohibitive, especially before the advent of our so-called "smart bombs." It was no doubt their lack of an offensive air capability that led the North Vietnamese to introduce into the ground war in the South large calibre rockets, heavy artillery, and heavy mortars, which often were employed against urban areas rather than specific military targets. These weapons constituted North Vietnamese "air power," to retaliate for U.S.-RVN air attacks in the North, which, although targeted against military objectives, could not completely avoid inflicting civilian casualties.

In their debate the JCS addressed the two major elements of the air war—an offensive against North Vietnam itself in terms of its war-making capacity and its will to carry on the war in the South, and an interdiction campaign to impede the flow of North Vietnamese troops, equipment, and supplies to South Vietnam via the Laotian panhandle or directly across the demilitarized zone. Our foremost airpower exponents, unwavering in their beliefs, were the Air Force and the Marine Corps, which believed that an allout air offensive not only could make North Vietnam incapable of further fighting, but could also compel its leaders to cease and desist in the South. The Army never fully shared this view, and it is doubtful that the Navy was completely convinced. North Vietnam did not possess the industrial development to justify strategic bombing, and practically all of its war materiel needed for either conventional or guerrilla warfare came from the Soviet Union or China. Historically, strategic bombing has achieved only limited success against even modern, industrialized states, as the U.S. Strategic Bombing Surveys conducted after World War II attest with respect to both the European and the Pacific theaters.[9] The Army was also keenly aware of the historically experienced limitations of air interdiction, particularly when conducted remotely from any ground operations. Consequently the Army was highly skeptical that such air operations would be effective in Southeast Asia, especially in view of the infiltration tactics and techniques used by the North Vietnamese, the dense nature of the terrain, and the highly redundant road-trail-waterway network found in the area. The Navy shared these reservations and moreover pointed out the extreme difficulty of stopping infiltration by sea where literally thousands of small junks and watercraft were available.

Yet despite the fact that unanimity did not really exist among the chiefs with respect to the air war, the JCS consistently submitted agreed recommendations to the secretary of defense and ultimately to the president. Why? One plausible explanation is that the JCS felt that the situation was growing more desperate, that strong military actions were required to save the day, and that therefore a unanimously supported position was necessary if their recommendations were to carry any weight with their civilian superiors. There is considerable logic to this rationale, but it has serious drawbacks as well. In circumstances as grave as committing the United States to war, it is dangerous to infer that an agreed course of action has been recommended when in fact there are serious differences of opinion as to how best to proceed. To conceal such basic differences existing among the chiefs from their civilian leadership was a disservice.

Wheeler favored the agreed-position approach and often persuaded the chiefs to forgo their objections in favor of a united view, on the theory that forwarding the split views of the JCS risked either accomplishing nothing or inviting the civilian authorities to make decisions on military matters which they were not as well qualified to make. But this argument does not hold water. Where there are fundamental differences of opinion among the chiefs, the political leaders should know so that they do not embark on a murky path with unclear consequences. There are times when doing nothing is better than doing the wrong thing. At any rate, the JCS persuaded themselves that they should pursue the air war solution on the grounds that all could agree at least that it was worth the effort and that there was no harm in trying it.[10]

CINCPAC consistently recommended and supported sustained air operations against North Vietnam but, recognizing the lack of truly strategic targets, initially emphasized the attack on lines of communications running through North Vietnam and the Laotian panhandle. U.S. leaders in Saigon did not fully share Washington's views as to the wisdom of air strikes in the North, but agreed, as did South Vietnamese leaders, that such attacks would raise the morale of the South Vietnamese.

In contrast, the employment of U.S. and RVN tactical airpower in support of the ground war in the South was not so controversial a subject as long as military targets were attacked and the risk of civilian casualties and damage was minimized. In the later war years after most U.S. forces had been withdrawn, U.S. airpower in support of South Vietnamese forces became a critical element of South Vietnam's ability to survive increasingly heavy and widespread enemy attacks employing modern, sophisticated armaments.

Just before the 1964 U.S. elections, the Viet Cong on 1 November mortared U.S. aircraft and facilities at the Bien Hoa airbase near Saigon, inflicting considerable damage. It appeared to be a deliberate act of escalation against the United States. The JCS wanted to retaliate with an allout air attack on North Vietnam and to introduce Marine and Army ground troops for the security of American personnel and facilities in the South. But President Johnson understandably demurred in taking any action until after the election, and still would not act when a Viet Cong bomb exploded in a U.S. billet in Saigon, the Brink Hotel, on Christmas Eve 1964, causing severe casualties. It was not until the 7 February 1965, enemy attack on the U.S. advisory compound and airfield at Camp Holloway near Pleiku in the Central Highlands that the president decided he had sufficient reason (some say pretext) to move. The resulting U.S.-RVN reprisal by air was swift and heavy against targets just north of the DMZ.

An amusing sidelight occurred when the JCS met to act on the president's instructions. Succumbing temporarily to the temptation to act as operations officers, the chiefs set to work drafting a message to CINC-PAC. As the minutes ticked by (it was about 3:00 P.M. in Washington, 9:00 A.M. in Honolulu, and 3:00 A.M. in the operational area in Southeast Asia) and questions came up as to the time of attack, the weather en route to and in the objective area, and other pertinent factors, the chiefs were making little progress writing their own operational order. Finally LeMay threw up his hands and bellowed, "For Christ's sake, what do we have a staff for? By the time we get this message out, it will be too late to do anything!" That broke the tension—we all laughed—and that sensible solution ended the JCS meeting. The Joint Staff did get the message out on time after Wheeler cleared it with the secretary of defense. The chairman also alerted CINCPAC, Admiral Ulysses S.G. Sharp, by secure voice telephone.

Undeterred by the U.S. air attack, the Viet Cong struck an even heavier blow on 11 February 1965 against a hotel in Qui Nhon used as an American troop billet. This in turn triggered what amounted to a sustained U.S. air war against North Vietnam, albeit of varying intensity and punctuated with numerous so-called "bombing pauses" calculated as much to appease domestic and international opinion as to obtain a more cooperative response from Hanoi. In mid-February 1965 the president publicly announced that the U.S. and RVN were engaged in an air offensive against North Vietnam, given the name "Rolling Thunder." A parallel air war was conducted against military targets in the Laotian panhandle. These latter operations, named "Barrel Roll," had already started on a limited scale in December 1964.[11] Recognizing that the United States and the North Vietnamese-Viet Cong were now directly at war with each other, the president made a corollary decision to bring American dependents home, and by Valentine's Day 1965 they had all departed.

A steady buildup of U.S. airpower based in South Vietnam and Thailand and on carriers at sea was soon underway. But the allout, constant pounding which the JCS consistently recommended was carried out on a graduated basis. B-52 strategic bombers of the Strategic Air Command (SAC) were added to the tactical air arsenal in June 1965. Command relationships were even more complicated, for these operations were conducted under the direct command of SAC.[12] The B-52s were employed primarily against enemy troops in the hinterlands away from populated areas. Their bombing accuracy was extraordinary, and when target intelligence was good and surprise was achieved the results were devastating. In fact, some intelligence reports indicated that this was the weapon feared most by the enemy.

Unfortunately, however, all too frequently the enemy had advance knowledge of the time and place of the strike and took effective defensive measures. It was uncanny how the Viet Cong and the North Vietnamese were able to defeat our security precautions, which were not as good as they should have been. Generally such security breaches occurred because of careless talk by Americans about pending operations over open, unsecure communication channels, although at times the penetration of U.S. operational headquarters by enemy agents was suspected. There was also the simple fact that SAC flight plans on world airways had to be reported to appropriate authorities en route as though our bombers were civilian air carriers.

With respect to the air war, U.S. political leaders, particularly in the 1965–67 period, kept very tight control over American military leaders. As a matter of fact, President Johnson would not delegate this control to anyone outside the White House, and for most of his presidency remained the target officer. Ironically, the commander-in-chief eventually approved practically all of the targets on the JCS-CINCPAC list, but the overall impact was lessened by the piecemeal application of airpower which lacked the mass, surprise, consistency, and sustained nature espoused by the JCS.

But even before the U.S. bombing offensive began in early 1965, and very probably before the Tonkin Gulf incidents of August 1964, the evidence indicates that Hanoi had already decided to escalate the war in the South, hoping to exploit the deteriorating situation following Diem's assassination. Individual North Vietnamese soldiers marched south to bolster Viet Cong units, along with complete North Vietnamese Army (NVA) combat and logistic units. The presence of NVA troop units in the South, although suspected earlier, was not fully confirmed by MACV intelligence until December 1964.[13]

Hanoi, beginning in mid-1964 and using materiel furnished by the Soviet Union and China, also decided to upgrade the Viet Cong, introducing among other weapons the famous Soviet AK-47 assault rifle. The first Viet Cong unit of division size, the renowned 9th Viet Cong Division, operating in the general area north of Saigon, was formed in the latter part of 1964.

Outgunned South Vietnamese forces were equipped with World War II vintage arms, including the U.S. M-1 rifle. Upgrading ARVN and paramilitary forces, however, lagged far behind and did not begin until late 1967, when the first sizable shipment of U.S. M-16 rifles arrived in South Vietnam. It should be noted that the Republic of Vietnam was divided administratively into forty-four provinces under the political, military, and administrative control of province chiefs, who acted as military governors. Province chiefs had their own full-time forces called Regional Forces (RF). Each province was further subdivided into districts under a district chief. The next lower entity was the village, which usually consisted of several hamlets. Popular Forces (PF) were the part-time militia organized for the relatively static local defense of hamlets and villages.

The "Rolling Thunder" operations of early 1965 had little effect on the war in the South, other than to raise South Vietnamese morale temporarily, and there was no letup from enemy pressure. Since U.S. airpower was the only means at hand to reverse the dangerous trend in the South, MACV's natural concern was to secure the more forward, exposed allied air bases in South Vietnam. Accordingly, early in 1965 a U.S. Marine Hawk Missile Bn was deployed for air defense of the U.S. Marine air base in the Danang area. Then in February 1965, concerned about the ground defense of the Danang air base, Westmoreland asked for two Marine infantry battalions, the first American ground combat troops destined for Vietnam. Ambassador Taylor was opposed to the plan, correctly foreseeing that once the United States assumed any ground combat role there would be an ever-growing U.S. commitment, an American tendency to take over the war, and a subsequent temptation for the South Vietnamese to "let Uncle Sam do it." Sensitive to the French failure, Taylor also saw grave problems for the American GI in adjusting to an oriental environment and a strange, unconventional war.[14]

But Washington approved Westmoreland's request and in early March both Marine battalions came ashore along with a headquarters ultimately known as the III Marine Amphibious Force. Employing the Marines ashore in the northern provinces of South Vietnam (in I Corps Tactical Zone) was consistent with CINCPAC's contingency plans for Southeast Asia, and Westmoreland basically agreed with the rationale provided by CINCPAC. This set the pattern for the entire war with respect to the role and employment of American Marines, committing them to a sustained land campaign totally removed from their normal amphibious role.

Meanwhile, in mid-February 1965 General Johnson, the Army chief of staff, sent me to the area, where I spent about a week in Thailand and Laos and two weeks in South Vietnam. The trip was a sobering eye opener for me. After private discussions with Westmoreland and his MACV chief of staff, Major General Richard G. Stilwell, I visited all four South Vietnamese corps tactical zones (CTZs), from I Corps in the north to IV Corps in the Delta, conferring with U.S. advisers and their counterpart ARVN commanders from corps to regimental level.

The overall picture was clear—unless the situation was reversed soon, South Vietnam would not survive. North-south roads and other communications lines, including the north-south railroad running along the coast, were cut in innumerable places by the Viet Cong, especially in the heavily populated coastal areas of I and II CTZs, and normal social and economic life was almost totally disrupted. In many areas the marketplace was dead and the schools were not operating. Political and social institutions were slowly being strangled, while demoralized government forces desperately tried to defend district and provincial capitals, many swollen with large numbers of refugees from subverted or contested areas in the countryside. In most areas government forces exercised control only in daylight hours, while a shadow Viet Cong government took over at night.

In III CTZ, a responsibility of III Corps (ARVN), which included Saigon and the upper Delta, typical Viet Cong operations, for example, might involve main force VC units secretly concentrating in one of the enemy war zones in the region, launching a surprise attack against a government installation, and then rapidly retreating into one of the numerous sanctuary base areas just across the Cambodian border. Viet Cong regular (main force) units operating in South Vietnam, as they became larger, more highly organized, and better equipped, needed safe base areas where they could rest, train, conduct political indoctrination, and prepare for further operations. The older base areas inside South Vietnam were often called "war zones." These bases were usually found within striking distance by foot troops of major population centers. Sometimes they boasted elaborate, concealed, or even deep underground facilities, such as command posts, ammunition and other supply dumps, and hospitals; and at times these installations were connected by tunnel complexes.

There was disturbing evidence of an enemy buildup in the northern provinces of I CTZ and of impending enemy plans to seize a large sector in the Central Highlands of II CTZ. South Vietnamese casualties were mounting, and ARVN troops, many discouraged, inept, and poorly led, simply could not handle the situation. To the Americans on the scene in Vietnam it seemed obvious that if the United States wanted to preserve the Republic of Vietnam, the only means available was to commit U.S. ground combat troops.

A critical weakness apparent in MACV at the time was the lack of an adequate U.S. intelligence capability that could focus on the war on the ground. Moreover, the South Vietnamese intelligence service, virtually destroyed when Diem was overthrown, had not yet recovered. The U.S. Army, which earlier had developed a credible ground order of battle on enemy forces in Southeast Asia, in the late 1950s shifted the responsibility for this task to U.S. Army, Pacific (USARPAC) in Hawaii, anticipating the loss of the Army's intelligence analytical capabilities to the Defense Intelligence Agency (DIA) when it was established in October 1961 with a U.S. Air Force officer as its first director. Predictably, DIA showed little interest in the subject. Then USARPAC, lacking the personnel resources and believing that MACV (established in February 1962) was assuming the responsibility, ceased work on the ground order of battle in Southeast Asia. The first MACV J-2 was an Air Force officer who was not interested in ground intelligence, so that area was relatively neglected until the summer of 1965 (after my visit to Vietnam) when the first experienced Army intelligence officer was assigned as J-2 MACV.

Thus a hiatus existed for about six years with respect to work on the ground order of battle in Southeast Asia. Considering the central importance of such intelligence, particularly in the kind of warfare being waged in Vietnam, this performance was inexcusable.

In early 1965, however, Westmoreland was no less worried about Saigon's political instability, with the attendant, never-ending nightmare of another coup. In a private lunch we had at his Saigon villa during this period, he seemed preoccupied with the coup threat and almost fatalistic about the prospect of an endless power struggle. Dressed in short-sleeved, olive drab, tropical worsted shirt and trousers, the handsome, well-built, and very youthful-looking Westmoreland was an impressive figure. Supremely self-confident, forceful, and incisive, with a classical jutting jaw and a long scar on his left cheek, he certainly looked the part of a four-star Army general. But Westmoreland was more than just a fine physical specimen; he was thoughtful, sensitive, and very shrewd. Many have underestimated him. One weakness was a preoccupation with his public image, not seeming to realize that a good record speaks for itself and that public impressions can be very fragile things.

Westmoreland was also a good judge of people and usually picked outstanding men for key command and staff jobs. Typical was his MACV chief of staff, Dick Stilwell, brilliant, tough, and soldierly, whose gaze could become uncomfortably penetrating. The blond, stocky Stilwell had one failing, shared with Westmoreland—both men were "workaholics." Stilwell was known to work until he fell asleep at his desk or in his chair, and often spent the night in his office, sleeping on a couch or on the floor.

Not long after I returned to the United States from Saigon, my boss, General Johnson, recommended to the JCS the commitment of one American division to defend the Central Highlands and hold coastal enclaves to the east, and a multinational four-division force, including U.S. troops, to man defensive positions south of the DMZ and to overwatch the Laotian border area to the west, thereby impeding the movement of enemy forces from the North into South Vietnam. After studying his report, the JCS in mid-March 1965 proposed sending two U.S. divisions and one South Korean division to South Vietnam for offensive combat operations, leaving the question of where and how to employ these forces for Westmoreland to decide. This was the chiefs' first recommendation for a major ground combat commitment in South Vietnam.[15]

Meanwhile, Westmoreland was faced with the immediate problem of assuring adequate security for the U.S. Air Force base at Bien Hoa near Saigon in III CTZ. He pressed for the deployment of a U.S. Army brigade for this task and suggested the 173rd Airborne Brigade stationed on Okinawa. Although its deployment was opposed by State, and General Taylor, our ambassador in Saigon, objected to the way the matter was handled, the decision was made to commit the brigade. In May 1965 it arrived in Bien Hoa, the first U.S. Army ground combat unit to fight in Vietnam. (The security of Tan Son Nhut, the other large air base in the Saigon area, which was used jointly by the Americans and the Vietnamese, remained the responsibility of the South Vietnamese.)

The specific role of U.S. ground troops and the tactics they would use were not clearly delineated, however. The question basically revolved around whether they would be used in a static defensive role, avoiding casualties and limiting their involvement, or in a mobile offensive role. A variation of the former, called by some the "enclave" concept, was advocated by Ambassador Taylor and would have allowed offensive operations in the vicinity of U.S. enclaves, or base areas generally near the coast. Taylor was concerned about the potentially disastrous psychological impact on the South Vietnamese if the Americans took over the fighting; moreover, he favored limiting U.S. involvement until a clearer picture of the situation emerged.[16] There was a brief period during the spring of 1965 when the offensive employment of American troops was restricted, but Westmoreland's persistent, forceful recommendations to "take the war to the enemy," using U.S. forces offensively while ARVN forces protected the populace, gained support and ultimate approval in Washington.

In a crucial July 1965 meeting in Saigon, McNamara and Westmoreland agreed on an American troop level of about three and one-half division equivalents (totalling about 200,000 troops) to be reached by the end of 1965, hoping that this would stabilize the ground situation.[17] Henry Cabot Lodge, already designated to take over in Saigon from Ambassador Taylor, accompanied McNamara to the meeting and agreed to the recommended force buildup.

These early U.S. force requirements, originating primarily from HQ MACV in Saigon and generally supported by the JCS, precipitated an intense but short internal government debate in Washington in July 1965. Apparently it was the only full-blown, top-level examination of U.S. objectives and strategy until after the enemy Tet offensive of 1968. The president's advisers at home were divided, and in Vietnam Ambassador Taylor was not enthusiastic. In fact, Taylor preferred a slower U.S. troop buildup and wanted to limit U.S. ground operations to small areas around specific U.S. enclaves. Finally, after almost continuous consultations in late July with his advisers, cabinet members, and congressional leaders, the president on 28 July 1965 approved a U.S. troop level of 175,000 and granted Westmoreland freedom to maneuver his forces as he saw fit.[18]

The die was now cast and the United States was committed to a showdown on Vietnamese soil. No longer was the United States pursuing the more limited objective of denying the enemy victory in the South and convincing him he could not win; the U.S. objective now was to defeat the enemy in the South, relying primarily on American troops. Unfortunately these actions gave the impression that the United States lacked confidence in the South Vietnamese government and its forces, and that the United States intended to win the war on its own.

During this period of escalating U.S. troop buildup, Hanoi responded with a stepped-up flow of forces from the North. (U.S. intelligence in April 1965 made its first, positive identification of a major NVA unit in the South—a regiment of the 325th NVA Division—located in the Central Highlands.) It was a fast-moving situation, and the JCS found themselves caught in the middle between a steady stream of requests from MACV for more troops and rising resistance to such requests surfacing in Washington.[19] The chiefs could see that there was a growing discrepancy between the total forces needed to meet U.S. commitments worldwide and the manpower base the civilian leadership was willing to provide.

In an effort to reconcile this imbalance within the U.S. defense establishment, the JCS made several proposals in August 1965. They advocated an overall strategic concept of U.S. military operations in Southeast Asia that visualized three tasks: (1) compel Hanoi to "cease and desist" in the South; (2) defeat the Viet Cong in South Vietnam and extend government control over all of the South; and (3) deter China from intervening and defeat any intervention should one occur. To support these tasks the JCS pressed for a partial mobilization (reserve callup) not only to provide a sustaining base for U.S. forces in Southeast Asia, but also to reconstitute a strategic reserve of U.S. forces at home.[20]

The chiefs visualized a sustained air and naval campaign against North Vietnam and its lines of communications to its forces in the South— roads, railroads, and waterways—to include a blockade of North Vietnam, as well as land and air actions in Laos and Cambodia to stop the movement of enemy troops and supplies. They also visualized a U.S. logistic effort in Thailand to deter any Chinese aggression by preparing a U.S. logistic base in advance of any commitment of American combat forces in Thailand. The chiefs consistently and doggedly pressed the adoption of this overall strategic concept on the secretary of defense and the president, but to no avail; their recommendations were never fully accepted.

In his book *A Soldier Reports* (1976), General Westmoreland described his strategy as essentially a war of attrition. He argued, quite rationally, that he had no alternative under the national policy adopted by the United States. He recognized that such a strategy meant a long, protracted struggle and that demonstrating progress in such an indefinite conflict to an impatient American people was extremely difficult.[21]

But to prevail in such a war of attrition assumes that one can inflict greater casualties than the enemy's manpower resources can replace and that eventually the enemy's strength—economic, societal, and military—will wither away. Yet at the height of the fighting in Vietnam, during the 1967–69 period, when casualties were highest on both sides, there was no compelling evidence that North Vietnam was hurting for manpower to keep on fighting. On the contrary, the indications were that the North could suffer frightful losses and still replace them quantitatively. There was no doubt a decline in the quality of enemy leadership, however; it takes time to develop leaders and there is no shortcut to experience, but raw manpower was not Hanoi's Achilles' heel.

In assessing North Vietnam's capabilities to fight a prolonged, grinding war of attrition, the CIA during the period 1964–72 consistently concluded that the North Vietnamese manpower base was adequate. (In 1967–68, North Vietnam's population exceeded eighteen million, while South Vietnam effectively controlled only about twelve million people.) The CIA pointed out that North Vietnam's own industry contributed only marginally to the war effort, practically all material support coming from the Soviet Union or China; that the diversion of substantial manpower to a very large air defense effort and to the large work force required to repair damage from U.S. air attacks was manageable; that North Vietnamese force levels had been readily expanded to keep pace with the allied troop buildup in the South; and that Hanoi's available manpower resources were clearly adequate to sustain the war indefinitely.[22]

Because of the peculiar geography of Vietnam, the unlimited mission of defending all of the South and defeating the enemy wherever found imposed a very severe logistic problem on the United States and had a synergistic effect in terms of the demand on American manpower and other resources. The elongated narrow conformation of the country, resembling a scimitar, with over 1,400 miles of coastline and about 900 miles of land border, but only 50 to 150 miles wide, results in little depth anywhere for the purpose of defense against overt attack; moreover, such a geographic configuration makes the country extremely vulnerable to infiltration from outside its borders. This geography, plus enemy tactics of making numerous cuts in South Vietnam's main roads and along its only railroad, running generally parallel to and close to the coast, add up to a logistic nightmare.

It simply was not feasible to establish one major logistic port-base area in the South from which supplies could flow overland to the rest of the country. In order to support large operations in every region it was necessary to establish a half-dozen major port-base areas, plus several more minor ones, from which supplies moved inland rather than parallel to the coast. The greatly increased demand for all kinds of logistic troops, port and transportation, engineer construction, communications, and medical units, as well as for security forces to defend these vulnerable areas, was inevitable.

This far-flung troop deployment-logistic problem was exacerbated by the construction of numerous bases for Vietnamese Civilian Irregular Defense Groups (CIDG) and U.S. Special Forces, most with their own C-130 capable airfields, throughout South Vietnam. Sited in isolated locations along the inland border or near enemy infiltration routes, these bases provided an important opportunity to acquire intelligence on enemy troop movements in the border areas. But the bases were extremely vulnerable to attack and difficult to reinforce with troops or support with tactical airpower because of their remoteness. Thus they constituted still another demand on resources, as well as a prime potential for American and South Vietnamese casualties. In terms of their overall contribution, the value of some of these bases was questionable, and a few were more of a liability than an asset. The large numbers of elite American special forces troopers absorbed in this mission drained off quality leadership and talents that could have been better used elsewhere as advisers or in U.S. units.

In any case, the kind of war that the United States had decided to fight within the boundaries of South Vietnam, coupled with the willingness and ability of North Vietnam to match any U.S. force increase, guaranteed a spiraling escalation of U.S. troop requirements. The JCS did their best to meet these needs from the limited resources available to the services, but the secretary of defense approved *only* those force levels that could be achieved without a reserve callup.[23] Thus a gap developed between the perceived troop requirements and approved force levels. The resulting frustration of the chiefs over the mobilization issue was particularly severe and reached crisis proportions in the fall of 1967, when the chiefs reportedly considered resignation en masse in protest.

In short, there seems to have been insufficient timely discussion in Washington as to how and for what purpose U.S. forces were to be employed in South Vietnam, that is, the U.S. strategy to be pursued in conducting the crucial ground war in a decisive way.

In his book, *Swords and Ploughshares*, Taylor comments frankly and with a little bitterness on this aspect. He makes several references to the 1965–68 period, when he served as special consultant to President Johnson. Taylor's first comment, referring to the latter part of 1965, expresses particular concern over the ramifications of the JCS concept for extending Saigon's control over all of South Vietnam, encompassing the "remote vastness of the Vietnamese frontiers" where the enemy would be close to his cross-border bases and where the terrain favored his unconventional tactics. Referring to the 1966–67 period, Taylor relates that each year Westmoreland submitted his campaign plan for the following year, but that it was not given any substantive review in Washington.[24]

Looking back at this period (1965–67), I have often wondered why General Taylor was seemingly unable to convince President Johnson that the U.S. strategy was a losing one. Taylor had been successively President Kennedy's special adviser, chairman of the JCS, U.S. ambassador to Saigon, and President Johnson's special consultant. (Taylor calls this latter position a "lame duck" consultant, partially answering my question.) Clearly Taylor not only knew the problems and pitfalls but also was in a position to wield great influence. The nagging question, though, remains—why was he not more successful in bringing about a sounder strategic approach to the war?

But by the end of 1966 McNamara did indeed recognize the open-ended nature of the U.S. ground force commitment and persuaded the president that a numerical limit should be placed on the number of U.S. forces in the theater of operations. And so by early 1967 a troop ceiling had been imposed on U.S. forces in South Vietnam, to be implemented by increments but not to be reached until June 1968.[25] This ceiling, set at 470,000, almost a half million American troops, nevertheless constituted a massive U.S. commitment. Significantly, that ceiling did more or less set the extent of our commitment, which peaked at approximately 550,000 in the aftermath of the enemy Tet offensive of 1968.

Historically, strategic concepts and initial operational planning for overseas expeditions are developed at the Washington level until the senior military commander is established overseas in the assigned theater of operations. Theater planning is obviously subject to limitations on the size, composition, and nature of the forces that can be made available. But it is Washington's responsibility to see that ends and means are kept in balance—that the strategic objectives under the strategic concept adopted are achievable with the forces and other resources expected to be available.

In the Vietnam War, however, the JCS (and the services) in a sense lost control of U.S. force generation. McNamara and Westmoreland, for example, might agree on the nature and composition of the force within a specific overall strength level without benefit of any JCS or service advice. But in the end the JCS and the services had to pick up the pieces; that is, determine the source of the additional combat forces and supporting units, determine their state of readiness and training for deployment overseas, and develop the movement plans in accordance with the priority of need in Vietnam.

From a global perspective, the JCS in a sense also lost control of the overall strategic direction of American armed forces as the burgeoning force demands of Southeast Asia quickly consumed the strategic reserves of forces in the United States previously earmarked for the reinforcement of Europe or Korea, or for an unforeseen contingency elsewhere. The inevitable result was a very serious strategic imbalance in U.S. force deployments worldwide.

The JCS seemed to be unable to articulate an effective military strategy that they could persuade the commander-in-chief and secretary of defense to adopt. In the end the theater commander—in effect, General Westmoreland—made successive requests for larger and larger force levels without benefit of an overall concept and plan. The chiefs (and the services), in turn, could only review these force requirements in a strategic vacuum without a firm feel for what the ultimate requirement might be, and without knowing what level of commitment would be acceptable to the American people and their elected leaders.

Finally, there was one glaring omission in the advice the JCS provided the president and the secretary of defense. It is an obvious omission, but more importantly, a profoundly significant one. Not once during the war did the JCS advise the commander-in-chief or the secretary of defense that the strategy being pursued most probably would fail and that the United States would be unable to achieve its objectives. The only explanation of this failure is that the chiefs were imbued with the "can do" spirit and could not bring themselves to make such a negative statement or to appear to be disloyal.[26]

2

1967: Corps Command, Vietnam

After the fateful decisions of 1965, American forces were deployed to Vietnam in a steady stream as fast as units could be brought to a state of combat readiness; and by mid-1967 American combat troops were heavily engaged in much of South Vietnam. In April 1965 I had been ordered from the Washington scene to the Dominican Republic to command the U.S. forces operating there during the period 1965–66.[1] My Dominican adventure was followed by a year (1966–67) commanding the XVIII Airborne Corps at Fort Bragg, North Carolina, where we were very much concerned with readying units of every description for service in Vietnam. Thus, during much of the 1965–1966 period I was out of the mainstream of developments that shaped the American intervention in the Vietnam War. Sooner or later, however, I expected to be ordered to Vietnam; the only questions were when and in what capacity.

In early 1967 President Johnson decided to replace Ambassador Lodge in Saigon with the renowned Ellsworth Bunker, our most experienced and respected diplomat at the time. Bunker and I had served together in the Dominican Republic during the 1965 crisis, when he bailed the United States (and President Johnson) out of a very difficult situation. Tall, slim, and urbane, Bunker was a superb diplomat with unlimited patience and tenacity, and with more than his share of physical and moral courage. His erect carriage and nimbleness on the tennis court belied his seventy-odd years at the time. One of the qualities I found most likeable was his earthy, New England sense of humor. Our relationship in the Dominican Republic was close and candid, and I developed a great admiration for this truly remarkable patriot. Once the Dominican problem seemed to be settled, we used to joke about which one of us would be ordered to Vietnam first.

Years later, in June 1981, Ambassador Bunker told me that in January 1967, when President Johnson asked him to go to Saigon, the president said that Bunker's mission would be to wind up the war for American troops as quickly as possible. The president apparently did not elaborate on what might constitute an acceptable South Vietnamese security posture which would allow U.S. troops to return home. It was a private conversation with only the two men present.[2]

Bunker's new assignment was announced just before the Guam conference of 20 March 1967, when President Johnson introduced his new team to the South Vietnamese leaders, Thieu and his vice president, Nguyen Cao Ky. (Whereas Thieu was an ARVN general, Ky was an air vice marshal in the Vietnamese Air Force.) Eugene Locke, a vigorous Texan with considerable background in overseeing U.S. economic aid in foreign lands, was to be Bunker's deputy, while Robert Komer, an aggressive, outspoken ex-CIA official, who had been handling Southeast Asia affairs on the National Security Council staff in the White House, was to be given the rank of ambassador and placed in charge of the pacification program. General Westmoreland would assume control of the pacification program from the U.S. mission in Saigon and Ambassador Komer would become a civilian deputy for pacification under Westmoreland. This unprecedented and far-reaching decision was not formally announced, however, until Bunker's arrival in Saigon on 25 May 1967.[3]

The Guam conferees discussed pacification, military operations, and other Republic of Vietnam government programs, with the principal focus on the prospects for the war and the new U.S. organization in Saigon. Westmoreland presented a grim assessment: unless North Vietnamese infiltration into the South could be stopped, the war could go on indefinitely. Nevertheless, the president clearly indicated his intentions: he would no longer go along with continuing escalation of the war by increasing U.S. troop commitments, or invading Laos or Cambodia to stop infiltration, or stepping up the bombing against North Vietnam; rather he intended to reduce the U.S. troop presence and shift the burden of the war to the South Vietnamese. According to Bunker, Westmoreland was quite aware of the president's intentions.[4] Later in the spring of 1967, General Westmoreland submitted his proposals for a minimum essential force of about 550,000 American military personnel and an optimum force of 670,000, the latter promising a greater chance of success over a shorter span of time. But the president, true to his Guam position of capping American troop strength, approved only the minimum force, with a ceiling of 525,000.

Bunker's revelations to me in June 1981 threw quite a different light on the period and came as a distinct surprise. In early 1967 it seemed clear enough that the president was unwilling to widen the war, that his objectives were limited, that he realized that the prospect of a protracted war was not going down well with the American people, and that he was deeply troubled about growing dissent. Nevertheless, I was under the impression in early 1967 that the president's determination to prosecute the war was strong and that he did not look for a lesser way out until much later in 1967, when Secretary of Defense McNamara, concluding that the ground war strategy had not worked, proposed a whole new approach to the war. McNamara's views no doubt had a great influence not only on the president's thinking but also on many other influential people near the president. In early 1968 the president's inside advisers, headed by Clark Clifford, the new secretary of defense, raised serious questions about U.S. policy toward Vietnam. And later in 1968 the so-called "wise men," a group of senior U.S. officials including former Secretary of State Dean Acheson, reviewed the Vietnam situation for President Johnson. The wise men responded by recommending a basic change in U.S. strategy.[5]

Senior American military and civilian officials in Washington in early 1967 were also debating the top military organization for U.S. forces in Vietnam. The Army chief of staff, General Johnson, wanted to establish a truly separate U.S. Army component commander (four stars) in Vietnam, leaving Westmoreland as the joint theater commander but divesting him of his Army command hat. Under this organization the deputy commander of MACV would remain at three-star level and a separate four-star field army commander would be established. The Air Force was much interested in the deputy MACV commander slot, but Secretary McNamara made it quite clear that only an Army officer would succeed Westmoreland as COMUSMACV. Later the Air Force settled for a double-hat arrangement whereby the commander of the 7th Air Force also functioned as MACV's deputy commander for air. Westmoreland, however, did not want a separate field army command established in Vietnam, and his desires prevailed. Moreover, he liked the arrangement of a four-star MACV deputy and definitely favored the Army vice chief of staff, General Creighton W. Abams, as his logical successor. And that's the way it went when Abrams's assignment to be deputy COMUSMACV was announced in April 1967.

Meanwhile in February 1967 I was ordered to proceed from Fort Bragg to Vietnam for a position not revealed to me at the time, apparently because the high-level debate over the ultimate U.S. organization in Vietnam had not yet been resolved. Arriving in Saigon in early March 1967, I reported to General Westmoreland, who assigned me to command II Field Force Vietnam (II FFV), actually a U.S. Army corps headquarters, given the field force designation to avoid confusion with the ARVN corps headquarters responsible for Vietnamese military operations. There were four ARVN corps headquarters, numbered I through IV from north to south, whose boundaries coincided with the four administrative areas established by the South Vietnamese government for overall political control of the country. These areas were called military regions (MRs), likewise numbered I through IV from north to south, with boundaries so drawn as to give each MR a cross-section of South Vietnam extending from the seacoast to the interior border with Laos or Cambodia. For military purposes the same areas were called corps tactical zones (CTZs). The ARVN corps commanders, three-star ARVN generals, were also military region governors responsible for civil administration. Exercising both political and military control, they enjoyed great authority and prestige. They reported directly to Saigon—the president at the palace on political matters, and the Joint General Staff (JGS) for military affairs.

U.S. field force boundaries coincided with ARVN corps boundaries, and the U.S. field force commanders, three-star generals, were double-hatted as the senior U.S. advisers to the ARVN corps commanders operating in their respective areas. Since General Westmoreland had opted to forgo operational control of South Vietnamese forces, this meant that within a corps tactical zone American and Vietnamese operations, although coordinated, were normally conducted independently of each other. Some CTZs also contained troops of other foreign nations, called Free World forces, which generally were assigned specific areas of operations. Since Westmoreland declined to seek operational control of these forces, their operations were conducted likewise on a coordinated basis rather than under the control of the U.S field force commander.

Increasing the complexity of command and control were the province and district chiefs, political heads of subordinate administrative areas within each military region, who conducted operations with their own regional or local forces, paramilitary in nature. These chiefs reported to the ARVN corps commanders and were responsible to them for military operations as well as for pacification.

In his book *A Soldier Reports*, Westmoreland presents a strong, practical case for his not seeking operational control of all forces operating in South Vietnam. He was leery of the connotation of French-type colonialism and wanted to encourage professional development of the South Vietnamese military. He particularly wanted to avoid the problems of dealing with an international staff in addition to his own U.S. staff. He felt, moreover, that, lacking any effective U.S. influence over the selection and promotion of senior South Vietnamese officers, he could not exercise genuine control of Vietnamese military operations. At any rate, despite its cumbersome nature, the cooperative command system worked, although more often than not there was a lack of close coordination.

The Free World forces—those of smaller nations, such as Australia, New Zealand, and Thailand (all operating in III CTZ)—considered themselves for all intents and purposes to be under U.S. operational control. The South Korean forces operating in II CTZ were quite a different matter. The first Korean commander in Vietnam, Lieutenant General Chae Myung Shin, set the pattern. Considering himself on the same level with COMUSMACV (General Westmoreland), he acted accordingly, with pre-

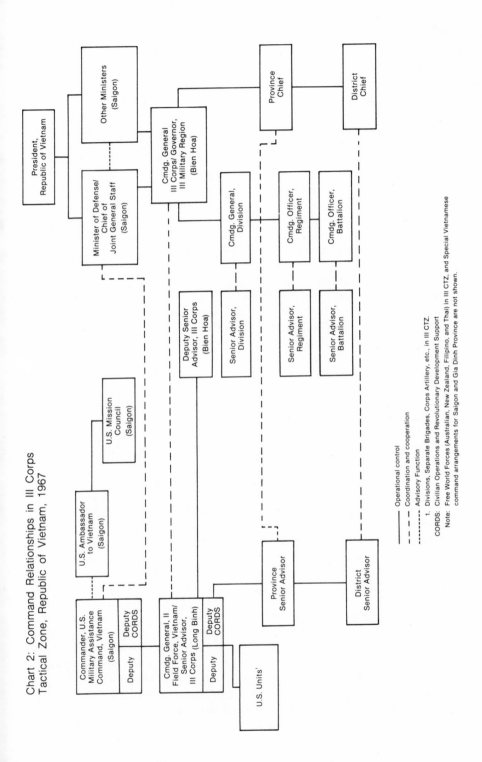

Chart 2: Command Relationships in III Corps
Tactical Zone, Republic of Vietnam, 1967

—————— Operational control

– – – – – Coordination and cooperation

· · · · · · · Advisory Function

1. Divisions, Separate Brigades, Corps Artillery, etc., in III CTZ.

CORDS: Civilian Operations and Revolutionary Development Support

Note: Free World Forces (Australian, New Zealand, Filipino, and Thai) in III CTZ, and Special Vietnamese command arrangements for Saigon and Gia Dinh Province are not shown.

dictable consequences. We never did get our full "money's worth" from the "ROKs." Although their troops fought bravely, carrying out their responsibilities in their assigned areas in a general commendable way, their leaders were loath to move very far away from their whitewashed base camps. They usually demanded all kinds of extra support—artillery, tanks, close air, and assault helicopter support—before they would undertake any operations outside of their normal areas. In their defense, however, it should be recognized that they were under heavy pressure from the ROK government to hold down Korean casualties.

In retrospect I believe that the advantages of having U.S. commanders exercise operational control over other national forces, especially South Vietnamese, would have far outweighed the drawbacks, for the fact is that we did not generate our best combined efforts. As a minimum we should have insisted on having a substantive voice in the selection, promotion, and removal of key South Vietnamese military commanders— for example, corps and division commanders and province and district chiefs. With this kind of clout, which we probably could have obtained had we made a major issue of it, we might have readily assumed operational control in situations requiring close coordination between U.S. and Vietnamese forces as, for example, an international force defending the DMZ.[6]

By March 1967 the buildup of U.S. airpower was essentially complete and included the Strategic Air Command (SAC) base at Utapao, Thailand. The U.S. ground buildup was well along, with five Army divisions, the equivalent of two Marine divisions, and four separate Army brigades in Vietnam. American ground units had seen their first heavy fighting in the summer of 1965 and had been conducting major operations in I, II, and III CTZs ever since. Within the borders of South Vietnam, American troop deployments, initially carried out in a piecemeal fashion because of the prevailing emergency situation, had settled down, allowing some consolidation. Our Navy and Coast Guard patrols offshore—working with the South Vietnamese Navy in operations called Market Time— had been highly successful in choking off enemy infiltration of supplies by sea. In addition, allied river patrol operations called Game Warden hindered enemy use of the vast inland waterways of South Vietnam. The total U.S. force level was now about 400,000 personnel.

It was also heartening to see the excellent progress made in organizing a strong U.S. ground intelligence capability in MACV under the aggressive leadership of the J-2, Major General Joseph A. McChristian, U.S. Army. The 525th Military Intelligence Group had been organized. It was a large, going outfit with a good grasp of the enemy situation in Vietnam and Laos. Likewise the 509th Radio Research Group (an element of the Army Security Agency) had been established and was providing outstanding support in intercepting and interpreting enemy radio communications. It was a highly centralized and closely held operation, however, and McChristian not only jealously guarded his assets, building up the MACV intelligence organization at the expense of the Army intelligence elements operating at field force (corps) and division levels, but also was reluctant to share the intelligence gathered. This policy, as I was to learn, resulted in an unusual intelligence relationship between lower headquarters—in my case II FFV—and higher headquarters, MACV.

The most remarkable development, however, had been the U.S. logistic effort, including the construction of a mature base structure. Well established base and port areas were in place in Danang in I CTZ, at Qui Nhon and Cam Ranh Bay in II CTZ, and in the Saigon and Long Binh areas of III CTZ. In I CTZ, the Danang air base had been greatly enlarged and a new air base built at Chu Lai; in II CTZ there were major air bases at Pleiku in the Highlands and at Tuy Hoa, Cam Ranh Bay, and An Khe on or near the coast. Bien Hoa and Tan Son Nhut air bases in III CTZ were involved in very heavy and sustained air operations. In the Delta, there were only small air fields in operation, such as the C-130 capable strip at Can Tho, but later a major jet air base was undertaken at Binh Tuy in the heart of IV CTZ. An extensive network of U.S. communications sites connected all U.S. facilities. Large numbers of U.S. Army aviation, engineer, communications, transportation, medical, supply, and maintenance troops were in place. In addition, several large U.S. contractors, for the most part employing indigenous labor, performed many major logistic functions at U.S. bases, while Korean contractors operated several of the largest ports. In sum, a logistic miracle had been wrought.

After a day of intense briefings at MACV Headquarters, I choppered to the command post of II FFV, locatd at the site of an old French plantation at Long Binh, about twenty miles east of Saigon. II FFV headquarters occupied a relatively small area, guarded by its own personnel but sited within a mammoth, sprawling U.S. logistic base. There I took command of II FFV, succeeding Lieutenant General Jack Seaman, an old friend and noted field artilleryman.

To my consternation I found that at five o'clock every evening the senior officers flew by helicopter to their quarters, a complex of villas and compounds in the nearby city of Bien Hoa, on the outskirts of which was located the ARVN III Corps headquarters. The choppers landed on a tiny pad built in a rice paddy on the edge of the II FFV compound in Bien Hoa. And early every morning at precisely the same time, the senior officers of II FFV and its supporting 12th Combat Aviation Group (also quartered in Bien Hoa) flew back to II FFV headquarters in Long Binh. It was a very insecure and risky procedure. Any enterprising Viet Cong could easily have hidden in the rice paddies and brought the choppers under close-in direct fire. Of even greater concern to me was the fact that the II FFV tactical operations center was simply not operational at night;

it should have been ready to handle an emergency situation twenty-four hours a day.

I spent only one night in the Bien Hoa villa and slept in the tactical operations center the next night, having ordered that the villas in Bien Hoa be vacated just as quickly as we could arrange for shelter in Long Binh. (This was the source of some grumbling for a while, but after the Tet offensive of 1968 the subject was never raised again because Bien Hoa was heavily assaulted in a surprise dawn attack and much of it occupied for a time. In my opinion, our people, had they remained in Bien Hoa, might easily have been wiped out. As it was, the ARVN III Corps headquarters and its associated American advisory group were besieged for several days before the enemy was driven out of the area.)

II FFV (a U.S. Army corps in reality) consisted of three divisions (the 1st, 9th, and 25th), three separate brigades (the 196th, 199th, and 173rd Airborne), the 11th Armored Cavalry Regiment, two groups of field artillery (medium and heavy artillery), and the 12th Combat Aviation Group. It was a formidable fighting force of about 70,000 men.

My ARVN counterpart was Lieutenant General Le Nguyen Khang, commanding general of III Corps, who also doubled as commandant of the Vietnamese Marine Corps. A slight, wiry man with dark-rimmed glasses, Khang habitually wore the camouflage field uniform of his marines. No doubt the most important aspect of his credentials was that he had the confidence of Thieu, to whom he was completely loyal. Outwardly he had all the earmarks of a professional military man, but I also felt that he would be readily involved in intrigue. We got along well and he was invariably cordial. He did, though, become very wary and sometimes a little agitated when I tried to get him to speak frankly about such unpleasant things as a poor unit performance, incompetent leadership, lack of training, or corruption on the part of his ARVN forces.

Full-time American military advisers, assigned to III Corps at division, regiment, and battalion levels, carried out the day-to-day advisory functions. Each advisory team was a small, self-contained mobile unit with its own communications that could accompany its supported ARVN unit anywhere in or out of combat. There were other U.S. advisory teams (composed of both military and civilian personnel) at the province and district levels serving at remote locations throughout III CTZ and reporting to the senior U.S. adviser for so-called civilian operations and revolutionary development support (CORDS) in III CTZ. Their thankless, dangerous, and difficult work generally went unrecognized and unappreciated. All too often the U.S. advisers were the unsung heroes in Vietnam, while American fighting units took the limelight and garnered most of the rewards. Since I was double-hatted as commanding general of II FFV and senior adviser to the commanding general of III Corps, I was provided with a U.S. Army colonel who functioned as the deputy senior adviser and lived with the corps advisory team within the III Corps compound at Bien Hoa. We were fortunate to have very experienced and competent advisers, particularly at corps and division level, as well as at province level.

During my brief tour in command of II FFV, I learned much about the nature of the war, especially in III CTZ. Like most American troops in Vietnam, the U.S. forces assigned to II FFV were well trained and well led; they carried out their assigned tasks in a highly professional manner. But the most pleasant surprise was to find myself working very closely with John Vann, the senior U.S. adviser for CORDS in III CTZ, with his headquarters in Bien Hoa. I had not seen him since he abruptly resigned from the Army in the fall of 1963. Finally accepted over a year later by the U.S. mission in Saigon for a job with the U.S. Agency for International Development in Vietnam, Vann had been assigned as a province chief adviser in the upper Delta in III CTZ. (The upper Delta of the Mekong River lies in the northeastern part of the Mekong Delta proper. Like the rest of the Delta, the upper region is mostly under water in the wet monsoon, and the sampan is the primary means of transportation. The major land route in the Delta, Highway 4 connects the region with the rest of South Vietnam and carries the bulk of the rice that feeds Saigon, located just northeast of the upper Delta.)

Vann had already earned a reputation for courage and competence. But he had also become a different sort of hero in the eyes of his CORDS associates for his hardnosed intolerance of U.S. or South Vietnamese bureaucratic incompetence that he perceived to be roadblocks to progress. He did not mind crossing swords with senior officials and had managed to irritate General Westmoreland by persistently challenging MACV policies Vann thought were impractical or counterproductive.

In any event, working with Vann was a memorable experience—a very sporty course. Fortunately for both of us, this feisty little dynamo was much in favor of the new organization that was to switch U.S. responsibility for pacification to MACV, and his staff and my II FFV staff were already planning together for the change. Under the new arrangement integrating civilian and military channels of authority, Vann was inserted into the chain of military command and thus became one of the first persons in U.S. military history to command military personnel while a civilian.

Vann was extremely knowledgeable about III CTZ, especially the upper Delta and the tough, Viet Cong-dominated provinces of Long An and Hau Nghia. He practiced what he preached by spending the night in district capitals, villages, and hamlets that were contested between the Saigon government and the Viet Cong. Moreover, he often traveled by jeep into contested areas, quite a different matter from flying into secure enclaves by helicopter.

Vann and I saw eye-to-eye on important things. We both opposed the U.S.-Vietnamese practice of moving people from contested rural areas off their ancestral land and into secure urban areas, where all too often they simply aggravated the slum nature of the overcrowded city. This was defended as a "scorched earth" type of policy for denying such areas to the local Viet Cong, but it had serious disadvantages and over the long term seemed to be the wrong thing to do. Vann and I also agreed that pacification was a job for Vietnamese forces, more or less exclusively, that the operational role of U.S. forces should be gradually reduced, and that primary emphasis should be placed on the development of the ARVN, the ultimate objective being to eliminate the need for U.S. troops.

In III CTZ we did not have much to work with in terms of regular South Vietnamese troops. The three ARVN divisions, the 5th, 25th, and 18th, were among ARVN's weak outfits at that time; some senior ARVN leaders were incompetent and others were corrupt. In one instance our advisory group discovered that the commanding general of 5th ARVN Division, using ARVN trucks and ARVN soldiers, was running a black market rubber business in cahoots with the French rubber plantation managers in his area. As already indicated, General Khang, the Commander of III Corps, was confident of his strong political position and did not want to listen to American counsel. In Gia Dinh, the province that contained Saigon, there was still another kind of situation, for the province chief had significant forces of his own and reported directly to the palace. In all, it was a complex and puzzling organization.

MACV headquarters excused many deficiencies of III Corps on the grounds that Thieu had to keep loyal, if inept or corrupt, leaders in the vicinity of Saigon to reduce the possibility of a coup, but this is not a satisfactory answer. In hindsight, stating it baldly, we lacked adequate intelligence concerning South Vietnamese leaders and their activities, and we influenced Thieu very little in the selection of top military leaders.

But perhaps the most disturbing aspect encountered was the extent of subversion within the South Vietnamese official structure. At times the government had been penetrated all the way from the palace down to small units in the fields. When I first visited the 25th ARVN Division headquarters at Duc Hoa, the division commander would discuss only trivial matters in his office; he took me outside well away from any building, with only the two of us present. Here he explained that he strongly suspected that his own Division G-2 (intelligence officer) was a Viet Cong agent; thus he did not dare discuss operational matters in his own command post.

In many ARVN units, battalion and regimental commanders would issue fictitious operations orders in writing, then at the last minute issue the real orders verbally in the field. It was also apparent that in some contested areas, a certain degree of accommodation existed between South

Vietnamese and local enemy forces, each operating in its own area, carefully avoiding the other's turf. It was at times suspected that this "cooperation" might exist even to the point of sharing access to government ammunition and other supplies, at different times and by prearrangement. This baffling situation was very difficult for Americans to understand, much less accept, especially for eager, bright-eyed young officers and noncommissioned officers on duty as unit and district advisers out in the "boonies."

While in command of II FFV, I learned first-hand the difficulty of defining the role of American forces in South Vietnam. Repeatedly demonstrating their vastly superior firepower and airmobility, our troops had proved that they could go anywhere in Vietnam and defeat any enemy units that decided to fight. It was also obvious that ARVN offensive capabilities were far inferior to ours.

But what was the proper role of U.S. troops? We recognized that pacification efforts (CORDS) were critically and centrally important to ultimate success, but there were many serious drawbacks to allowing U.S. units to become too closely involved. Following this course would discourage and preempt the efforts of our South Vietnamese ally, whose forces had to do the job in the final analysis. The mere presence of U.S. combat forces in their large base camps—for example, the 25th Division at Cu Chi and the 1st Division (the Big Red One) at Di An, a few miles north of Saigon—was a major asset for the pacification mission; but when these troops moved out on other missions, even if only for a few weeks, they left a void, and pacification deteriorated. Unfortunately this happened all too often.

In Gia Dinh Province surrounding Saigon, we experimented with the 199th Infantry Brigade (one of II FFV's separate brigades) in various U.S. Army-ARVN experiments in joint organization. Mixed U.S. Army-ARVN units, organized at squad, platoon, rifle company, and battalion level, were tested operationally. When mixed formations of U.S. Army and ARVN units conducted operations in the field, though, there were wide cultural, arms, equipment, and procedural gaps, and the results were not particularly promising.

The most suitable tactical role for U.S. forces seemed to be one of taking on the regular, so-called main force units of the enemy. Originally they were exclusively Viet Cong in makeup but eventually became predominantly North Vietnamese Army (NVA) as Viet Cong casualties mounted, the war escalated, and more and more NVA troops were sent south. But the United States, having decided to limit the ground war to South Vietnam, and therefore unable to block enemy forces moving through Laos, could not prevent an enemy buildup within or on the borders of South Vietnam. So the rub was bringing the enemy forces to battle, for they had no definite, recognizable, overt positions. They remained either "underground" (often literally) within South Vietnamese borders, or back in base sanctuaries in Cambodia or Laos, going on the attack only when they so decided, seeking to surprise a preselected victim. Thus the enemy clearly had the initiative; and, given the way the United States had decided to fight the war in a passive defense of South Vietnam, American forces found themselves in the unenviable situation of having to react and dance to the enemy's tune.

Our greatest battle successes occurred when the enemy chose to attack a U.S. unit well dug in and prepared to defend its position. As enemy forces learned about the devastating impact of greatly superior U.S. firepower, both ground- and air-delivered, they became less inclined to attack an American unit unless they could hit one moving overland, surprise one unprepared, or ambush a unit making a helicopter air assault into a landing zone. Although our infantry bore the brunt of direct enemy assaults, our artillery, armor, aviation, engineer, military police, signal, and even logistic troops became proficient at beating off NVA infantry attempting to overrun their positions.

This, then, was the rationale behind the offensive operations conducted by American units, often called "search and destroy" operations. It was tough, risky business, for our troops, moving into and searching a hostile area, were exposed to enemy ambush, mines, and booby traps. Frequently they suffered casualties without ever seeing or contacting the enemy. After our troops had stopped moving, usually before daylight ended, and had prepared their defensive positions for the night, they often hoped for an enemy attack and an opportunity to inflict heavy casualties.

An early exponent of this offensive-defensive tactic was Major General William DePuy, J-3 (Plans and Operations officer), HQ MACV, who perfected it when he took command of the 1st Division, one of II FFV's assigned units. When one of his units planned an air assault into an unknown landing zone, DePuy insisted on heavy preparatory fires, all that he could muster—mortars, artillery, attack helicopters (gunships), and tactical air. Making his battalions stick together, he discouraged rifle companies from moving out of mutually supporting range or being sent on independent missions. He made his battalions stop early enough in the afternoon to prepare extensive positions, digging in deep and reinforcing them with all available materials on hand, and making certain that artillery supporting fires had been registered before nightfall. Slow and methodical as this process was, it nevertheless paid off in minimizing U.S. casualties. The enemy learned the hard way that it did not pay to pick on a Big Red One battalion.

This technique had several significant weaknesses. For a good chance of success, it required—but did not always have—reasonably accurate intelligence about the enemy's movements and likely tactical objectives. It also demanded flawless execution and imaginative measures that would deceive the enemy, but unfortunately our air assault operations were often an open book. Finally, a major weakness was that it surrendered the night to the enemy. Night operations were particularly difficult and exceedingly dangerous for American troops in Vietnam, but to preclude them by design was a self-imposed handicap that gave the enemy an uncontested advantage.

A different approach was used by another II FFV division, the 25th Division, initially commanded by Major General Fred Weyand. The 25th preferred staying in an area long enough to dominate it thoroughly, gradually extending its control of secured ground. The division made certain that South Vietnamese forces could continue to maintain security before the U.S. forces present were allowed to move away on a new mission.

During the period from February to May 1967, II FFV conducted two multidivision operations: the first was called Junction City; the second, Manhattan. (Both were named after small cities near Fort Riley, Kansas, the home base of the 1st Division.) The largest operations attempted in South Vietnam, they had mixed results. Junction City was designed, first, to penetrate War Zone C, a large, uninhabited, jungle-covered (full of valuable teak and mahogany), and hitherto unchallenged enemy base area northwest of Saigon and contiguous to the Cambodian border; and second, to seal off a large part of the war zone, disrupting enemy activity and destroying any enemy troops uncovered. The Central Office for South Vietnam (COSVN), the top enemy headquarters in South Vietnam, was believed to be in the area. Manhattan, a somewhat smaller operation, was targeted against the enemy's Long Nguyen base area, which encompassed the large Michelin rubber plantation about thirty miles northwest of Saigon.

The battle of Ap Gu, the last big battle of Junction City, occurred in northern War Zone C very close to the Cambodian border on 31 March and 1 April 1967 when a regiment of the 9th V.C. Division attacked the 1st Battalion, 26th Infantry of the 1st Infantry Division (Big Red One), commanded by a then little-known Lieutenant Colonel Alexander M. Haig, Jr. Haig's battalion, well dug in with overhead cover and having preregistered its supporting artillery fire, had been ready when the enemy hit just before dawn. Heavy close air support and massed artillery fire were immediately brought to bear. When I arrived by chopper not long after daylight, the battle was over, and dead enemy soldiers and the debris of combat were strewn throughout the battalion position. Some of the greatest carnage had been wrought a short distance from the American position, where our tactical fighter-bombers caught some of the enemy in close formation in an open area. Enemy remnants had broken off the action and were believed to be heading for their sanctuary base across the border. Fortunately, our casualties were light, only a fraction of the more than 500 NVA soldiers killed. Our troops were in good spirits, cleaning their weapons and rebuilding damaged positions, while others had the unpleasant duty of collecting dead bodies. Out of necessity, there was a mass burial overseen by a Big Red One chaplain, who administered the proper rites.

Later that day when I got back to my command post at Long Binh, I received a phone call from General Westmoreland, who earlier had ordered an all-out pursuit of the fleeing enemy and was totally dissatisfied with the response. I praised the performance of our troops, trying to defend the lack of pursuit. The enemy had disappeared into the jungle, had not been picked up by our air reconnaissance, and had probably reached the Cambodian border in a very short time. There was also the risk of our blindly pursuing forces being ambushed and suffering unnecessary casualties. But Westmoreland did not accept my excuses and chewed me out royally. In principle, he was right. Although the practicality of pursuit was dubious, the psychological importance of immediate pursuit—making every possible effort to finish off a defeated foe—was difficult to dispute.

Operations Junction City and Manhattan again demonstrated that no enemy base area was secure from U.S. forces and that, in the dry season, U.S. armor and mechanized troops could also operate successfully in many areas of South Vietnam. Enemy base complexes were violently disrupted, as was the enemy's overall headquarters, COSVN. Thereafter, the enemy decided to move COSVN to Cambodia and to rely primarily on Cambodian sanctuaries for bases, training centers, supply depots, and hospitals.

A closely held second phase of Junction City involved a concealed, stay-behind force, the 196th Infantry Brigade (Separate), to operate in War Zone C after the other U.S. forces had been withdrawn. It worked—but the phase was ended early when the brigade was sent north to counter the enemy buildup in I CTZ.

On the negative side, these large operations were of questionable utility, for they involved large numbers of troops, only a few of whom were actually engaged in combat, and they consumed large amounts of U.S. resources. Vast, heavily vegetated areas were involved, and it was simply not feasible to seal them off, search them completely, and police them permanently. During Junction City two Vietnamese CIDG-U.S. Special Forces camps and several C-130 capable air strips were constructed deep in War Zone C. Such camps were, however, a dubious asset. They gave the enemy, located nearby in Cambodian sanctuaries, vulnerable, isolated targets that were easy to attack but very difficult for our forces to reinforce and support because their base camps were located some distance away. The CIDG was composed essentially of mercenaries organized into company-size units by the CIA in the early 1960s to man fortified outposts, charged primarily with border surveillance. They were composed mostly of Montagnards or other native inhabitants of remote regions. Later the CIDG units were transferred to the U.S. Army Special Forces, and their combined camps, complete with the families of the civilian irregulars, became known at CIDG-Special Forces bases. South Vietnamese Special Forces officered the CIDG companies. At the height of its development, the CIDG numbered almost 50,000 troops organized into over 100 camps.

The so-called main force mission led us in II FFV to encourage our U.S. divisions to move further north toward Cambodia, closer to the less populated border areas and farther from the heavily populated areas to the south. The 1st Division did move its headquarters and part of the division to Lai Khe, considerably farther north and much closer to the border, while the 25th Division developed a forward base and command post at Tay Ninh just south of War Zone C.

The 9th Division, based at Bear Cat southeast of Saigon, was in a different situation, as it was in the process of moving its center of gravity into IV CTZ, the Delta, largely underwater, where unoccupied dry land was almost nonexistent. To solve the problem, base areas were created on land by dredging dirt from the rivers and canals, and one brigade of the division was based afloat. The latter became the Army (ground) element of the novel U.S. Mobile Riverine Force, a joint Army-Navy undertaking that developed a unique mode of operation to overcome the inherent operational obstacles and difficulties posed by the Delta.

But one of our basic problems in II FFV's area was the lack of depth between the Cambodian border and the heavily populated areas of Saigon and the upper Delta. Distances to the border were short, and enemy infantry had several covered, high-speed approach routes for reaching Saigon in a matter of only hours. The Parrot's Beak salient, due west of Saigon, was only twenty-five miles away. We were caught in a dilemma. We would have liked to confine the enemy forces to their Cambodian bases and deny them access to Vietnamese base areas closer to their objectives in South Vietnam, but the territory concerned was too vast to seal off or cover by surveillance. Especially at night, it was too easy for the enemy to bypass our troop positions and get past us undetected. This was to be driven home to us hard at the time of the enemy Tet offensive of 1968.

It was also very apparent that the war was a small unit affair, mostly of rifle companies and battalions. Higher headquarters—brigade, division, and corps (field force)—were more in the business of allocating resources and support to their subordinate units and coordinating their operations than of actively maneuvering subordinate units in a tactical sense. Thus II FFV's role was primarily one of deciding priorities of effort with respect to such matters as ammunition for divisional artillery, reinforcing fires from II FFV artillery, and additional engineer and helicopter support obtained from nondivisional units. It led to some intense competition between units and some rather high-keyed rivalry between such proud old outfits as the 1st and 25th divisions.

I felt, nonetheless, that regardless of its pragmatic role, II FFV to function as a corps tactical-type headquarters should at least look and act the part of a combat-oriented outfit, setting the example for its assigned troops. So should division and brigade headquarters, and the base camps of these echelons should resemble austere, lean combat units, not "rear echelon commando" units complete with Red Cross girls and librarians.

In this connection, excellent tactical communications and helicopter mobility tended to make the fighting too remote for field force, division, and brigade commanders. They could readily visit subordinate units in enemy contact, or expecting contact, in a matter of a few hours by chopper and then return to the relative quiet of their own command posts the same day. Such travel on the ground would take many hours or even days, particularly over unsecured territory. Higher echelon commanders in Vietnam had to guard against this syndrome, which all too easily could generate an unreal, unhealthy atmosphere, resulting in a lack of appreciation for the true situation on the ground.

The routine use of the helicopter as an aerial command and reconnaissance vehicle by many senior American tactical commanders resulted at times in gross oversupervision of, and sometimes unwarranted interference with, subordinate commanders, in particular company and battalion commanders. In some divisions it was standard practice to keep an assistant division commander continuously airborne during daylight hours over units in active or imminent enemy contact. The senior officer in the helicopter could monitor simultaneously the command radio nets of several command echelons on the ground (for example, company, battalion, and brigade) and could enter any of these nets whenever he wished.

The results generally were not very good. The perspective of the observer in the air, even at low altitudes and slow speeds, is drastically different from the view at ground level and can be dangerously misleading. The noise and often dust from the helicopter are dead giveaways, and superfluous radio chatter can endanger the men on the ground by revealing locations and movements of friendly units. Airborne leaders lack a feel for the terrain and the tactical situation that can be gained only by leaders well forward on the ground. Attempting to direct ground fire and maneuver from the air is even more unwise. It demoralizes the leaders and troops on the ground, stifles initiative, and inhibits the development of a strong sense of responsibility. Many ground commanders reacted by turning off or tuning out their radios; they simply ignored the requests for situation updates as well as the orders emanating from their chopper-borne superiors. In short, it was becoming a pernicious practice that caused more harm than good.

Overzealous leadership at division level also resulted in bypassing intermediate commanders, further weakening the chain of command. This was especially hard on brigade commanders (colonels who normally did not have helicopters at their disposal), and in some divisions this echelon was squeezed out of the tactical chain and became more of an administrative echelon. In II FFV, the 1st Division was particularly bad about directing operations from helicopters, and I pointedly tried to discourage the practice without directly ordering that it be stopped.

As II FFV commander, I also had to learn how to operate under General Westmoreland and his MACV staff. It was an unusual setup. Westmoreland and his intelligence chief liked to size up the enemy from their perspective and then tell each subordinate corps (field force) commander what to expect in his area. This was a switch from normal procedure, where intelligence information flows from lower to higher headquarters. Field commanders should usually know more about the enemy in their areas than the higher echelons do. But MACV tightly controlled access to information obtained electronically, and the intelligence derived through such means was estimated to amount to about 80 percent of the data collected. These circumstances made this reversal of the flow of intelligence information inevitable.

With respect to operational planning, Westmoreland encouraged a sort of competition among his subordinate commanders, each vying for more forces or support, the commander with the most convincing case getting the most resources. Lieutenant General Stanley R. Larsen, the crafty, combat-wise leader of I FFV, was a master at this game and had Westmoreland's ear. This practice can be risky, however, as commanders who exaggerate their situations can gain advantage over those commanders who try to be objective and factual, resulting in the commitment of scarce assets to less important objectives.

But despite some deep misgivings about the U.S. strategy being pursued, as well as the organizational and operational difficulties facing us, I enthusiastically supported the missions assigned to II FFV by MACV. I confided my misgivings to only a very few persons; one of those was General Abrams. The first time was in April 1967, when he visited Vietnam just before he became deputy COMUSMACV. We spent a day and a night with the 1st Infantry Division, whose command post was at Lai Khe, and sat up most of the night talking. Although he listened carefully, Abrams seemed unimpressed.

The second instance was a short time later, soon after he joined as Westmoreland's deputy. Again Abrams listened carefully, but his reaction was that it was really too late to change U.S. strategy. As for any major changes within MACV, the pattern was set in concrete. He felt that Westmoreland, with far more continuity of experience in Vietnam, had made up his mind and that his job as Westmoreland's deputy was to support him in every possible way. But in an unguarded moment during the long conversation, Abrams did say that he too was dismayed by the U.S.-Vietnamese organizational and operational setup that had evolved. Much later, in hindsight, it occurred to me that Abrams at this time was no doubt aware of President Johnson's intention to scale down U.S. operations and to shift the burden to the South Vietnamese. Moreover, Westmoreland had made Abrams's primary responsibility the improvement of South Vietnamese performance. This loyalty to Westmoreland was typical of Abrams, who was first and last a soldier. Earlier, as vice chief of staff to General Johnson, he had served in exactly the same way— loyalty to his chief was his first commandment.

Early in May 1967 Ambassador Bunker visited us at II FFV HQ in Long Binh. It was his first real trip to the field since his arrival, but unfortunately his visit was marred by a series of mishaps that were in some ways funny but could easily have had tragic consequences. For his afternoon visit he was due at the II FFV chopper pad at one o'clock, coming in via a MACV Huey taking off from Tan Son Nhut. Our people knew when his party departed, but then they simply disappeared. Thirty hectic minutes later a "Jolly Green Giant" search and rescue helicopter of the USAF approached the landing pad of an Army transportation unit next door to our headquarters. On the hunch that it might be carrying our missing ambassador, I quickly jeeped over to the neighboring pad (made of oiled dirt in contrast to our asphalt setup) just in time to greet the ambassador as he climbed down from this giant chopper in a white Palm Beach suit, clutching his fine Panama straw hat. After dumping him unceremoniously out in the dirt, the chopper lifted off, covering us all with very dirty, oily dust. But the good-natured, unflappable Bunker with his shy grin took it all in stride, and it was just plain fun to see this grand old diplomatic warrior again.

When we got back to my command post, we immediately let a most anxious HQ MACV know that the ambassador was safely on the ground. Then we got the rather comic story. MACV had a sound, special procedure for the security and transportation of such VIPs in Vietnam, but the MACV Huey unit charged with the mission had broken every rule in the book. First, there was no second "chase ship" following the VIP-carrying aircraft. Second, there was no copilot, as the ambassador was seated in the copilot's seat. Third, a *Time-Life* photographer with all kinds of cameras, light meters, and other paraphernalia hanging all over him, was allowed to move around in the interior compartment of the Huey, taking photos in flight. That was the fatal mistake. A loose camera flipped the fuel switch located on the control panel between the pilot and the copilot, and the pilot, believing he had an engine failure (the HU1 is single-engined), immediately went into autorotation. This happened over Highway 1A, a new American-built highway between Saigon and Long

Binh, a very busy road, loaded at the time with heavy military traffic, much of it U.S. The Huey was very fortunate to crash-land on the highway without colliding with a vehicle. Hearing the Huey pilot's "May Day," the pilot of the USAF Jolly Green Giant, on a training flight, immediately landed near the Huey. The Air Force pilot, unfamiliar with the MACV setup, did not know who Ambassador Bunker was and had never heard of II FFV or our headquarters at the "Plantation" in Long Binh. But he was able to deliver Bunker next door to his destination!

Needless to say, General Westmoreland was chagrined about the incident, particularly so since a similar incident had occurred several years before when a lone Huey flying Ambassador Lodge went down near Viet Cong country deep in the Delta before the pilot could let someone know their whereabouts. Many long hours passed before the rescue of the ambassador, who could have been captured by the Viet Cong. HQ MACV had laid out very specific instructions to prevent a recurrence and now it had happened again. Much hell was raised in Saigon over the second incident.

We did our best to assure Mr. Bunker that the U.S. Army in Vietnam did indeed know what it was doing. Though we had a good private laugh about it, we both knew it was no laughing matter. I also told him that the next time he wanted to visit, we would pick him up in Saigon with our own choppers.

In my office adjacent to our tactical operations center I privately briefed the ambassador on the situation in the II FFV-III Corps area. I stressed my private reservations about the feasibility of our pacifying South Vietnam, given the depth of the insurgency and our passive defense strategy that could not prevent the infiltration of large forces from North Vietnam into the South. I voiced the thought that a clear-cut decision over the insurgents might not be possible and that eventually an accommodation between the two sides might have to be negotiated unless U.S. strategy was fundamentally changed. Having said that, however, I expressed confidence in our ability, using U.S. troops of II FFV, to deny the invading NVA troops freedom to operate as they pleased in III CTZ. MACV's concept of operations was to force the main force units of the enemy back to the Cambodian border, well away from populated areas, thus allowing South Vietnamese forces to get on with the job of pacification. Little did I realize that only eight months later, the enemy was to thwart our plan by slipping past our forces into these populated areas, while the local populace stood by without revealing the presence of the enemy. This, of course, was at the time of Tet 1968.

After our meeting, Ambassador Bunker and I flew by chopper to several forward infantry units of the 1st Division operating in the Loc Ninh area among the rubber plantations along Highway 13, which runs north from Saigon to the Cambodian border. Bunker enjoyed talking to various young soldiers and was struck by their quiet acceptance of dangerous work that had to be done. We then flew to a squadron of the 11th Armored Cavalry Regiment operating in the southeastern edge of War Zone C. Since it was getting late in the afternoon, the squadron was preparing defensive positions to protect its armored vehicles for the night. We traveled by jeep around the perimeter of the position, carved out of heavily canopied rain forest, and the ambassador had a first-hand view of tanks, armored personnel carriers, and self-propelled artillery, all equipped with special protection from enemy land mines. He gained some insight into how we coped with difficult terrain and a tough, skillful, well-armed guerrilla enemy.

After returning Bunker safely to Saigon, I began to reflect on where we had taken him that afternoon and wondered whether I had not pulled a dumb trick by exposing our number one representative in Southeast Asia to unnecessary danger. But I rationalized our trip with the thought that there was no other way for him to get even a glimmer of the kind of war we found ourselves caught up in. One thing we were sure of, however, the ambassador thoroughly enjoyed himself despite the inauspicious start of his first visit to the field.

About this time General Westmoreland broke the news that he was moving me to HQ U.S. Army, Vietnam (USARV), located at Tan Son Nhut Air Base near Saigon, where I would be his Army deputy. I raised every objection I could think of, including that I was professionally unqualified and temperamentally unsuited for this predominantly logistic support job. But Westmoreland was adamant, maintaining that he wanted his USARV deputy to be the senior three-star Army general in Vietnam, senior to his field force commanders, and that meant Palmer. It was apparent that Westmoreland wanted Weyand, who had commanded the 25th Division and knew III CTZ well, to command II FFV. I made no secret of the fact that I was deeply unhappy to be taken out of the operational chain of command in Vietnam, but of course I obeyed the order.

3

1967-1968:
Army HQ, Vietnam

At headquarters, U.S. Army, Vietnam, I replaced a very fine soldier, Lieutenant General Jean Engler, perhaps the most respected logistician in the U.S. Army at the time. When I arrived on the scene many horrendous logistic problems had already been largely solved. It is easy to point out deficiencies in hindsight, so the remarks that follow are offered in a constructive spirit and are not intended to detract from the thousands of talented, hard-working, dedicated support people who made large-scale U.S. operations in Vietnam possible.

HQ USARV had a strong staff. Brigadier General Robert Taber was my chief of staff and Brigadier General Frank Linnell was deputy chief of staff for operations. Both were seasoned combat veterans and experienced paratroopers; we had all served together during the 1965–66 crisis in the Dominican Republic. Our deputy chief of staff for administration was Brigadier General Earle Cole, an experienced Adjutant General Corps officer. The USARV staff made an outstanding team which could have readily handled tactical operational matters as well as administrative and logistic affairs. Early in my tenure, I strongly recommended to General Westmoreland that USARV be redesignated as a field army with operational control of all U.S. Army units in Vietnam. Indeed, USARV functioned in many important respects as an operational field army, but it was not destined to become a full-fledged one.

As General Westmoreland's U.S. Army deputy I discharged many, but not all, of his Army responsibilities toward the approximately 350,000 Army troops in the theater at the time. Specifically I had administrative command (*not* operational command, which was the direct responsibility of Westmoreland as COMUSMACV, the joint commander) of the Army divisions, brigades, and other tactical units totaling almost 175,000 men (roughly half of the Army forces in Vietnam), but exercised complete command, including operational command, of the other half. This other half was basically the logistics component—1st Logistic Command, 1st Aviation Brigade, Engineer Command, 18th Military Police Brigade, 44th Medical Brigade, and 1st Signal Brigade. Most of these troops had a combat support role and at times even a minor direct combat role.

Overall, USARV had an immense logistics job supporting in one way or another almost one million military personnel. This included the U.S. Army troops; about 50,000 U.S. Air Force and 11,000 U.S. Navy personnel; over 50,000 allied troops; and Vietnamese forces numbering over one-half million at that time. USARV also hired about 72,000 local nationals and roughly 7,000 third-country nationals, mostly Koreans and Filipinos. About one-third of this civilian work force belonged to large experienced contractors and performed major overhaul and rebuild functions, provided power, maintained depots, and operated ports for our forces. Finally, a large construction contractor under the direction of the Department of the Navy and employing another 15,000 civilians, did much of the military-oriented vertical construction (building) in Vietnam. On top of this, USARV supported and supervised the numerous troop morale support activities operating in the theater, such as the USO, Red Cross, and post exchange system. Needless to say, this complex of interrelated support activities was subject to great pressures and temptations, and caused more than its share of headaches to responsible commanders.

At USARV, in accordance with General Westmoreland's personal guidance, our responsibilities toward U.S. Army forces stressed three broad areas: (1) force structure, seeking the best possible combat effectiveness from our limited manpower; (2) base development and overall logistic posture; and (3) combat developments, that is, the rapid assimilation and dissemination of new equipment, as well as novel tactics and techniques, especially those demonstrated successfully by our own operating forces. There was much to be done in all three of these areas, and I can mention only a few highlights.

With respect to manpower, our basic problem was to stay within a tight troop ceiling imposed by the secretary of defense and to see that the highest priority missions had similar priority for their manpower needs. This was not easy because of the natural tendency in any organization to let overstrengths accumulate at higher echelons, with chronic understrengths at the cutting edge in the field, especially in the infantry outfits that absorb over 90 percent of the battle casualties. Some of our solutions were not very popular, but we did manage to keep our combat units operational.

As the number of U.S Army troops committed to battle rose during the period, Army casualty rates and material losses increased, reaching all-time levels in the November 1967–April 1968 period. In Vietnam the

Army simply was not getting enough men through the replacement system; where to pinpoint the responsibility and place the blame was difficult, if not impossible.

This problem of maintaining an adequate and timely flow of combat loss replacements from the United States to units in Vietnam brought on the only serious confrontation I ever had with my old friend and West Point classmate, General Abrams. The enemy's dry monsoon offensive of 1967–68 had started in November 1967 along the border, with heavy fighting over the provincial capitals of Song Be and Loc Ninh in III CTZ. A particularly bloody conflict had been fought at Dakto in II CTZ, where the 173rd Airborne Brigade suffered severe casualties. In late November 1967 Abrams had just returned to HQ MACV after a visit to the 173rd Airborne Brigade, finding it quite understrength, and called for me.

Late that night I flew in to HQ MACV from Long Binh; the weather was atrocious and we had been shot at by either some trigger-happy local RF/PF troops or unfriendly Viet Cong. So I entered Abrams's office in a rather foul mood and found him alone and brooding at his desk in an even fouler mood. He kept me standing while he glared at me for a full minute without saying a word. Then, in a typical Abrams volcanic fashion, he exploded in a torrent of cursing and verbal abuse. He was especially vehement about Earle Cole, who was in charge of USARV personnel matters. Since no amount of explanations would satisfy Abrams, I interrupted him with equally bad-tempered words, told him to go to hell, and stormed out of his office. Fortunately, he realized that he had gone too far and ran after me to ask me to come back. The closest he could come to an apology was to say, "You shouldn't let my goddam temper get your goat." We then both cooled off and I departed for Long Binh.

Another major handicap was the large "hump" in rotation of personnel caused by the one-year tour. If nothing was done about it, a fighting division could find itself suddenly very unready, with the mass departure of experienced men and the mass infusion of green replacements. Our solution was not very popular, but it was better than doing nothing. We paired off like units but with different dates of arrival in Vietnam, and simply swapped large numbers of officers, noncommissioned officers, and junior enlisted men. In this way we were able to achieve an acceptable rate of attrition of experienced people, but at significant cost in unit cohesion and troop morale, which were hurt by such arbitrary personnel transfers.

The most pernicious policy encountered was the base camp idea. The manpower it soaked up was appalling, not to mention the waste of material resources and the handicap of having to defend and take care of these albatrosses. We found one separate infantry brigade, operating by itself a long distance from the headquarters to which it reported, that habitually kept almost one-third of its strength, fighting and support, in an elaborate base camp that could have carried out support missions for a much large force. It made little sense. Base camps occupied large areas which generated correspondingly large security requirements and almost immobilized the parent unit.

The solution was obvious—all units should be required to live tactically in the field, avoiding any construction; and essential rear area functions, such as returning wounded or sick men to their units, should be handled by small facilities serving not just one brigade or one division but all the forces in a large area. But bad habits are hard to overcome and we never did reduce the rear area echelons to the minimum feasible size. Nevertheless we did consolidate a good many base camps and in the process "scarfed up" huge amounts of excess parts and supplies, including large, complex items such as a complete sawmill, which some units had brought to Vietnam without authorization but had never put to good use.

The major justification given for the big base camp syndrome was the notion, shared by numerous senior U.S. civilian and military officials, that somehow our troops would perform better if they had at least reasonable access to the basic amenities of home. There was a similar rationale for the one-year tour in Vietnam for all military personnel—conscript, volunteer, or career. My personal opinion is that we tend to sell our youth short and that, contrary to popular notions, most American soldiers will serve under difficult conditions and will fight well when they understand the necessity for it.

One spectacular success which greatly helped the personnel, training, and logistic managers charged with maintaining our fighting ranks, was the standardization of so-called TOEs (tables of organization), which prescribed the specific people and equipment each unit was authorized. To meet the peculiar requirements of Vietnam, the Department of the Army instituted a system of MTOEs (modified TOEs), which authorized specific changes in standard TOEs for numerous units. But the system got out of hand. In Vietnam we found fifteen different organizations for infantry battalions, twelve different TOEs for light artillery battalions, seventy for infantry rifle companies, and sixty-two for light artillery batteries. After much debate, USARV established for the first time one standard organization for each like unit serving in Vietnam. Needless to say this brought great cheers from the personnel, training, and logistic managers responsible for sustaining our army troops in Vietnam. It also got some applause from our field commanders.

Logistically one of our great headaches was to sort out the mountains of supplies shipped to Vietnam during the early periods before logistic facilities and personnel were on hand to receive, identify, and store this flood of material. Part of the problem had been caused by the automatic resupply philosophy, espoused by the Army in World War II, Korea, and now Vietnam, under which every conceivable item was shipped in large quantities without any firm grasp of what the actual requirement was. Another related policy was the establishment of large on-the-ground stockage objectives for the theater, seeking to build up in Vietnam large amounts of every class of supply, from rations and ammunition to spare parts and construction materials, as a hedge against the disruption of the long supply line from the continental United States or the loss of supplies in Vietnam from enemy action or natural disaster. In Vietnam some logistic managers doubled or even tripled requirements that had been carefully calculated for a particular item simply because they were afraid to risk being caught short. The logistician's natural tendency to play things safe can be counterproductive if it overwhelms the supply system to the point where no one has an adequate handle on the kinds and amounts of supplies on hand.

In late 1966 and early 1967 the confidence of our troop units in the supply system had reached such a low ebb that each U.S. division in Vietnam was maintaining a large "liaison section" (50–100 men) at one or more major port-base areas, whose mission was to search constantly through the great mass of stuff on the ground, looking for items their outfits needed or might need. Once having located such desired items, the liaison group then made out a pro forma requisition and delivered the items with their own means of transportation, ground and air, to their parent unit. This, of course, is *not* how the supply system is supposed to work. Moreover, it is a wasteful, selfish practice which does not necessarily utilize the supplies in question in the most equitable and efficient manner. We were able to improve the whole performance of the system and to eliminate the liaison sections without stirring up hard feelings in our combat outfits—no mean accomplishment.

Base development and construction standards constituted another major problem. It soon became very obvious that we were overbuilding in terms of bases and that construction was too sophisticated, out of line with the austere Vietnamese environment. Priorities and standards were out of balance. In the Pleiku area, for example, we found combat engineers of a U.S. division building concrete sidewalks in the division's base camp when the major ammunition supply point and major fuel dump supporting the division were impassable mud holes in the rainy season. We eliminated a lot of planned construction and saved many millions of dollars and priceless engineering effort in the process.

On the U.S. advisory mission side, the accelerated expansion of the ARVN, Regional Forces, and Popular Forces (especially after Tet 1968) caused a corresponding increase in American advisers. The task of supporting our advisers became too big for MACV to handle and consequently was turned over to USARV. In areas like the Delta and much of

II CTZ, where the advisers could not be readily satellited on U.S. Army units for support, we had to develop a separate logistic system. CORDS was also expanding, and USARV became involved in the support of many U.S. civilian agencies and civilian advisers—a new and different mission. Likewise we were often asked to assist the Vietnamese logistic system when it could not keep up with the expanding Vietnamese forces.

In this connection, when I took over USARV, the headquarters was responsible for the U.S. logistic advisory mission; we retained that mission until 15 March 1968. But in mid-1967 I believed it to be such an important responsibility, on a par with our mission of supporting U.S. forces, that I elevated USARV's logistic advisory group to a general staff section, called the Military Assistance Section, reporting directly to my chief of staff.

We found many things wrong with the ARVN logistics system, including a crying lack of modernization and a grossly inadequate logistic force structure. Visiting the area logistic commands—one in each CTZ except II CTZ, which had two, one in the highlands, and one on the coast—was an eye opener. They were incredibly antiquated and primitive. I also visited many of the administrative and logistic support companies, generally operating at the province level, which supported the RF/PF in the area. Again they seemed hopelessly inadequate.

Nevertheless, we were able to overcome many of their critical shortages and deficiencies by the simple device of transferring excess vehicles and equipment from American units, thus saving many months of lead time needed to process things through the normal military assistance program. USARV helped in many other logistic areas, such as ammunition supply and heavy handling equipment, and initiated a comprehensive logistic modernization program. But perhaps the most damaging aspect of the situation was the tendency for senior Vietnamese commanders, especially corps commanders, to hoard resources, misuse them, or divert them to their favorite units while starving those in disfavor. In short, I could see a long road ahead of us in instilling in the Vietnamese our philosophy of logistic support; namely, placing the emphasis on aggressively pushing support from the rear and seeing that the supplies got to the troops that needed them.

But despite our best efforts and protests from our entire logistics advisory group, MACV decided to divest USARV of all advisory responsibilities and concentrate them at MACV level. Abrams, whom Westmoreland had placed in complete and personal charge of all U.S. advisory matters, with the mission of improving Vietnamese performance as quickly as possible, supported this move. It could be argued that this centralized control was the right way to go, but in MACV headquarters, military assistance responsibilities were fragmented among twenty-odd staff sections, all of which had other major tasks to handle. I had always felt that there should be a separate MAAG under a senior officer reporting directly to Westmoreland, and that there was no better way to achieve the cohesive, overall direction and singleness of purpose needed to upgrade the Vietnamese armed forces. Even after the mission was transferred, I believed that USARV could contribute to the logistic advisory effort in a major way, but it was not to be.

But my personal inclinations lay on the operations side, and I continually tried to engage USARV headquarters as far as possible in what would be the normal responsibilities of a field army—tactical, logistic, and administrative. Westmoreland was very understanding and let us get more and more into the operational side, including comprehensive, full-scale continency planning. Thus we became deeply involved in developing detailed operational plans for possible offensive operations against NVA forces in Laos and Cambodia in the event Bunker and Westmoreland secured approval to conduct major operations outside South Vietnam's borders. We even conducted logistic feasibility tests of our plans, since logistics was the key limiting factor with respect to the magnitude, range, and nature of our contemplated operations in extremely difficult country. Indeed, our logistic capabilities dictated the scheme of maneuver we selected. MACV could not adequately perform such planning, because only USARV possessed the essential in-depth technical competence.

In point of fact, USARV performed many of the important functions of a field army. With five corps-level commands to support, USARV refereed the spirited competition for resources among them and decided on corps allocations of such items as tactical air support and nondivisional artillery, engineer, assault helicopter, and armor support. The 1st Logistics Command operated basically as a field army support command, while the Engineer Command performed both the combat and construction engineer function of a field army engineer. The 1st Aviation Brigade carried out both operational and logistic field army aviation tasks. And the 1st Signal Brigade performed both theater and field army communications functions. And of course we took care of all the other normal support missions of a field army—medical, personnel replacement, military police, transportation, ammunition, fuel, rations, and all other supplies, and all kinds and levels of repair and maintenance. We even established an artillery section, which performed as a full-fledged field army artillery staff doing such tasks as organizing a counter-battery organization along the DMZ.

Intelligence was an area to which USARV could have contributed substantively by improving and expanding the intelligence capabilities of major Army combat units, particularly division and separate brigades. We at USARV believed that skilled intelligence personnel and capabilities were too highly centralized at MACV level and we wanted to spread the wealth a little by transferring some of these assets to lower echelons of intelligence, but we were unable to make our case with the MACV J-2. We did make some headway, nevertheless, in speeding up the passing of tactically valuable but fleeting intelligence obtained by MACV from signal intercepts to the immediately concerned field commanders.

At Westmoreland's urging we accelerated the move of HQ USARV in the summer of 1967 out of the Saigon area to new facilities at Long Binh, but I was uncomfortable with the ambitious construction nearing completion there, in particular the individual quarters built for general officers on the USARV staff. I would have much preferred to live in a small tent. Although it was far too late to change the basic character of the construction, we were able to eliminate many nonessentials.

Shortly before we moved out of Saigon, McNamara in June 1967 visited Vietnam to consult with Westmoreland on MACV's latest request for additional forces. The conferences were held at USARV headquarters. Holding forth in a large, crowded conference room, McNamara put on a dazzling performance as he listened to a comprehensive series of MACV briefings, asking sharp questions and making pungent comments. The secretary's private reaction was not known, for we were not privy to Westmoreland's "one-on-one" meetings with him.

A short time later we learned that President Johnson in July 1967 raised the projected June 1968 troop ceiling from 470,000 to 525,000. But it also became perfectly clear that our civilian and military leaders were far apart on the need to mobilize and on the objectives of the war in South Vietnam. Late in 1967 McNamara advised the president that to continue the war at a high level of intensity was not in the best interests of the United States, and recommended the reduction of U.S. air and ground operations. This no doubt influenced President Johnson's decision to replace McNamara with Clark Clifford as secretary of defense in March 1968.[1]

The strong-minded and seemingly insensitive McNamara gave an impression, perhaps unintentional, of arrogance, but underneath this hard exterior was a sensitive man. He had the perception to see that something was seriously awry in Vietnam, and the courage, right or wrong, to change his mind about the war. Several years later, in June 1971, part of the basis of McNamara's disenchantment was revealed in great detail when the *New York Times* published what became known as *The Pentagon Papers,* based on a highly classified, voluminous official study from the Office of the Secretary of Defense entitled "History of U.S. Decision-making Process in Vietnam." Commissioned by Secretary McNamara in June 1967 and not completed until January 1969, it was prepared secretly by a team of about forty civilian and military officials knowledgeable about Vietnam. Some of the authors were bitter, outspoken critics of the war, and their bias is reflected in some parts of the report.

McNamara's successor, the suave and impressive Clifford, before he became secretary of defense, visited Saigon in July 1967 with General Taylor during a fruitless trip through the Far East designed to obtain more support from our allies in the Pacific. At the time we had no inkling that Clifford was to play a key role later in Washington in determining the Johnson administration's outlook on the war.

During the course of 1967, political pressures on President Johnson increased in the United States, and concrete indications that our war efforts were making progress became more and more urgent. After ducking several direct invitations from the president to make a public appearance at home, Westmoreland returned to Washington and addressed a joint session of the Congress on 28 April 1967. In a dramatic speech he stated that the allies would prevail and praised the performance of American troops in Vietnam.[2]

Although this speech helped raise spirits on the home front for a while, the president continued to feel the heat from steadily rising domestic dissent. As a result, in November 1967 he summoned both Bunker and Westmoreland home to make public appearances and to testify before the Congress in support of the war effort. Since it was obvious that Westmoreland was being used for political purposes, many of us in Vietnam at the time resented having our field commander put on the spot in this manner. Westmoreland enjoyed these occasions, however, and would return to Saigon still "up on cloud nine."

During this latter trip, Westmoreland addressed the National Press Club on 21 November, and made his first public explanation of his strategy. Realizing the growing discontent at home with a prolonged war, Westmoreland offered the prospect of phasing down the American commitment while turning over more of the burden to South Vietnam. His tone was upbeat, and in answer to a question after the speech he stated that it might be possible to phase down U.S. troop levels two years hence, or in November 1969.[3] Voicing a specific time element was unfortunate, however, because it raised expectations, and the unforeseen shock of the enemy's Tet offensive was just around the corner.

Well before Tet 1968, my chief of staff at USARV, General Taber, was very skeptical about any suggestions that the Viet Cong were so hard-pressed in III and IV CTZs that they had been forced to break up into small groups and lie low. Taber had been a U.S. military attaché in Indochina in the early 1950s and was one of the few Americans to visit Dien Bien Phu before it fell in 1954. His estimate of the French situation in Vietnam at that time was pessimistic, sharply different from the optimistic estimate supported by the U.S. MAAG chief in Saigon. Taber had seen the French repeatedly deceived by the Viet Minh into thinking that enemy forces were in trouble when in fact they were gearing up to take the offensive again. Thus he believed that the current lull clearly meant that Hanoi was preparing to launch a major offensive. As it was, however, HQ MACV did not regard such an eventuality as highly probable until one week before Hanoi began its Tet offensive.

When the Tet offensive hit the Long Binh area before daylight on 31 January 1968, I was very proud of the performance of HQ USARV and the many support-type units which manned the huge perimeter protecting the base. Battalion-size VC attacks struck hard at our clerks and mechanics at several points, but their defenses were never penetrated. HQ II FFV in the north-central area of the same perimeter, however, was so hard pressed that most of the 11th Armored Cavalry Regiment had to be called in to keep the II FFV command post from being overrun.

At the beginning of the Tet offensive, allied troops in the southern CTZs were forewarned when some enemy forces, apparently by mistake, jumped the gun and began their attacks 24 hours ahead of schedule, on 30 January. These early attacks occurred at Nha Trang and Qui Nhon in the coastal area of II CTZ; at Ban Me Thuot, Kontum City, and Pleiku in the Central Highlands, II CTZ; and near Danang in I CTZ. This pattern of attacks indicated a planned, possibly country-wide offensive generally aimed at the large urban areas, province and district capitals. Despite these warnings, however, enemy troops surprised numerous South Vietnamese military installations when the main attacks occurred on 31 January. A major factor favoring the enemy was that practically all ARVN and RF/PF units were at very low strength, since many of the soldiers had been given home leave for the Tet holidays. American units, on the other hand, were not affected by Tet, a Vietnamese holiday that is the equivalent of our Fourth of July, Thanksgiving, Christmas, and Easter all rolled into one glorious period of celebration.

One of USARV's pre-Tet missions was to act as MACV's alternate command post, if that ever became necessary, and during the Tet fighting we demonstrated our ability to operate around the clock. HQ MACV was only partially operational for several days after the Tet offensive broke because many MACV staff personnel, billeted all over Saigon, were prevented from getting to work by enemy activity within the city.

The American embassy was also rudely disrupted by enemy action. Before dawn on 31 January a Viet Cong assault unit blew a hole in the wall surrounding the embassy compound in Saigon and stormed into the grounds. Alerted to the danger, U.S. guards immediately escorted Ambassador Bunker from his living quarters inside the compound to a safe-house in a different part of Saigon. U.S. Army military police and U.S. Marine guards valiantly defended the embassy until troops from the 101st Airborne Division arrived by "Huey" helicopters, landing on the roof of the chancery. Surviving enemy soldiers were driven from the grounds, but not before a terrific fire fight made a shambles of the first two floors of the chancery.

HQ U.S. 7th Air Force, on the other hand, also located at Tan Son Nhut airfield on the outskirts of Saigon, was well prepared for the attack. The commander, General William W. Momyer, insisted that his senior officers and NCOs be billeted near their operational stations; his foresight and dedicated outlook paid off handsomely.

U.S. Air Force personnel at Bien Hoa air base just east of Saigon, however, were not so well off, finding themselves in the middle of a first-class ground battle. American fighter aircraft at the base were unable to launch a single sortie for about forty-eight hours until 101st Airborne Division troopers finally drove off the enemy and the airfield could become operational again. It was a highly embarrasssing, if not galling, experience for our Air Force compatriots because during this period Army attack helicopters (Huey Cobras) flew scores of sorties in support of the U.S. and ARVN troops engaged in clearing the Bien Hoa area.

Before Tet, I used to be kidded a lot about invariably coming to HQ MACV in my field uniform, but after Tet it was a different story when the headquarters area took on the appearance of a fortress. A local defense force was formed, comprised of men from all the services, dressed in special jungle camouflage uniforms and armed with M-16 rifles. Nick-named the "MACV Tigers," the force was a welcome idea but slightly late.

Nevertheless, during Tet, MACV maintained control of the overall direction of operations, and the basic command and communications network in South Vietnam functioned effectively. But USARV, through its "vertical" commands, including the aviation brigade, logistics command, military police brigade, engineer command, medical brigade, and signal brigade, had sources of information on the combat and logistic situation throughout South Vietnam which were not immediately available to MACV. In many areas, including Saigon, USARV support troops—military police, aviation mechanics, construction engineers, supply clerks, and communications specialists—found themselves fighting like infantry. Thus during the first few days of Tet, USARV support troops played a valuable role in gathering comprehensive, timely information on the situation for the use of MACV, CINCPAC, and the JCS, and contributed directly to the military defeat of the enemy.

Prior to the Tet 1968 offensive, American and South Vietnamese officials alike shared the feeling that the enemy was planning something big during the dry monsoon that began in October 1967. We were no doubt deceived about the nature of the expected offensive by the bloody frontier attacks in I, II, and III CTZs in November 1967. The enemy buildup near the end of 1967 in northwestern I CTZ, prior to Hanoi's all-out effort in 1968 to take Khe Sanh, reinforced the deception. In the Mekong Delta (IV CTZ), things were too quiet in the fall of 1967. One hypothesis was that allied operations had so weakened Viet Cong forces in the area that they had broken up into small groups and gone underground. But the eruption of large-unit enemy attacks throughout the Delta on 31 January 1968 served to confirm the differing view that enemy forces had simply kept quiet while they prepared for the Tet offensive.

And so while we were expecting big trouble at the time of Tet, we were surprised by the timing (judging that it would come *after* Tet), by the nature of the enemy attacks aimed at the large urban centers, by the enemy's ability to launch coordinated, almost simultaneous major attacks country-wide, and by the total weight of the offensive. It dwarfed all previous enemy efforts. Taking advantage of the Tet celebrations, the enemy had managed to infiltrate large units around allied forces and emerge with little warning at the edge of or inside almost every major city in the country.

A retrospective review of our intelligence performance just prior to Tet 1968 reveals that major differences existed within the U.S. intelligence community with respect to estimated enemy strength in South Vietnam at the time. Generally the MACV J-2 (intelligence officer) and the Defense Intelligence Agency (DIA) supported a considerably lower estimate than did the CIA. This led to an intelligence conference at HQ CINCPAC in Honolulu in the fall of 1967 which produced enemy strength estimates somewhat higher than MACV-DIA's but still significantly lower than the CIA's. In turn this became the basis for a special national intelligence estimate published in Washington in November 1967 which stated that regular force strength (VC and NVA) in the South had declined slightly, to roughly 120,000, while guerrilla forces had suffered a substantial reduction. Some CIA analysts supported an increasing rather than decreasing regular force, especially VC, and contended that guerrilla forces were likewise increasing rather than decreasing. Reportedly Richard Helms, the director of Central Intelligence, reluctantly agreed to the figures in the interest of giving the president an agreed national estimate on enemy strength.

In Vietnam at the time I was generally aware of this intelligence dispute. During the immediate Tet period I was also very much aware of public allegations of a major intelligence failure, some critics at home even going so far as to allege deliberate understating of enemy capabilities on the part of MACV in order to claim progress in "winning" the war. We all knew, of course, that there was pressure from Washington to show progress and that 1968 was a presidential election year, but deliberate manipulation of intelligence is neither a fair nor a true judgment. Nevertheless, in hindsight I feel that the November 1967 agreed national estimate of enemy strength—generally lower than the CIA's estimate, which was later confirmed[4]—probably helped reinforce the feeling in Vietnam prior to Tet 1968 that the enemy was not capable of conducting major, near-simultaneous, country-wide attacks. In turn, this may have contributed to the tactical surprise achieved by Hanoi.

Estimating enemy strength in a partly conventional, partly guerrilla, highly unorthodox war like Vietnam is extremely complex and difficult. At best such estimates are "best guesses." There are just too many highly uncertain factors. Estimating the strength of regular, so-called "main force" and "local force" units, VC and NVA, is relatively straightforward, but for other categories—part-time guerrillas, local militia (self-defense forces), civilians forced to act as ammunition bearers or in other support roles in an engagement, political cadres in the villages and hamlets, and the like— it is a far different matter. What categories had sufficient military capability to be counted as enemy soldiers? A related issue concerns the enemy casualties that should be counted in adjusting enemy troop strength. A regular NVA soldier stripped of his uniform for a sapper (demolition) mission is indistinguishable from a local guerrilla, local militiaman, or a local civilian impressed into carrying ammunition.

Nevertheless it seems clear that MACV and the U.S. embassy, probably dating from the 1963–64 period, consistently understated the growing dimension of Viet Cong part-time guerrillas and emerging regular main and local force units. Many American and South Vietnamese officials simply did not understand the nature of the insurgency and the need for close civilian-military coordination between Vietnamese special police and military intelligence at every level from the district on up to Saigon if a complete picture of the enemy was to be obtained. This was the origin of the order-of-battle controversy that went on within the intelligence community from the mid 1960s to the early 1970s.

The rate of infiltration down the Ho Chi Minh Trail to the South was also at issue. Basic intelligence on infiltrating units came from signal intercepts, but MACV quite properly did not accept such evidence for inclusion in the MACV order of battle (the detailed listing of various elements of the enemy forces) without positive collateral evidence, such as a unit identification from a POW, or a captured document. As a result, there was a time lag, sometimes of several months, after receipt of an intercept about a unit before MACV adjusted its order of battle. This conservative methodology meant that MACV's enemy strength estimates were often out of date.

In short, overall estimated enemy strength figures were the sum of various force and personnel estimates of widely varying validity. But as a final observation, I would note that overestimating enemy forces is potentially as risky as *under*estimating them; either could lead to poor decisions, with disastrous results for one's own strategy, force planning, and tactical operations.

At the time of the enemy Tet offensive of 1968, none of us realized the ultimate significance of this period in the war and the profound impact that it would have on the United States. Although it ended up as an allied military victory in Vietnam, at home it resulted in a stunning political and psychological defeat for the United States and the Republic of Vietnam. For Hanoi, it was the reverse, a military defeat in the field of large proportions, which included almost total annihilation of the underground Viet Cong political structure in South Vietnam, but, of far greater import, a decisive political victory. Thereafter, Hanoi relied mainly on the North Vietnamese Army to conquer South Vietnam.

In the United States, concern for the besieged U.S. Marine combat base at Khe Sanh, fanned in the media by amateur "military" analysts likening the situation to Dien Bien Phu, magnified the psychological effect of Tet. The enemy did go all out to take Khe Sanh and undoubtedly this was a major element of Hanoi's Tet offensive. Senior military professionals in Vietnam, however, unanimously agreed that U.S. forces could and would hold the base against all comers. There was simply no comparison between the two cases. Overwhelming air- and ground-delivered firepower, coupled with resupply and reinforcement capabilities by air, regardless of weather and visibility conditions, were U.S. cards that the enemy could not match. Yet undue fear of Khe Sanh's loss persisted until the enemy began withdrawing in March 1968 and the area was cleared by 1st Cavalry Division airmobile operations in conjunction with a Marine ground linkup in April 1968.

Another aggravating factor was the request made by Westmoreland not long after the Teg offensive had begun for a little over 200,000 additional American troops. Intended to be phased over a period of time to allow MACV to exploit the enemy defeat in Vietnam and to provide a strategic reserve in the United States for the JCS, the request was interpreted by many influential members of Congress and governmental officials in Washington to mean that more troops were urgently needed to meet an emergency situation. The timing was particularly unfortunate because it played into the hands of the war critics. Regrettably, General Wheeler, who engineered and in reality was responsible for Westmoreland's abortive request, did little to set the record straight.

On the plus side, the enemy violation of Tet outraged large segments of the South Vietnamese population, who definitely decided that their loyalties lay with Saigon and started lending active support to the government, even to the point of informing South Vietnamese officials when VC or NVA personnel were in their area. One indication of this feeling lay in the behavior of our Vietnamese civilian work force. When the initial enemy attacks occurred, our workers failed to show up in many areas for reasons not entirely clear to us at the time. Our large civilian contractors were similarly affected. As a result we lost some ground in our logistic operations, road construction and improvement efforts, and other construction projects. But within a few days the work force numbers were back to pre-Tet levels.

At any rate, for the first time the Saigon government felt confident enough of popular support to order general mobilization, and numerous young men volunteered to serve in the armed forces. This was a very significant improvement because it meant that the government could now not only maintain its regular toops and other security forces, but also expand their strength. In fact, President Thieu went so far as to launch the formation of a very large people's self-defense force countrywide, and to provide them with arms and ammunition.

On the negative side, Tet was a major catalyst in solidifying disenchantment in the United States with the war, culminating in President Johnson's partial bombing halt of 31 March 1968 and his withdrawal as a future presidential candidate. Tet was not the only catalyst, however. It was no coincidence that the groundswell of American middle-class turning against the war started when middle-class college-age youths began to be drafted in large numbers for duty in Vietnam in 1967–68. But the turning point was Tet. Thereafter the Johnson administration desperately tried to make peace with Hanoi, talks finally beginning in Paris in May 1968.[5]

President Johnson's decisions were profoundly influenced by the views and recommendations of the Clifford group established by the president on 28 Febtary 1968 to take a whole new look at the war and the options open to the United States. The group included Rusk, McNamara (Clifford succeeded him as secretary of defense on 1 March), the director of Central Intelligence (Richard Helms), and General Maxwell D. Taylor. Clifford's report for the group, delivered on 4 March, was pessimistic in tone; its thrust was to caution against any deeper American commitment and to look to the South Vietnamese to carry through on the war. In effect, it was a recommendation for a U.S. disengagement.[6]

The Clifford group was no doubt fully aware of the pessimistic and highly critical nature of the voluminous study of the war commissioned by McNamara in June 1967, subsequently leaked to the *New York Times,* and published as *The Pentagon Papers* in June 1971. The majority view of the president's advisory group known as the "wise men," which included Dean Acheson, George Ball, McGeorge Bundy, Cyrus Vance, and retired Generals Matthew Ridgway and Maxwell Taylor, likewise embodied some form of U.S. disengagement from the war.[7]

In April 1968 the president announced that Abrams would succeed Westmoreland. Abrams took command of MACV in June 1968 and Westmoreland returned to the United States, succeeding General Johnson as the chief of staff, U.S. Army, on 3 July 1968.

Earlier in consultation with the outgoing chief of staff, Westmoreland had selected me to be his vice chief of staff. It was a great honor but I was reluctant to leave Vietnam with so much yet to be done. This was no doubt to be my last job in the field with troops, and I took leave of our gallant forces in Vietnam in a depressed mood. In Washington, late in July 1968, I was sworn in and once again found myself serving as Westmoreland's deputy—this time for the entire U.S. Army worldwide.

4

1968-1969:
The Transition Years

It turned out to be my lot to serve out the final years of direct American involvement in the Vietnam War as the Army vice chief of staff in Washington. In this capacity, I could view those years from the perspective both of the JCS and of the highest command level of the Army, not to mention the civilian stewardship of the Army and the Department of Defense.

While in Vietnam I had not fully appreciated the seriousness of dissent back home, in particular the magnitude of the riots in the United States in the spring of 1968 following the assassination of Martin Luther King on 4 April, when federal troops had to be employed in Washington, Chicago, and Baltimore to restore order. In all, there were major disturbances in 125 cities in 29 states. In such civil disorders the Department of the Army functions as the executive agent for the secretary of defense in providing military support to civil authority when local and state security forces can no longer handle the situation, and must therefore work very closely with the Department of Justice. So as vice chief of staff I was to become intimately familiar with this peculiar Army responsibility when during the later war years violent attempts to disrupt the government were mounted in Washington.

One aspect of this Army mission, however, was particularly disturbing—the question of gathering information on potential disorders within the United States, in effect a domestic intelligence function. I learned that earlier the Department of Justice had called upon the Army to take on this task, apparently after the FBI very sensibly declined to do so, and the Army had dutifully complied. But it was a dubious mission for the military, and our civilian superiors in the Department of Defense were slow to recognize the constitutional pitfalls involved. By the time they did, a large amount of information on various American nationals had been accumulated and placed in military intelligence computers, and some undercover intelligence operations had been conducted which were very probably illegal. It took many months to track down and eliminate the computerized data, and this became a major headache.

But it was highly disillusioning to see the Army pilloried publicly for "spying on civilians" when it had done precisely what higher civilian authority had requested. It was even more disappointing to see our civilian masters run for cover and let the military take the blame. There is no simple answer to this dilemma for the military man, because if he declines to carry out an order of questionable legality he can be replaced by someone who is willing to do so. Thus it comes back to the responsible political leaders. If in their judgment the situation requires such drastic action, then those leaders must publicly assume the responsibility for the consequences.

But even after American involvement in Vietnam peaked in 1968–69 and then began to wane in 1970–71, and although power had been transferred from a Democratic to a Republican administration, dissent and organized civil disorders continued in the United States. These were particularly trying days for the Army. It bore the brunt of combat in Vietnam, and at home was publicly villified by the press, on the campuses, and even in the churches, for fighting an "immoral" war. At the same time, the Army was being called upon repeatedly to reinforce civilian law enforcement agencies.

It was bad enough for our citizen soldiers returning home, but for career Army officers and noncommissioned officers rotating to Vietnam on successive tours of duty, the war was a recurring nightmare. Their families felt even greater pressure as a new drug culture, the abdication of authority in our high schools and colleges, and a new permissiveness in our society all arrived almost simultaneously. The plight of the wives of career soldiers is poignantly told in Thomas Fleming's historical novel *The Officers' Wives*.[1]

A draft system rightly perceived by our youth to be grossly unfair, coupled with a disastrous political decision to opt for "guns and butter" rather than mobilization, created an explosive domestic situation. It was clear to anyone interested that the draft was unfair to the less advantaged, particularly to black males. In the 1961–66 period, Department of Defense statistics showed that blacks were more likely to be drafted and sent to Vietnam, more apt to serve in high-risk infantry combat units, and consequently more apt to be killed or wounded in battle. Although black casualty rates were in line with the proportion of blacks in combat units in Vietnam, black casualties amounted to almost one-fourth of U.S. Army enlisted losses at a time when blacks composed approximately 11 percent of the U.S. general population between nineteen and twenty-one years of age.[2]

The Nixon administration early in its tenure initiated legislative proposals to correct the most glaring injustices of the draft. In late November 1969 the draft lottery law was enacted; among other things it precluded arbitrary actions by local draft boards. Soon afterward most of the previously authorized exemptions from the draft were eliminated. But it was too late to soften the deep resentment in the United States to the way the draft had been applied. The damage was already done.

These difficulties at home were sharply reflected in the attitudes of some of our troops in Vietnam. Morale began to decline and disciplinary problems began to rise during the later years of the war. One of the most devastating manifestations of such a deterioration was the appearance in 1969 (peaking in 1971) of so-called "fragging" incidents, mostly involving disgruntled young soldiers who used fragmentation hand grenades against the establishment represented by their leaders. Relatively few incidents had racial overtones. Generally night sneak attacks, they usually occurred in the base camps of service type units and were often directed at career NCOs ("lifers," in the jargon of the draftees) and junior officers. Regardless of their views on the war and their perceived grievances, the soldiers involved in these cowardly attacks were committing nothing less than assault with intent to do bodily harm.

Our armed forces have had serious disciplinary problems in past American wars, even in the two world wars that enjoyed relatively positive domestic support in the United States. All services have had substantial desertion rates that went up as the war grew longer. Some soldiers and marines have refused to obey orders in combat situations in which their lives were at risk, some airmen have refused to fly combat missions, and some sailors have jumped ship to escape hazardous duty. In that context, Vietnam was no different from past wars. In numbers, desertion rates in Vietnam were comparable to those experienced during the later years of World War II.[3]

Although strong leadership, realistic training, and first-class weapons and equipment help make good warriors, armies and navies from the beginning of organized societies have all had to rely on strict discipline backed up by punitive legal sanctions to enforce that discipline swiftly and impartially, especially in time of war. Without such a punitive military code it is probably a moot question whether troops would fight a tough, determined enemy at the risk of their own lives. It is true that fighting men in reality fight for their own small units—squads and platoons—and their buddies, or their homes and families, rather than some abstract concept of love of country. And it can be demonstrated that the esteem of his peers, what his squadmates think of him, mean a great deal to the soldier and act in effect like another sanction shoring up his conduct on the battlefield. But the larger sanctions enforced by his society still loom in the background.

In the case of the Vietnam War, however, low morale at home weakened these sanctions in the combat zone and made it even more difficult for small-unit leaders and higher commanders to get their troops to respond to orders that entailed physical danger. Even so, to its everlasting credit the U.S. Army did not fail in its duties despite the unprecendented, enormous pressures of the period.

At the same time that societal troubles were erupting at home, the Army was plagued by a series of seemingly endless internal problems of a serious nature. My Lai, which surfaced in March 1969, and the Green Beret incident of July 1969 were two which demanded the intense attention of the high command, including ultimately the commander-in-chief himself.

Ironically, the Army's Special Forces took the heat on the Green Beret affair, which involved the death of a foreign intelligence agent in Vietnam, although the people directly responsible were intelligence personnel assigned to Special Forces, operating under J-2, MACV. The Green Beret case probably could have been handled quietly without attracting national attention in the United States had not General Abrams become incensed over what he perceived to be a coverup in the 5th Special Forces Group, where the intelligence personnel were assigned. The USARV HQ put the senior officers of the group in solitary confinement in the "LBJ" (Long Binh jail) without benefit of due process. The press learned of the affair and exposed the officers' plight, which forced Secretary of the Army Resor to intervene. Eventually the White House declared that it was not in the national interest to prosecute the case any further.

The My Lai tragedy was quite a different matter. Bursting upon the Army's highest officials without warning, it involved a small infantry unit in the Americal Division operating in I CTZ and occurred in March 1968, when both General Westmoreland and I were still in Vietnam. We—indeed, everyone except those involved—were totally ignorant about the matter until it surfaced a year later, when senior officials in Washington received letters and photographs vividly depicting the incident from a former soldier (a combat photographer) of the division. Exhaustive investigations were immediately launched by the Army, and eventually formal courts-martial, or other administrative actions of a punitive nature, were conducted where the evidence so warranted.

Reflecting on the affair in the light of my own experiences and those of countless others who served in Vietnam, I am convinced that My Lai was an aberration. Americans did indeed commit war crimes in the course of the protracted Vietnam War, but no more in proportion to the numbers of people involved than have occurred in past wars. In Vietnam, allegations normally were promptly and thoroughly investigated by impartial personnel, and where substantiated (somewhat less than 50 percent of the time), appropriate punitive actions were taken. But these crimes were mostly individual in nature, with only a very few committed by two or three men together.

My Lai, on the other hand, involved actions committed by a unit under control of its leaders, in a systematic, organized way and then deliberately concealed. To make matters far worse, allegations of misdeeds did reach senior officers of the division, including the division commander, but were not adequately investigated. The American Division, operating in the northernmost military region in South Vietnam, was farther removed from HQ USARV and HQ MACV than any other U.S. Army forces. This contributed significantly to the fact that the dark secret lay hidden for over a year.

Exploring why it happened and probing the broader implications of the episode are quite beyond the scope of this book. The most objective, comprehensive, and balanced exposé of war crimes in Vietnam in general and of My Lai in particular appears in Professor Guenter Lewy's book, *America in Vietnam,*[4] which I commend to the interested reader. On the other hand, the so-called Peers Report (W.R. Peers, *The My Lai Inquiry*)[5] in my opinion lacks objectivity and balance. Lieutenant General Peers, directed to make the inquiry by General Westmoreland and Secretary Resor in November 1969, organized a large panel of military and civilian (Department of the Army employees) investigators which essentially completed its work in March 1970. After Secretary Resor added two prominent civilian criminal lawyers to the panel in December 1969, the court of inquiry took on a "star chamber" aspect. Persons under investigation were not allowed to be present when witnesses were examined, or to cross-examine witnesses, or to have legal counsel. Subsequently the proceedings were considered by many observers to be highly improper and the inquiry panel, declining to cooperate with congressional investigations underway, incurred the wrath of the House Armed Services Committee. More significantly, the court of inquiry's activities complicated and hampered the formal investigation of specific offenses charged against individuals under the Articles of War. But the most unfortunate aspect of the Peers inquiry was that it was exploited by many to promote sensational headlines and to excite further anti-Vietnam feelings in the United States.

Serious drug and racial disharmony problems also surfaced in the Army as our Vietnamese involvement began to wind down. Widespread drug abuse became evident among American soldiers in Vietnam about a month after the Cambodian invasion began in the spring of 1970. A short time later farspread use of drugs appeared in U.S. forces serving in Germany. How this apparent drug explosion came about we could never satisfactorily explain. One thesis attributed it to a well planned and executed Mafia operation, but this could not be demonstrated. Another thesis blamed Hanoi for the phenomenon. A simpler explanation is that in the beginning small unit leaders chose to look the other way until finally durg use was so prevalent that it could no longer be ignored. As soon as commanders started reporting drug use to higher headquarters, it created the illusion of a sudden appearance. To aggravate the drug situation in Germany, racial disorders also were severe among the troops of the U.S. Seventh Army.

By the summer of 1968, near the peak of U.S. force levels in Southeast Asia, it had become very clear that President Johnson had lost any stomach for the war and was determined to negotiate a political settlement with Hanoi. For understandable and legitimate political reasons, he wanted to accomplish this before our national elections in November. There ensued an almost frenzied round of White House meetings in which the president frantically sought support from his cabinet members, close advisers, and congressional leaders for a negotiated agreement which would deescalate the conflict and eventually lead to a peaceful ending. It was this desperate kind of negotiating that led to the complete bombing halt of 31 October 1968, on the shaky basis of the famous informal, unwritten "understandings" between the United States and North Vietnam, which Hanoi neither accepted nor rejected at the time of the bombing halt but later completely ignored.

Twice during October 1968, filling in for General Westmoreland, who could not be present, I attended meetings held by the president in the Cabinet Room of the White House concerning the question of a total bombing cessation. The first, on 14 October, was attended by Secretary of Defense Clifford; the JCS (General Wheeler, chairman; General McConnell, chief of staff, U.S. Air Force; Admiral Thomas H. Moorer, chief of Naval Operations; General Leonard F. Chapman, commandant, U.S. Marine Corps; and myself, representing the U.S. Army); W.W. Rostow, national security adviser to the president; and Senator Richard B. Russell. The second meeting, on 31 October, was an expanded cabinet meeting which the JCS also attended. Neither one was a true discussion or a very fruitful session. The first meeting was especially disconcerting for two reasons. First, the presidential photographer was present the entire time, taking an unending series of snapshots of the president from every conceivable angle. It was impossible to ignore the photographer's presence. Second, the president was in constant motion, receiving or making telephone calls, pressing the buzzer under the top of the desk to give orders for all kinds of tasks, and frequently interrupting anyone trying to articulate his views. The atmosphere was hardly conducive to a meaningful discussion, and it was obvious that the president was paying scant attention to what his visitors had to say. At both meetings the unmistakable impression was that of a pro forma gathering designed to support the claim of undivided support for the bombing halt that the president had obviously settled upon long beforehand.

At the first meeting Secretary Clifford and General Wheeler supported the rationale for the decision, while the service chiefs unequivocally pointed out the uncertainty of the so-called understandings and the one-sided nature of the matter—Hanoi had conceded nothing. But there was one view stated that the president could not ignore. Senator Russell looked him in the eye and said in effect that the president indeed had the authority but must accept full responsibility for the decision, and that he (Senator Russell) would not share such responsibility because he felt that the president was making a serious mistake.

The second meeting was a remarkable performance. The president stated what he intended to do and then polled the cabinet members and others present, including the service secretaries, one by one, as to their views. There were no substantive comments in response, each person indicating his full support. It was obvious that if anyone had any differing views or reservations, he was not about to state them in such a forum. This meeting was apparently the principal basis for the "unanimous" support for the bombing halt decision described by President Johnson in his book *The Vantage Point*.[6]

Shortly thereafter, in November 1968, Richard M. Nixon won a narrow victory at the polls. The people had spoken, but their message was perhaps more a repudiation of the Johnson administration than an enthusiastic endorsement of Nixon. More importantly, while the new secretary of defense, Melvin R. Laird, clearly interpreted the election as a mandate to get the nation out of Vietnam, it was not at all clear that President Nixon shared this view.

In South Vietnam, allied forces helped hold the country together during the last half of 1968 by repulsing several enemy mini-offensives and getting pacification moving again as the nation recovered from the effects of the heavy fighting during and after Tet. Ambassador Bunker, his deputy, the highly experienced and competent Ambassador Samuel Berger, and General Abrams made a strong, effective, and intelligent team. Abrams concentrated on pacification and on improving the South Vietnamese armed forces, while Bunker and Berger worked with President Thieu and his government to strengthen the economy, achieve political stability, and improve overall performance.

Berger strongly advocated that the United States apply more pressure on President Thieu and other senior Vietnamese officials to weed out incompetent or corrupt leaders in the armed forces and the government. Berger and I discussed this matter on several occasions, and I heartily supported his views. But Bunker and Abrams believed that the South Vietnamese governmental fabric was fragile, and therefore felt that increasing such pressure would be unduly risky.

Berger, replacing Gene Locke as the deputy U.S. mission chief in Saigon, earlier had served as U.S. ambassador to South Korea (1961–

64), where he succeeded in restoring political stability and in laying the foundation for the striking economic development of the country in subsequent years. His untimely death in February 1980 was a great loss.

In November 1968, William E. Colby (later to become the director of Central Intelligence) became Abrams's deputy for pacification, replacing Komer, who had been appointed U.S. ambassador to Turkey. In sharp contrast to Komer's aggressive, outspoken manner, Colby was quiet and thoughtful. A career CIA official, he had served several times in Vietnam, including one tour as the CIA station chief in Saigon and another as a senior CORDS official. He had also helped the South Vietnamese organize Project Phoenix, targeted against the Viet Cong political organization. George Jacobson, Ambassador Bunker's special assistant for pacification, became Colby's deputy at this time. He and Colby made a strong team.

The first Nixon administration included a strong secretary of defense, the shrewd and able Laird, with unequalled background gained from his long experience in the Congress. By preagreement, Laird served for four years and then voluntarily left the position in late January 1973. Melvin Laird was a political animal to the marrow of his bones. He was adept at manipulating the JCS and the service secretaries, not to mention the Congress, and more often than not got his own way. He could use one line with the JCS, a somewhat different one with the service secretaries, and a third version in dealing with key members of the Congress, many of whom were close personal friends; meanwhile, all the time he skillfully kept his options open. His relations with the White House were generally adversarial in nature, but regardless of how issues were settled, he did not lose his contagious good humor, and gracefully accepted the final decisions of the president, even though in some instances he may have strongly opposed him. An example was the all-volunteer force concept which President Nixon decided to implement for domestic political reasons, despite the fact that every member of his cabinet, according to Secretary Laird, opposed the idea (although not all for the same reasons). Laird was strongly opposed, but just as firmly supported Nixon's decision. The new secretary of defense made this very clear to the JCS at one of his first meetings with the chiefs in January 1969.

Stanley R. Resor, who had become secretary of the Army under President Johnson on 7 July 1965, was held over under the new administration until 30 June 1971, a record-breaking six years. Hardworking and energetic, Resor became intimately familiar with the administrative details of running the Army. This proud, intelligent man possessed uncompromising integrity and strongly resisted political pressure that he felt to be improper. He was also one of the most knowledgeable Americans with respect to Southeast Asia, and steadfastly supported U.S. policy in Vietnam. He whole-heartedly supported the critically important pacification program and greatly improved the quality and prestige of the U.S. military advisers (mostly Army) serving in Vietnam.

Robert F. Froehlke, who succeeded Resor on 1 July 1971, did a good job in providing continuity as the civilian leader of the Army during a critical period in American history. Willing to question traditional "sacred cows," Froehlke was a breath of fresh air for a weary American Army tired of a steady diet of bad news. Although he was very close to Laird, having managed several of his congressional campaigns and coming from the same part of Wisconsin, Froehlke resisted undue "guidance" from Laird and was his own man in managing the Army.

The JCS lineup at the start of the new administration found General Wheeler continuing as the chairman until 2 July 1970. In all he served for six years. (By law the term of the chairman of the JCS is two years; the president can, however, extend that term for an additional two years, subject to confirmation by the Senate. In wartime, there is no limit to the number of such extensions.) Wheeler was a fine chairman, who literally gave his life to the country. The great responsibilities and pressures of the job broke his health and he died not long after he retired. He was highly respected and had the ear of the president, but he was overshadowed by such men as McNamara, the constant and courageous Dean Rusk, who never wavered from his support of U.S. policy, and the eccentrically brilliant NSC adviser to the president, Henry Kissinger.

Wheeler was succeeded by Admiral Thomas H. Moorer, who moved up from the CNO job and served two terms as chairman of the JCS from 3 July 1970 to 30 June 1974. A hearty, bluff naval aviator, Moorer was quite a different chairman. His background was primarily a naval one with little joint experience, in contrast to Wheeler's predominantly staff background with considerable experience in the joint arena. There was one noticeable difference in their modus operandi—where General Wheeler religiously kept the other chiefs closely informed on all developments in the national security area, debriefing them in detail on the numerous intergovernmental meetings attended only by the chairman, Admiral Moorer was less inclined to do so.

This tendency was heightened by a definite trend under the new secretary of defense to make the JCS chairman more and more a single chief of staff in terms of day-to-day operations. This trend was inevitable, particularly in the fast-moving operational environment of wartime, but it risked creating a climate in which the other chiefs found themselves less and less informed, if not isolated, on operational matters. It put the onus on each individual chief to keep himself up to speed, but this is difficult when the Joint Staff works exclusively for the chairman with respect to current operations.

Moorer was an effective chairman in many ways, but the hostilities in Southeast Asia puzzled him. He had difficulty in handling the strange-sounding Vietnamese place and family names. But, of far more significance, he could not appreciate the deeper subtleties of the war.

In contrast to the two-year term of the CJCS, the service chiefs by law are appointed for a four-year term, the congressional intent being to shield the chiefs from undue political pressure. (The Congress recognized, on the other hand, that the CJCS is in reality a member of the administration and therefore gave the president more flexibility with respect to the chairman's tenure.) The service chief lineup at the time was as follows.

General Westmoreland, the Army chief of staff, who was to serve from 3 July 1968 to 30 June 1972, guided the U.S. Army through a crucial period—withdrawing from active hostilities in Vietnam, trying to restore high standards of ethics and professionalism, and adjusting to the changing environment of the post-Vietnam era. Because of the unpopularity of the war, the administration considered Westmoreland a political liability and treated him accordingly. Both major political parties regarded him as a significant presidential threat because he was so well known nationally and internationally. A proud, sensitive South Carolinian, but always a Christian gentleman, Westmoreland was deeply hurt by the slights accorded him by administration officials, who rarely consulted him on Vietnam affairs. But he carried on with great forbearance and in good humor, and rarely complained. Indeed, I cannot recall a single instance when Westmoreland got genuinely angry and lost his temper, much less resorted to even mild swearing. In retrospect, I wonder whether he would not have fared better had he blown off some steam occasionally. The army benefited greatly by his leadership.

It was my good fortune to serve as his vice chief, his alter ego. Early in his tour of duty, General Westmoreland decided to travel extensively; given the unsettled conditions of the time, his visits to Army troops throughout the United States and overseas were a necessary stabilizing factor. For my part, I became very familiar not only with the Army's internal affairs but also with the JCS arena.

Admiral Elmo R. Zumwalt, Jr., succeeded Admiral Moorer as chief of naval operations on 1 July 1970 and served until 19 June 1974. He was neither his predecessor's nor the Navy's sentimental choice for the job, as he was relatively very junior and lacked major command experience. But he was bright and energetic, and his duty at sea with the fleet and his systems analysis background were big pluses in dealing with the civilian bureaucracy in Defense. At JCS sessions he was sometimes naive (particularly with respect to the conduct of the war) and often an irritant, but I admired his courage in tackling deep-seated internal problems of the Navy. He was also farsighted and innovative in shaping the Navy of the future, and his sound influence on naval technological and doctrinal areas will bear fruit in the long run.

General John D. Ryan succeeded General McConnell as chief of staff, U.S. Air Force, on 1 August 1969 and served until 31 July 1973. Ryan, a leading expert and proponent of strategic air power, had an unexcelled combat record. Well liked and admired, he was the favorite choice of the Air Force for the job. In the joint arena his aggressive, impatient nature made it difficult for him to sit still during any prolonged debate and he had little use for the art of compromise. But the other chiefs never had any doubt as to where he stood on an issue.

General Leonard F. Chapman had succeeded General Green as commandant, U.S. Marine Corps, on 1 January 1968 and served until 31 December 1971. A quiet, articulate, and thoughtful man, Chapman was a steadying influence on JCS deliberations and could hold his own in any company. But his "Mr. Nice Guy" approach to real world issues was not in character with the traditional Marine Corps image. It was a relief when Chapman abandoned his serene composure under pressure and got his hands dirty along with the other chiefs grappling with difficult problems.

During the transition period the new administration early in 1969 conducted a thorough review of senior U.S. policymakers' views on the war. The results were mixed, finding our senior civilian and military leaders in the Pacific and the JCS in Washington reasonably optimistic about achieving a satisfactory ending, while our civilian leaders in the federal government leaned more to the pessimistic side. Likewise, the intelligence community was not in complete accord in estimating enemy capabilities and prospects. But the administration lost no time in adopting its own strategy of "Vietnamization" (a term coined by Laird) of the war, which was to be concurrent with a U.S. dissengagement from South Vietnam. In Vietnam, John Paul Vann had favored such an approach for years, and in Washington Secretary of Defense Laird was its leading proponent.

Although President Johnson had likewise wanted to Vietnamize the fighting, he visualized a residual allied force in Vietnam and hoped to negotiate a settlement with Hanoi before withdrawing any U.S. troops. President Nixon's negotiating strategy was quite different. He sought to Vietnamize the war by a steady buildup and improvement of South Vietnamese forces and institutions, at the same time bringing military pressure on the enemy, while slowly but steadily withdrawing American troops. Nixon counted on the success of Vietnamization, hoping that both Moscow and Peking would begin to cool about supporting the war, and wanted to strengthen the U.S.-RVN position before negotiating seriously at the bargaining table. It was this hard-nosed strategy that lay behind the president's decisions to order the "secret" bombing of the enemy's sanctuaries in Cambodia in March 1969, the invasion of Cambodia in the spring of 1970, the invasion of Laos in February 1971, and the closing of Haiphong harbor in May 1972.

Supporting this strategy posed somewhat different problems for each military service. While the number of Army soldiers and Marines in combat steadily dropped in Vietnam, the Air Force and the Navy were faced with an even heavier combat commitment in carrying out a sustained air offensive against North Vietnam and periodically providing allout tactical air support to hard-pressed South Vietnamese troops. At the height of this late-in-the-day air action, President Nixon failed to appreciate why the Air Force could not send more tactical fighter squadrons to Vietnam and Thailand, and the Navy, more carriers on the line in the South China Sea. The "details" of creating more combat-ready air crews, additional sea-worthy aircraft carriers with their fighting ship complements, more bombs, ammunition, and spare parts (all well beyond the programmed budget levels requested by the secretary of defense), not to mention the fact that our air bases in Southeast Asia were already saturated and all of the ser-vices were already expending more operations and maintenance funds than had been appropriated by the Congress—all these mundane but nonetheless essential matters simply escaped our commander-in-chief.

Concurrently the authorized manpower strength for each service was being cut back to pre-Vietnam force levels or below. This phasedown was further accelerated by the administration's decision to shift rapidly to an all-volunteer force and to eliminate the draft. From mid-1969 on, draft calls were steadily reduced. On 27 January 1973 a "zero draft" condition was reached and Mr. Laird announced the end of draft calls.

At the same time, the services were struggling to keep authorized force structure levels (the numbers of divisions, air wings, and carrier battle groups, etc.) at the minimum required to meet our strategic com-mitments worldwide. The Office of the Secretary of Defense and the Of-fice of Management and the Budget at the time were fully committed to driving the Army down to nine or ten active divisions, totally inadequate to meet minimal U.S. force requirements (treaty commitments for the most part) in NATO Europe and elsewhere, requirements determined prior to the Vietnam War to be a minimum of sixteen active Army divisions. The Army lost the bureaucratic battle to remain at the sixteen-division level, but thanks to strong White House support, did manage to hold the line at thirteen-plus divisions. Fortunately for our nation succeeding de-fense secretaries persuaded the administration and the Congress to support a sixteen-division active Army structure, although three of the divisions were not fully active but included major elements from the National Guard and Army Reserve. Unfortunately, the resources needed to man, equip, and sustain sixteen active divisions have never been provided to the Army.

Several other interrelated issues arose in connection with the admin-istration's concept of winding down the war for the United States. There were the questions of the rate and timing of the withdrawal of U.S. troops, of the phased reduction of overall U.S. force levels, of when and under what circumstances South Vietnamese forces could hold their own against North Vietnam, and of what residual American presence was required and might be allowed to remain in South Vietnam. The administration sought to phase the reduction of American troops in accordance with MACV's estimate of South Vietnamese capabilities, tempered by the amount of domestic pressure being generated to bring our forces home.

Maintaining the readiness of U.S. forces worldwide became very difficult for all the services, in particular the Army, as draft calls, for political purposes, were often reduced below the numbers requested by the military departments. The failure to mobilize the reserves and provide adequate manpower had almost disastrous consequences for the services, especially their career forces, who found themselves serving repetitive tours of duty in Southeast Asia with little respite in between.

Outside Vietnam, with the manpower available the Army simply could neither maintain units at authorized strength nor properly man key officer and NCO leadership positions, especially in units stationed in the United States and Europe. The result was a drastic drop in combat readiness, lowered morale, and deteriorating discipline. In Europe the key officer and NCO leaders were not in place long enough to get on top of difficult morale problems and control their troops effectively. Despite the outstanding leadership of its commander, General James H. Polk, the proud, well trained, and combat-ready Seventh Army in Germany was in effect, over time, destroyed as a fighting force. Nevertheless, Polk's successors, Lieutenant General A. S. Collins (February–June 1971) and General M. S. Davison (1971–75), who about a year earlier had led our forces in the invasion of Cambodia, managed to meet, if only marginally, our NATO commitments. Fortunately for the United States, the Soviet Union had other fish to fry at the time and opted not to create any crises in Europe.

In South Vietnam, as American troops realized that the United States was disengaging from the war, the challenge to American troop leadership was unparalleled in our history. It is a great tribute to that leadership to note that the American Army in Vietnam held together and continued to perform effectively overall, despite serious disciplinary and morale problems.

Gauging South Vietnamese capabilities as American forces withdrew was a dicey thing. So long as there was a strong U.S. advisory element present, the consensus among American military men held that there was at least a 50-50 chance for South Vietnam to "hack it" against their very tough, determined, and able North Vietnamese foes. American advisers were the backbone of the greater part of the South Vietnamese Army and frequently acted as the de facto leaders of ARVN units in battle. Abrams called our advisers the "glue" that held the South Vietnamese armed forces together. At any rate, all eyes were on the ARVN forces in the field, searching for clues as to their ultimate performance. From the professional military man's point of view this was the key factor, and the more time available to correct well known ARVN deficiencies in such vital things as leadership and training, the better were South Vietnam's chances for survival.

5

1969-1971: Vietnamization

Although the Vietnamization process and the disengagement of U.S. troops from the war began in earnest in the latter part of 1969, few people realized how soon or where the mettle of South Vietnamese forces would be put to the test. The new strategy of Vietnamizing the war, while at the same time bringing greater military pressure to bear on Hanoi and steadily withdrawing U.S. forces, turned on the ability of the South Vietnamese to carry on the war on their own. In this sense the new strategy was a gamble, betting that the South could hold its own with the North. Combined U.S.-RVN cross-border offensive operations against North Vietnamese forces in Cambodia in the spring of 1970 and RVN operations into Laos early in the following year were to be harbingers of the ultimate test to come in 1975.

But the first testing came much earlier, when the enemy conducted a country-wide offensive in February 1969, causing a surge in allied casualties, and hit Saigon in March 1969 with an indiscriminate rocket attack. COMUSMACV and the JCS had long favored bombing the enemy's base sanctuaries along the unpopulated Vietnamese border, but the proposal had not been supported by U.S. civilian leaders for fear of widening the war. Even after President Nixon had decided to launch such an attack, it took some time to persuade Secretary of Defense Laird and Secretary of State William Rogers to go along, and the first B-52 strike was not made until 18 March 1969.[1] Regrettably, tasteless code names, called the "menu series," were given to each strike—names like "breakfast," "dessert," "snack" and the like. This was the beginning of the so-called "secret bombing" of Cambodia, Sihanouk reportedly acquiescing unofficially, and Hanoi choosing not to react for political reasons of its own. The bombing went on with some regularity into the late summer of 1969 and then intermittently until the allied incursion into Cambodia in May 1970, after which U.S. air attacks were conducted openly.

The White House decision to conceal the air attacks was based on reasons which are suspect, in my view. It was done partly to preserve the myth of Cambodia's neutrality, which had been long since fractured by the large presence of NVA troops, unofficially sanctioned by the Sihanouk regime in Phnom Penh. And it was done partly to avoid domestic repercussions in the United States.

The White House staff devised an elaborate scheme to cover the operations. Secret records were kept separate from regular reports, which covered up the true nature of the operations, and great pains were taken to conceal the expenditure of munitions. Knowledge of the operations was kept on a very close-hold basis. In the Pentagon only the secretary of defense, the JCS, a handful on the Joint Staff, and the service DCSOPS were privy to the secret arrangements. Although the service vice chiefs of staff were not intended to know, I soon stumbled onto the operations at a JCS meeting where I was representing the Army chief of staff. General McConnell, the Air Force chief, began grumbling about the operation, labeling the effort to conceal the bombing "stupid," and the other chiefs present chimed in. It didn't take me long to deduce what had been taking place.

Although the service secretaries were not on the need-to-know list, Secretary of the Army Resor began asking questions of the Army staff when major leaks about the attacks first appeared in the press. We decided to disregard the prohibition and thereafter kept Resor reasonably well informed. My conscience did not bother me, for there is a statutory requirement for the service chief of staff to keep his service secretary informed on all significant JCS matters. Stan Resor and I were on close, friendly terms and it was only natural that he would look to me as Westmoreland's alter ego to see that this particular chore got done. Then Brigadier General Donn R. Pepke, assistant DCSOPS for the Army, at least once a week personally briefed Resor on the status of active JCS matters.

Some time later the other service secretaries were to deny publicly any knowledge of the attacks. I find this difficult to accept, particularly with respect to the secretary of the Air Force, Robert Seamans. Surely Seamans must have had some inkling of these operations by USAF B-52s under the Strategic Air Command which went on for over a year.

Secretary of the Navy John Chaffee, on the other hand, might be excused because he was running for governor of Rhode Island at the time and did not have his heart in the Navy job. Moreover, Chaffee had to hustle to keep pace with the irrepressible CNO, Admiral Zumwalt. Chaffee's successor, John Warner, strongly believed that a service secretary should not only be aware of service operations but should feel a sense of responsibility for them. Strong, forceful, and articulate, Warner made a fine secretary. He refused to let Zumwalt ignore him and soon made it quite clear who was running the U.S. Navy.

At the time I believed the decision to operate in secrecy was a bad mistake, and I feel so even more strongly in retrospect. It placed the military in an impossible position, having literally to lie publicly about a perfectly legitimate wartime operation. It made a mockery of any congressional oversight, for only a handful of members of Congress were informed and they had no realistic appreciation of the extent or the implications of the bombings. These congressional leaders should have challenged the decision. It had nothing to do with keeping the operations secret from the enemy, who had to know all about them, nor did the decision have anything to do with enhancing the safety of the combat aircrews making the attacks. In the event of American casualties, how was the Air Force to explain the circumstances to their families?

This matter goes to the very heart of the basic problem posed by the Vietnam War—the failure of our political leaders to grasp why it was necessary to go to war. In the absence of that understanding, it was difficult if not impossible for our government to explain the war to the American people and get them directly and personally involved. War involves fighting by the armed forces in overt operations under rules laid down by the Geneva Convention and acceded to by most civilized nations. To place our uniformed military personnel in any other position is unfair to them, dishonors the military code of ethics, and constitutes a gross breach of trust on the part of their government. War must be perceived as legitimate in the eyes of the people and of the warriors entrusted to do the fighting. For these same reasons I have always firmly opposed employing U.S. military personnel in covert operations which the government can credibly deny. This is not what the military man takes the oath of service for.

It was the secret bombing of Cambodia which probably cemented the adversary-type relations between Secretary of Defense Laird and the Nixon White House. In any event, it was Laird who questioned and often opposed White House initiatives that did not seem to fit his concept of U.S. disengagement from and Vietnamization of the war as rapidly as could be prudently accomplished. Laird moreover had a far more intimate and accurate appreciation of the temper of the American people, the extent of dissent in certain segments, and what was politically feasible. He also knew how easily American public opinion could be swayed by media unsympathetic to the war, and how thin public support was for a protracted conflict. So Laird pushed for faster and larger U.S. troop withdrawals and lower draft calls, and continually pointed out the budgetary constraints on U.S. operations in Southeast Asia, especially as the war dragged on inconclusively and congressional support weakened.

Very much attuned to the domestic political consequences, Laird opposed widening the war in any way. This led to the president's bypassing or finessing him on numerous occasions and at times resulted in orders going from the White House directly to the CJCS, followed by countermanding orders from the secretary of defense. Obviously this was an intolerable situation, especially for the CJCS and the service chiefs, who are sworn to carry out the orders of their commander-in-chief and yet at the same time know full well that the statutory chain of command runs from the commander-in-chief through the secretary of defense.

Laird's problems with the White House coincided with the rapid growth of influence exercised by the president's national security advisor, Henry Kissinger, and his assistant, Alexander M. Haig, whose stature likewise increased rapidly. When Nixon became president, Haig was a U.S. Army lieutenant colonel who had been selected for promotion to colonel but not yet promoted. Initially the Army nominated several other colonels to Kissinger for the job—men with much wider experience and broader background than Haig, but Kissinger rejected them all. Finally Kissinger made it clear that Haig, and no one else, was his specific choice for the job. Later we learned that Dr. F.G. Kraemer, a special assistant to the Army's DCSOPS and a long and close friend of Kissinger, had urged him to ask for Haig. Kraemer was impressed with Haig's brilliance and thought he would be temperamentally quite compatible with Kissinger.

Thereafter, Haig's rise in the army was meteoric. He was promoted quickly to brigadier general and then major general, skipped the grade of lieutenant general, and four years later, in January 1973, was promoted by the president to full general—four stars. This was all without benefit of a single day in a military job since his command of a battalion as a lieutenant colonel in 1967, his job in the White House hardly qualifying as a military one. Possessing extraordinary talent and energy, and driven by an insatiable personal ambition, Haig nevertheless served his country well during a period of extraordinary trouble and turbulence.

With the adoption of the new Vietnamization strategy, it became paramount to make every possible disruptive effort against the enemy, particularly his logistic and troop reinforcement system, while substantial numbers of U.S. combat troops were still in the country. This basic purpose lay behind the cross-border operations into Cambodia and Laos. Cambodia was more or less off limits to major operations by allied forces, however, until Sihanouk's overthrow in March 1970. Sihanouk had allowed the historically hated Vietnamese (both North and South) to use Cambodia as a forward base, yet he continued to proclaim his country's neutrality. Hanoi's high-handed treatment of Cambodians in the border area, a faltering economy, and notorious corruption in the royal family led to Sihanouk's undoing. He was on a prolonged vacation in Paris when his premier, Lon Nol, took over the country in mid-March 1970 and promptly invited the NVA and the Viet Cong to leave. Hanoi reacted swiftly and forcefully to this new situation, which jeopardized the elaborate network of NVA bases that extended along the entire Cambodian-Vietnamese border. As we were able to confirm later, supplies flowing from North to South Vietnam at this time came mainly by sea through the port of Sihanoukville and thence cross-country to the border bases in Cambodia and Laos. An uncooperative Cambodia meant that resupply by sea through Cambodia would be denied, that the NVA would have to insure the security of their Cambodian border bases, and that their forces in the South would now have to be sustained solely via the Ho Chi Minh Trail through Laos.

So the NVA and the Khmer Rouge (the communist insurgents in Cambodia) launched a wave of attacks to seize a safe strip of Cambodian territory ten to fifteen kilometers wide practically all along the South Vietnamese frontier, as well as to secure the lines of communications leading into these base areas. Although the JCS estimated at the time that it could contain the internal Khmer Rouge threat, the small, inexperienced Cambodian army was helpless against the qualitatively vastly superior North Vietnamese, who were well on their way to seizing control of Cambodia east of the Mekong River and positioning themselves to cut off all access to Phnom Penh. Not surprisingly, Lon Nol asked Washington for help.

The collapse of Cambodia would be a disastrous blow to South Vietnamese prospects for survival, and it was this situation, reinforced by the necessity to gain time for Vietnamization and to safeguard the withdrawal of U.S. forces, that led to the presidential decision to launch a major allied offensive against the NVA's bases in Cambodia. The intent presumably was to occupy Cambodian territory only for a limited time with the objective of inflicting heavy casualties on the enemy, destroying his base areas and supplies, and setting back his offensive plans until the next dry season (October 1970–May 1971). Earlier our top military leaders would have been elated by the prospect of such an offensive, but the hour was now very late—this move should have been made years earlier, in 1966 or 1967. Moreover, the decisive objective lay in the panhandle of Laos, not in Cambodia.

To understand the rhythm of the war's course in Vietnam, one must be familiar with the ebb and tide of the annual dry and wet monsoons. In most of Indochina the dry monsoon extends from mid-October to mid-May, while the rainy season runs from mid-May to mid-October. There are major variations in this pattern in the northern part of South Vietnam, specifically I and II CTZs. Here the high mountains shield the coastal plains from the rains brought in by the wet monsoon (May to October), yet during the dry monsoon (October to May) these northern provinces get most of their annual precipitation in the form of a persistent drizzle accompanied by treacherous fog, which can materialize very suddenly. The French called this condition "crachin." It slowed down overland movement and made flying hazardous, even by helicopter.

For both sides the dry monsoon generally meant favorable weather for offensive operations. The North Vietnamese would send their troop reinforcements, war materiel, and supplies down the Ho Chi Minh Trail to their base areas just north of the DMZ and in Laos and Cambodia during the wet monsoon in preparation for launching their annual offensive sometime in the dry season. The allies, on the other hand, would seek to disrupt the enemy buildup during the rainy season, mostly by U.S. air attacks, and would spoil his dry monsoon offensives by intercepting his troops reentering South Vietnam, and by seeking to neutralize or destroy them before they reached the populated areas.

While the situation worsened in Cambodia, the JCS and the services in concert with MACV were deeply involved in carrying out an orderly, phased withdrawal of U.S. forces according to approved plans. By April 1970 about 115,000 American servicemen (about 60,000 Army, the rest Marine) had already been withdrawn. The flow of replacements to remaining units was also greatly curtailed. Roughly one-fourth of the Army's combat forces and one-half of the Marine combat units in Vietnam were included in this initial phase of the withdrawal.

Concurrently with these troop withdrawals, substantial reductions in U.S. tactical air and B-52 operations had been ordered, along with associated cuts in the funding of such operations. These reductions, coupled with orders from Laird to Abrams in October 1969 to cease all offensive operations by American ground combat forces, meant that U.S. air strikes, especially by B-52s, had become in reality Abrams's strategic reserve in Vietnam. He was to use them skillfully in that role with devastating effect. In these circumstances the possibility of offensive operations by U.S. ground forces in Vietnam seemed far remote to those of us in uniform who were aware of the facts at the time.

The president's decision to send forces into Cambodia was taken late in April 1970 after about a week of furious consultations.[2] When queried by Washington, Bunker and Abrams agreed on the need to take offensive action, employing both American and South Vietnamese forces, and the JCS concurred. Lukewarm in their support because it came so late in the day, the JCS played a minimal role in the Cambodian operation, which was conceived in the White House and planned and executed in the theater of operations. Both Secretaries Laird and Rogers generally were opposed to such operations, especially if U.S. troops were employed, but Nixon was determined to make the move. In hindsight, it seems clear that few if any of our leaders at the time anticipated the sharp reaction to the Cambodian operation that was to take place at home.

In Vietnam the orders to invade Cambodia hit U.S. field commanders with little warning and little time to plan. In fact, in II CTZ, the U.S. 4th Division had almost completed its move out of the Central Highlands to the coast for further movement back to the United States when the electrifying word arrived. Lieutenant General Arthur S. Collins, Jr., the tough, combat-wise commander of I FFV, who controlled all U.S. combat forces in the zone, managed to assemble an American brigade and, despite difficult logistic problems, move it into the border area. He then organized U.S. and Vietnamese attacks across the border in only slightly more than forty-eight hours—an incredibly short time under the circumstances. This quick response of U.S. forces to sudden orders that temporarily reversed their disengagement activities was a dramatic demonstration of the need to remain flexible in wartime and a great tribute to the professional qualities of our military leaders.

The main allied attack, however, was not made from II CTZ but was launched from III CTZ on 1 May 1970 with another but secondary effort launched from IV CTZ. In III CTZ, Lieutenant General Michael S. Davison, the able commander of II FFV, organized and executed a large, coordinated U.S.-ARVN cross-border attack in remarkably short order, while ARVN troops from IV CTZ moved against other NVA bases farther south along the border. The advance seldom went farther than ten to fifteen kilometers inside Cambodia, although hundreds of square kilometers were searched in the border region. Allied forces also cleared both banks of the Mekong River all the way to Phnom Penh, about sixty kilometers by river. By then the advent of the wet monsoon and the domestic outcry at home made it prudent to terminate the operations, and by 1 July all allied forces were back in South Vietnam.

The immediate operational results of these combined American-Vietnamese actions lasting two months were mixed. On the Cambodian side of the border enemy forces were routed and their hospitals were soon full of casualties. Large quantities of enemy arms, ammunition, food, and other supplies were captured, and many of the enemy's primary base areas were destroyed. The unexpected allied attack forced the enemy to move its top headquarters to safer areas, and consequently numerous documents and records of high intelligence value were captured during the drive. Unfortunately a decision to conduct a heavy B-52 strike just prior to the allied assault across the border gave things away and allowed many enemy personnel to escape.

The performance of III Corps ARVN troops under the inspiring leadership of Lieutenant General Do Cao Tri was especially encouraging, but this promising commander was killed the following year in a helicopter crash inside Cambodia. ARVN troops from IV Corps also performed well, but in II Corps the performance of senior ARVN leaders and their commands was deeply disappointing. Indeed, some American officers present, in particular Collins, the highly respected I FFV commander, concluded that ARVN was not up to handling the NVA and that it would take a long time to develop a reliable ARVN fighting force, at least in II CTZ.

For the United States and its allies, the initial consequences of the

Cambodian incursion were favorable. Overall enemy offensive plans were set back; indeed, the enemy delayed mounting any major operations in III and IV CTZs for almost two years. Phnom Penh and the Lon Nol regime appeared safe for the present, and the port of Sihanoukville was closed to Hanoi. In South Vietnam ARVN morale was visibly raised and ARVN troops took over the "big war" in the border area while U.S. troops moved to the coast and the American troop withdrawal resumed. In turn, this led to a dramatic decrease in American casualties.

On the negotiating front the successful operation also raised the president's confidence in Saigon enough to propose with Thieu's concurrence a "stand-still cease-fire" in October 1970, essentially the format ultimately reached in late 1972.[3] The significant implication of this proposal was that NVA forces would remain in South Vietnam if allied forces were unable to expell them. In effect the proposal was a very important concession on the part of the United States and South Vietnam.

But, as during Tet of 1968, the domestic repercussions at home resulted in a major political and psychological setback for the administration. The Cambodia operation triggered massive antiwar sentiment and civil disorders in the United States, culminating in the tragedy at Kent State on 4 May 1970, another trying ordeal for the U.S. Army. Although the Ohio National Guard troops involved had not been federalized but were under the command of the governor of Ohio, the active Army was responsible for overseeing National Guard training, which encompassed both combat missions and duty in civil disturbances. Immediately after the tragedy the secretary of the Army, as the Department of Defense executive agent for such matters, directed a comprehensive review of the rules of engagement for all active and reserve forces engaged in civil disorders and urged all state adjutant generals to follow suit for the National Guard, emphasizing that live ammunition would be used only as a last resort in dire circumstances. Army doctrine had always stressed this point, and ball ammunition was normally kept in the soldier's ammunition pouch rather than in the magazine of his individual weapon. This was a basic precaution to preclude unnecessary injury as a result of jumpy trigger fingers or the accidental discharge of weapons. I am convinced that the Kent State incident would not have occurred had well trained and well led troops been involved. Kent State should not have happened. Unfortunately it did.

The cross-border Cambodian action also marked the beginning of a series of congressional resolutions and legislative initiatives that were to limit severely the executive power of the president. In this instance the Congress forbade the use of American advisers in Cambodia and limited the amount of U.S. military aid for Cambodia. By the end of 1970 the Congress had imposed a legal prohibition on the expenditure of funds for any American ground troops operating outside Vietnam.

The repercussions from the Cambodian operation also became a major factor in accelerating the withdrawal of U.S. forces. Congressional defense budget reductions, which were not contested by Secretary Laird, and lowered draft calls, which in contrast had Laird's strong support, made it mandatory that U.S. troop strength in Vietnam be rapidly reduced. This kind of ambivalence did not make the service chiefs' tasks any easier. Their budgets were constrained and they had large responsibilities in other parts of the world, not to mention the central task of rebuilding their respective services after almost a decade of a seemingly endless, costly war.

Moreover, it was difficult to maintain much service enthusiasm for a war which was being de-Americanized. This was particularly true of the Navy, which wanted out of the South China Sea as soon as possible. Indeed, this attitude permanently soured relations between General Abrams and the Navy.

On the other hand, the Air Force could do no wrong in Abrams's eyes. He felt a very strong sense of comaraderie with the Air Force combat crews in the area, who never let him down, whether it was in close support of American or Vietnamese troops in the South, on interdiction missions in the region, or in the air offensive over North Vietnam. The bond became even stronger as U.S. ground troops departed and Abrams had to rely more and more upon B-52 strikes and other tactical air support.

In this connection there was a great difference between the prospects for survival of U.S. aircrews (mostly Air Force, Army, and Marine) in the South and U.S. aviators (Air Force, Navy, and Marine) downed over North Vietnam. The former shared the untold misery of the ground troops captured or missing in the South, and few survived, while the POWs in the North mostly survived their ordeal. The hero's welcome accorded our pilots released from POW camps in Hanoi after the cease-fire was well deserved, but left a feeling of being forgotten and ignored for those still missing in action in Southeast Asia that persists today. This feeling is deeply shared by the hundreds of thousands of Americans of all services who served in Vietnam, not to mention the families of the 50,000 who died there.

Looking back, the Cambodian incursion of May 1970 was the second major turning point of the war, in my view. Tet 1968 ended any hope of a U.S.-imposed solution to the war, while Cambodia 1970 fatally wounded South Vietnam's chances to survive and remain free. Consider how the gains from Cambodia boomeranged:

(1) Although the operation bought much valuable time for the allies, the loss forced Hanoi to rely entirely on cross-country routes from the North for the maintenance of its forces in the South. In effect the Ho Chi Minh Trail became the jugular vein for the NVA effort in all South Viet-

nam. As a consequence Hanoi expanded its initially primitive routes into a wide network of all-weather roads and way stations that could handle even tanks and other heavy equipment. In the end, this logistic capability enabled Hanoi to overrun the South with massive conventional assaults. Hanoi was also compelled to beef up the ground and air defense of its logistic structure and, as we learned later, to move the center of gravity of its supply dumps further west out of harm's way.

(2) Although NVA capabilities against the heavily populated areas of III and IV CTZs were greatly reduced, the nature of ARVN was such that Saigon could not take advantage of this development by shifting some ARVN troops northward. ARVN was a territorially based and supported army. The families of ARVN soldiers lived near their home stations and were partially sustained by local ARVN resources—housing, for example. Historically ARVN regiments and divisions had not performed well when deployed any great distance from their families. In the Vietnamese culture, particularly in the South, family ties were stronger than loyalty to ARVN or the government, and if the families needed help when so separated, the soldiers simply deserted. The elite airborne and marine divisions, based in the Saigon area, on the other hand, were the nation's strategic reserve and were accustomed to being deployed in areas far from home for varying periods. But even these troops were susceptible to the same syndrome if the period became protracted. So ARVN faced the paradox of an excess of troops in the southern areas that could not be effectively employed in the northern CTZs, where the enemy threat was now permanently greater. Thus the military gains from Cambodia could not be fully exploited, at least without the presence of American combat troops in the northern provinces.

(3) Politically, Cambodia not only spelled a downward spiral of public and congressional support for U.S. operations in Southeast Asia, which finally became proscribed, but also eventually resulted in a drastic diminution in U.S. military advisory effort and military aid for South Vietnam. This was probably the most damaging blow of all for Saigon.

The foregoing discussion obviously raises the question of Cambodia's ultimate fate. American judgment had always been that if South Vietnam were conquered by the North, Cambodia would surely follow very shortly thereafter. The widening of the war in May 1970 led to the weakening of the Cambodian regime, since Hanoi, initially unfriendly to Pol Pot and the Khmer Rouge, threw in with them because the North Vietnamese badly needed additional communist forces. (It should also be borne in mind that from Hanoi's point of view the struggle from the beginning was wider, involving all of Indochina.) Thereafter the Lon Nol government struggled for five years against both North Vietnamese and Khmer Rouge foes with only minimal U.S. assistance. Finally, when South Vietnamese defenses crumbled in I and II CTZ in March–April of 1975, Lon

Nol gave up the unequal contest, and Phnom Penh fell to Pol Pot on 16 April 1975, two weeks before the fall of Saigon. Phnom Penh's conquest, with scarcely a protest from the Americans, was dramatic evidence that the United States was prepared to abandon Indochina.

One can speculate as to whether Pol Pot's ensuing attempt to exterminate the urban-dwelling elements of the Cambodian people on a wholesale basis might have been prevented. But that seems quite problematical. Lon Nol deposed Sihanouk on his own without the knowledge or help of the United States, and the Cambodian incursion came later. Even had the Cambodian situation developed quite differently, there is no assurance that the ultimately victorious North Vietnamese could have prevented Pol Pot's coming to power and the unparalleled horrors that followed.

But going back to the fall of 1970, domestic pressures at home had already compelled an accelerated schedule of U.S. troop withdrawal which would reduce our forces to roughly 180,000 (about one-third of the peak U.S. strength) by the end of the following year, 1971. Moreover, it was anticipated that by the summer of 1972 only a small, residual, logistic-type U.S. force of about 50,000 personnel would remain. Thus the dry season of 1970–71 (October–May) would be the last opportunity for South Vietnam to take the offensive and buy more time for its own survival. This was the basic rationale that led to the White House proposal to launch an incursion into Laos in March 1971.[4]

Almost from the beginning General Westmoreland had sought authority to conduct operations into the panhandle of Laos to cut and physically block the numerous infiltration trails and waterways comprising the Ho Chi Minh Trail. Significantly, both Ambassadors Lodge and Bunker strongly supported such operations. Westmoreland also liked the idea of an international force to defend a line running south of the DMZ and extending across the Laotian panhandle, as did General Cao Van Vien, chief of the Vietnamese Joint General Staff. (General Vien, with long combat experience in the South Vietnamese Army, was a fine soldier and an extraordinary military leader. He remained loyal to President Thieu, supported American policy to the best of his ability, cooperated willingly with the American high command, MACV, and took care of his soldiers—all together no mean list of accomplishments. He survived the war and was granted asylum in the United States, where he has been engaged, among other things, in writing a history of the war for the U.S. Army Center for Military History. On 20 January 1982 Vien became a naturalized American citizen in an Alexandria, Virginia, courtroom. In my opinion, our country gained a brave, decent man.)

Still another proposal, developed in detail by the U.S. Army staff under General Johnson, encompassed a regional development project for Southeast Asia, involving South Vietnam, Laos, and Thailand. Called the Pan-SEA (Pan-Southeast Asia) Pike, this plan proposed a major road-construction peoject, improving Route 9 (which runs south of and parallel to the DMZ from the South Vietnamese coast to the Laotian border), and extending the road across the Laotian panhandle to hook up with a highway in Thailand. Allied engineers, including contingents from any willing Western European ally, were to be protected by allied combat troops, thereby constituting an antiinfiltration screen of sorts.

During the period 1966–68, while he was in command in Vietnam, General Westmoreland had several plans, large and small, developed involving different objectives and various schemes of maneuver for operations into Laos, as well as some involving both Laos and Cambodia. At HQ USARV we had even gone so far as to discuss some of these plans with the senior American and ARVN field commanders in I CTZ. The last such plan was developed in early 1968 while I was deputy commander of USARV. Our USARV senior planner, Colonel John Collins, prepared a sound plan that we were convinced not only would work operationally but also was logistically feasible.

In the 1966–67 period Westmoreland felt that he had insufficient forces, either combat or logistic, to launch any major cross-border operations and still maintain the operations required to gain the initiative over the enemy in South Vietnam. He therefore did not press very hard for authority to expand the ground war into Laos. Ironically, when in 1968 there were forces available, the political climate at home would not permit such a move. Nevertheless, in the earlier 1960s Westmoreland did receive authority to make small, harassing-type raids into the Laotian panhandle, employing American and South Vietnamese special forces and using U.S. helicopters to insert the troopers. Unfortunately, some of these raids were of marginal value and it was questionable whether they were worth the cost in highly skilled and trained men, not to mention high-cost helicopters.

But as it came to pass, the primary ground efforts against the Ho Chi Minh Trail turned out to be the U.S.-supported and directed operations (though not acknowledged by the United States) utilizing Meo tribesmen from the area. Although these efforts were relatively minor pinpricks to Hanoi, they were a life or death matter to the Meo tribes. These gallant people fought a long, remarkable campaign against impossible odds, but in the end they became expendable. It was another tragedy of the war.

The more immediate origins of the March 1971 incursion into Laos, namely the White House, illustrate how completely President Nixon and his NSC staff dominated the overall control and conduct of both the war and the closely interrelated negotiations to end the war. This was, of course, a proper role for the president, who was ultimately committed to terminate American involvement, had the necessary authority, bore the executive responsibility for U.S. actions, and was accountable to the American people. What was so different, however, was the role of the president's national security adviser, Henry Kissinger, who became for all intents and purposes the de facto chairman of the JCS, who managed to poach on the territory of the secretary of defense, and who in essence usurped the responsibilities of the secretary of state.[5]

The JCS for the most part could now only react to Kissinger initiatives, usually surfaced with minimum warning and time for review. It was frustration over this state of affairs that led to the famous case of the U.S. Navy yeoman on Kissinger's staff who surreptitiously furnished copies of NSC staff papers to Admiral Moorer, the CJCS. The service chiefs, with far less access to the day-to-day actions of the Joint Staff than Admiral Moorer, had to rely on the chairman to keep them posted. General Westmoreland, by far the most knowledgeable member of the JCS on Vietnamese matters, was basically ignored by both Laird and Kissinger, and had access to them only on those rare occasions when he was the acting chairman during Moorer's absence.

Laird, however, was a formidable adversary for the White House, and Kissinger found that it was extremely difficult to outmaneuver this wily bureaucrat with such highly developed political instincts. Kissinger might gain a temporary advantage over Laird on some issue of an operational nature, such as the timing and extent of U.S. troop withdrawals from Vietnam, but Laird with his congressional connections and his overall control of defense manpower, hardware procurement, budgets, and the like, could usually find means to modify at least the operative outcome. The service chiefs were caught in the middle, trying to meet the operational requirements generated by the White House in the face of the real world constraints on defense, manpower, money, and material.

But the U.S. leaders who carried the brunt of this infighting were Bunker and Abrams, particularly the latter, who might receive orders directly from the White House, or from Laird, as well as through the normal joint military channels from Washington. Moreover, there were times when such instructions to Abrams were conflicting. Over time, Abrams developed a unique way of coping with this problem. In his living quarters at Tan Son Nhut airbase, not far from HQ MACV, Abrams's routine practice in the evening was to stay up very late sipping scotch and water and listening to Wagnerian operas played in stereo at maximum volume. He would sit back in his chair for hours with his eyes closed without speaking a word while he soaked in the music. He explained that in this way he was better prepared to respond to the inevitable urgent and sometimes contradictory messages that daily arrived from Washington, and that it helped him maintain his sanity. When I visited Vietnam I stayed with him, but I found it difficult to remain awake so late and would go to bed with the wild strains of the "Ride of the Valkyries" thundering against my eardrums.

Alexander Haig soon became an essential and integral part of Kissinger's political-military apparatus which "ran" the intertwined Vietnam war and the negotiations for a cease-fire. He made his first official visit to Vietnam in the latter part of January 1970 to make a personal assessment of the political and military situations in light of the initial U.S. troop withdrawals. His second trip was in December 1970 to discuss the White House proposals for the second allied cross-border operations with Ambassador Bunker, General Abrams, and President Thieu. (Typically, Laird made his own separate trip to Saigon in January 1971 for the same purpose.) Haig's third visit, in mid-March 1971 was to make a personal assessment of the Laotian operation that had started in February. Haig had his own small, hand-picked team of advisers, mostly young, bright, but relatively inexperienced U.S. Army officers, who accompanied him.

By this time, Haig had the confidence of both the president and Kissinger, and, incredibly, his military assessments of the situation in Vietnam were given more weight than the judgments of General Abrams, other responsible commanders in the field, and the Joint Chiefs of Staff, the latter being the statutory senior military advisers to the president, the secretary of defense, and the NSC. This development was difficult to accept, but it was an accurate reflection of the extraordinary power and arrogance of Kissinger and his NSC staff. In any event, the president and Kissinger thereafter were to send Haig to Saigon on numerous occasions to assess the political and military situations first-hand, to consult with Bunker and Abrams, to act as a personal emissary of the president in conveying messages to President Thieu, and to report back on the reactions obtained.

Serious consultations and planning for the Laotian venture originated in the White House beginning in December 1970. White House thinking originally considered an amphibious thrust into North Vietnam, aimed at Vinh, but then finally proposed another incursion into Cambodia. Ambassador Bunker and General Abrams, with President Thieu's agreement, countered with a proposal for a far bolder and riskier attack into Laos. (Several years later, General Frederick C. Weyand, Abrams's deputy in Vietnam at the time, told me that he was extremely dubious about the proposal.) After weeks of skillful maneuvering the president and his NSC advisers managed to get all U.S. principals aboard—Laird, Rogers, Helms, and Moorer—for an attack into Laos in early February 1971 via Route 9, just south of the DMZ. Another operation would be launched from III CTZ into Cambodia to destroy a major enemy base being developed in the Chup rubber plantation. Prince Souvanna Phouma's agreement was obtained through Ambassador G. McM. Godley in Vietnam.[6]

The objectives of the Laotian operation were to seize the logistic complex in the Tchepone area, located at a very strategic junction of supply routes along the Ho Chi Minh Trail and about fifty kilometers by road from the border with South Vietnam; and then, during the remainder of the dry season, to interdict the Trail and destroy the logistic facilities in the area. A successful campaign, it was hoped, might buy as much as two years' time for the allies, assuming that the enemy would need about one year to rebuild his logistic structure to support an offensive in the following dry season (October 1972–May 1973).

Again, knowledge of the plan was on a very close-hold basis in Washington and only a handful of people in the Pentagon and State were aware of it. Although Admiral Moorer as the chairman of the JCS was kept abreast of the status of the planning, the service chiefs were only dimly aware of the bare outlines of the operation. Detailed planning was accomplished in Vietnam, where need-to-know was also strictly limited. Indeed, the commanders and forces involved had only a bare minimum of time for essential preparations but lacked enough time to disseminate the latest tactical intelligence to the ground and aviation units making the assaults, obviously a serious disadvantage.

The green light was given from Washington late in January 1971 and only days later, on 30 January, phase I began. This entailed the securing by U.S. forces of Route 9 inside South Vietnam to the border. The penetration into Laos, phase II, was to begin on 8 February. As luck would have it, HQ MACV on 3 February made the mistake of briefing the Saigon press on the impending operation with an embargo until it jumped off, but the news promptly leaked and spread rapidly. This was the first inkling of the planned operation for most of us assigned to duty at the Pentagon. But the bad news, of course, was that the enemy, already keenly aware of his total dependence on the Ho Chi Minh Trail, and generally expecting an attack against it sooner or later, was now undoubtedly alerted to the specific intentions of the allies.

LAMSON 719, the South Vietnamese designation given the operation, involved some of their very best troops—the 1st ARVN Division, 1st Armored Brigade, and three ranger battalions from I Corps; and most of the elite Airborne Division and Marine Division from the Joint General Staff's strategic reserve. The overall commander of LAMSON 719 was Lieutenant General Hoang Xuan Lam, commanding general of I Corps, whose reputation as a combat commander was only mediocre, but who was considered to be a loyal, capable administrator.

In December 1970 the U.S. Congress had imposed a legal prohibition on the expenditure of funds for any American ground forces operating outside of Vietnam. This meant that the ground operations would have to be conducted solely by South Vietnamese troops, enemy propaganda labeling them as cannon fodder exploited by the American imperialists. Moreover, no American advisers were permitted to accompany ARVN units into Laos. U.S. forces were, however, allowed to support LAMSON 719 with tactical air, helicopters, and long-range artillery operating from South Vietnamese bases.

The prohibition of American advisers was a new and potentially critical obstacle to closely coordinated operations, since ARVN commanders were accustomed to counting on their American counterparts in arranging for U.S. air, assault helicopter, heavy artillery, and logistic support. Moreover, the language problem greatly hindered effective close air support by U.S. fighter-bombers and attack helicopters because of the lack of English-speaking Vietnamese forward air controllers.

Senior American and South Vietnamese leaders were quite aware that the risks were great in committing South Vietnamese ground forces to a major offensive more or less completely on their own. But the stakes were high. Hanoi was busily replacing the casualties resulting from the May 1970 Cambodian operation and was pushing supplies south during the dry season; February and March 1971 were expected to be the peak activity months before the heavy rains came in May. Allied leaders also knew that the NVA had strong main force units, infantry, armor, and heavy artillery, in addition to numerous service troops stationed along the Trail. In fact, the enemy could concentrate a force in the Tchepone area which would be a good deal larger than the invading South Vietnamese force.

Our leaders also knew that very formidable ground-based air defenses, including surface-to-airmissles, were deployed along the Trail and were particularly thick in the Tchepone area. The terrain, combining the higher elevations of the Annamite Mountains with dense jungle (mostly single or double canopy), was also an allied liability. Natural clearings were rare and helicopter landing zones usually had to be carved out of the dense tree and vegetation growth. This meant that the relatively few natural landing zones would very likely be heavily defended. Finally, allied leaders knew that although it was the dry season, sudden, unexpected rains could occur in this very rugged region of Laos which might persist for some time and severely inhibit both ground movement and air operations, even by choppers.

Looking at the situation in cold objectivity, it did look very much like sending a boy to do a man's job in an extremely hostile environment. But General Abrams was counting heavily on U.S. B-52 strikes, suppressive fires by tactical air against air defenses, and the tactical mobility provided by assault helicopters with their own armed escort helicopters to even the odds. With luck, a successful campaign was a distinct possibility. Nevertheless, it was a big gamble. Failure would bring Vietnamization into serious question and might result either in keeping U.S. forces in Vietnam longer, or in generating such pressure at home as to cause the United States to abandon its hapless ally.

Yet in a strategic sense the Laotian operation was a sound move. Its strategic objective was decisive in nature—striking at the enemy's lifeline to the South and seeking to block physically, if only temporarily, his main invasion route to South Vietnam. Furthermore, Abrams's audacious plan was quite in keeping with his background and temperament. He had been brought up in the school of thought of the U.S. cavalry/armor that "fortune favors the bold." He also had great faith that the artful but violent use of mobility, firepower, and what cavalrymen and tankers call "shock action" could carry the day against even the most determined foe. By shock action he no doubt had in mind the massive weight of U.S. airpower, whose psychological effect could be as devastating as its destructive impact. Only a MacArthur or a Patton would have made such a daring move; an Eisenhower or a Bradley would not even have considered it.

The concept for LAMSON 719 was a complex one requiring reliable command communications for the coordinated control and direction of the forces, as well as skillful execution.[7] The U.S. 101st Airborne Division was to secure Route 9 to the Laotian border, reoccupying the old fire support base site at Khe Sanh, the scene of heavy, protracted fighting back in 1968. Later, at this location, a U.S. command post was established to coordinate all helicopter air assaults, close air support, long-range artillery support, and resupply operations using stocks brought forward to the combat base.

Elements of the 1st ARVN Division, reinforced by armor, would make the main effort, up the jungle-covered river valley along the axis of Route 9 into Laos to seize the Tchepone area in the heart of the enemy's Base Area 604. The advance would consist of a series of leap-frogging overland and helicopter air assaults. The flanks were to be protected on the north by airborne and ranger battalions, air-assaulted into key hilltop positions, and by similar operations along the sheer escarpment to the south of Route 9, conducted by other elements of the 1st ARVN Division. Marine units were later to take over the southern flank while the 1st ARVN Division made the final assaults into the Tchepone area, which was to be reached in about five days.

Originally, the plan was to remain in the objective area for several months (until the arrival of heavy rains in May), searching for and destroying enemy supply caches and any forces protecting them. No one had any illusions, however, about the overwhelming probability that the NVA would fight to the finish to keep their jugular vein from being severed, and that there would be no relatively easy scattering of surprised enemy forces followed by deliberate search-and-destroy operations in the enemy's base areas, as had occurred in Cambodia in May 1970.

Although LAMSON 719 jumped off on schedule on 8 February, just about everything went wrong from the beginning, and Lady Luck deserted the allied side. Bad weather limited the tactical air support the first day and heavy rains on 9 February turned Route 9 into a quagmire. Intermittent rains threw repeated crimps into planned operations, and at times heavy fog kept all aircraft, even choppers, on the ground.

Foul weather was particularly hard on resupply operations by helicopters, as it forced them to lower altitudes, where enemy air defenses
were especially deadly. Daily, resupply Army Hueys escorted by Army
Cobras (attack helicopters) flew a gauntlet of fire down Route 9 to South
Vietnamese troops needing ammunition or other critical items, and evacuated the badly wounded. Daily every aircraft flying these missions was
hit by groundfire at least once.

By 20 February the attack had almost stalled far short of the objective
area, and the enemy was reacting violently in great strength. Supported
by heavy artillery and tanks, the enemy threw repeated frontal assaults
against ranger and airborne troop positions on the northern flank. When
South Vietnamese troops were thus thrown on the defensive, several critical weaknesses were revealed. Selection of positions was poor and the
essential link between infantry units and supporting artillery broke down.
Consequently, units were often dependent on fighter bombers or attack
helicopters for badly needed fire support.

After days of heavy fighting and fierce resistance by the greatly out-
numbered South Vietnamese defenders (roughly 2 to 1 in infantry), the
NVA by 3 March controlled the high ground on the north of Highway
9.[8] But it was at a heavy cost to the enemy, as U.S. B-52 formations
struck repeatedly, inflicting casualties that MACV estimated to be one
combat effective NVA regiment a week.

At this juncture, the allied advance appeared to be indefinitely stalled,
but undaunted South Vietnamese airborne troops, now in the valley floor,
established new fire support bases on the northern flank on 4 March, and
by 6 March ARVN battalions air-assaulted onto several key positions just
south and north of the key road junction at Tchepone.[9] But these exposed
positions with no flank security were in a very precarious situation. Meanwhile, South Vietnamese marines had replaced the ARVN battalions on
the southern escarpment.

Although Abrams strongly urged President Thieu to reinforce his be-
leaguered forces that had finally reached the objective area, and to fight
it out to a decision with the NVA, Thieu on 9 March decided to terminate
LAMSON 719. He had cogent reasons for his action. His senior commanders in Laos had made similar recommendations, feeling that they
had insufficient strength to hold their positions. All concerned wanted to
remain in the area for another two months but considered that the risks
were too great. Thieu was unwilling to reinforce his troops in Laos and
accept more casualties. Nor could he afford to lose one of his very best
divisions and the bulk of his strategic reserve. Abrams privately felt that
Thieu lost his nerve, and never quite forgave him. But Thieu's decision
was understandable and probably prudent in the longer run. He strongly

believed that the heaviest offensives from the north were yet to come, early in 1972, and that he could not afford the severe casualties that were implicit in a prolonged campaign in Laos.

So General Lam began a retrograde movement, the most difficult of all military operations, especially when under pressure from numerically larger enemy forces. The NVA now had the major assault elements of four divisions converging on the area. The withdrawal took twelve days and became a nightmare by the time it ended. Northernmost airborne troops were withdrawn by helicopter first, as airborne and armored forces in the valley withdrew along Route 9, experiencing repeated ambushes on the way. The marines in the southwest came under extremely heavy attack until finally withdrawn in helicopter operations that completed the retreat on 22 March. It had been a close call, for the enemy went all out to encircle and destroy the South Vietnamese force. As it was, U.S. air support and assault helicopter operations staved off disaster and allowed South Vietnamese troops to leave Laos generally intact and in fairly good order.

Concurrently, the attack against the NVA base in the Chup rubber plantation in Cambodia had been launched from III CTZ. In the early fighting, however, when the colorful III Corps commander, Lieutenant General Tri, was killed in a chopper crash, his ARVN troops lost heart and the campaign petered out.

The military results of the Laos campaign were mixed. Heavy casualties (over 12,000 killed) were inflicted on the NVA units involved, which would now require much time and many replacements to recover. General Lam's forces also suffered severe casualties, about one-fifth of the total assault elements committed being killed or wounded, but much fewer than the enemy's losses. South Vietnamese performance was spotty— some units fought extremely well, others did poorly. Indeed, some of South Vietnam's best troops had broken under heavy, sustained assaults by some of the best and most experienced troops in the North Vietnamese Army.

Serious weaknesses in ARVN's ability to command and control their forces were apparent, and the degradation of effectiveness caused by the absence of American advisers was also quite noticeable. Even more serious, however, was heavy South Vietnamese dependence on external U.S. fire support, the weight of which they could not match within their own means. These factors did not bode well for the future. Thus it was no surprise to learn that the Saigon high command was shaken as the implications of LAMSON 719 struck home.

On the U.S. side, planning had not been adequate initially and many improvisations had to be made as the campaign progressed. But in the end, U.S. support was carried out in a very professional and effective way despite the fact that the American personnel involved inside Laos—the pilots and aircrews—were not supporting fellow American GIs but Vietnamese soldiers from a totally different culture.

Slightly over one hundred U.S. Army choppers were lost in combat with roughly the same number of Army pilots and crewmen killed or missing in action and several hundred others wounded. The USAF lost seven fighter-bombers, and four pilots were killed in action. To put these helicopter combat losses in better perspective, it should be remembered that our assault (troop-carrying) and attack helicopters were operating against an extremely dense and effective low-altitude air defense system that had the advantage of being able to concentrate on the natural flight routes imposed by the mountainous terrain, especially in marginal weather. During LAMSON 719, many thousands of helicopter sorties were flown in this hostile environment. The loss rate was only one-quarter of 1 percent for every thousand sorties, which compares quite favorably with the loss rate experienced by high performance aircarft in Southeast Asia during the same period.[10]

The viability of airmobile operations in heavy close combat, as was the case in Laos, continues to be debated to the present date. In my judgment the operation in Laos earned a positive vote of confidence for the concept, but it also demonstrated that good intelligence on enemy air defenses, air superiority, intense tactical air support, imaginative cover and deception techniques, and skillful helicopter flying tactics and techniques must all be on hand to make success possible.

Overall, LAMSON 719 temporarily disrupted the enemy's main lines of communications to the South and at least initially gave Hanoi some anxious moments, while it generally raised morale in South Vietnam. Hanoi, however, was able to sustain a sufficient flow of supplies through Laos to support its forces in the South, even at the height of the fighting. Nevertheless the Laotian venture was an important factor in delaying the next major offensive of the North Vietnamese until a year later, in the spring of 1972. But there were other factors in that delay, such as the need to correct NVA operational deficiencies, notably the lack of coordinated infantry-tank actions. The cross-border operations of 1970 and 1971, taken together, probably saved the South Vietnamese forces from defeat in 1972, when South Vietnamese ground forces and American airpower were just barely able to stop the enemy.

In hindsight, on the other hand, one might make the case that the Laotian venture was a mistake. It revealed to the enemy grave weaknesses in our South Vietnamese allies, not the least of which was their dependence on U.S. advisers and U.S. air support. Significantly, Hanoi must have recognized Saigon's lack of any substantial strategic reserve and its inability to shift forces rapidly within South Vietnam. But Hanoi also had to recognize that even with their greater familiarity with the terrain and their larger numbers, North Vietnamese soldiers had no easy time of it.

LAMSON 719 may have also encouraged Saigon to hang on to every square foot of SVN territory when a lesser objective might have been more prudent. In truth, Saigon's desire to defend every province resulted in a very vulnerable overextension of South Vietnamese forces.

In Washington the course of the Laotian campaign caused much pain and anxiety at the White House, expecially within the NSC staff. Kissinger willingly assumed a field marshal role when things went well, but, not understanding the nature of war and its treacherous uncertainties, became irritable and upset when LAMSON 719 stalled. He gave Abrams a hard time, although Abrams wisely did not attempt to respond in detail to the flood of White House queries. At the climax of the crisis Kissinger could stand it no longer and sent his trusted "deputy field marshall" Haig to assess the situation personally.

At home, domestic reaction was not as sharp as in May 1970 during the Cambodian incursion. Nevertheless, during and well after the operation, multiple efforts to limit the president's discretionary power to conduct military operations escalated in the Congress, and pressure from the media on the subject likewise intensified sharply. There were six weeks of demonstrations in Washington against U.S. involvement in the war during April and May 1971, culminating on May Day with a deliberate effort to bring the federal government to a halt. Expecting more than the city could handle, the mayor of the District of Columbia asked for and got federal help. Thus, the U.S. Army once more found itself in charge of protecting the federal government from civil disobedience, disruption, and destructive vandalism. By then the Army's Military District of Washington, the D.C. National Guard, the mayor's office, and the D.C. operations center were quite used to working together. So May Day 1971 went by without any major disruptions despite the efforts of several thousand professional agitators, who did their best to transform the much larger number of peaceful demonstrators into a rampaging mob.

Concurrently with these events and the continuing reduction of U.S. force levels in Vietnam, a successful pacification program was evolving under MACV and the South Vietnamese government. Military operations in support of pacification focused on attacking the enemy's real Achilles' heel, the logistic system. Whereas in conventional warefare supplies are brought up from the rear or stockpiled to the rear of the front lines, in this unconventional part of the war in the South, the enemy had to "prepare the battlefield," namely, establish concealed supply caches and communications stations in advance. The allied watchword was to "work the system," finding and seizing forward supply caches, disrupting the messengers, radio communications, and resupply couriers that not only provided the support for any main-force attacks but that also kept the Viet Cong underground political and administrative structure resupplied and informed.

These tactics, coupled with the upgrading and expansion of ARVN and Regional and Popular Forces, as well as the creation of an armed People's Self-Defense Force, really paid off. By the end of 1970, and certainly by mid-1971, the pacification campaign was well on the way to success. Ambassador Bunker to this day insists that this essential and integral part of the war had been won in 1971. Indeed, this was obviously a major factor in Hanoi's decision to rely on all-out conventional warfare to subjugate the South.

6

1972-1973:
Cease-Fire Achieved

As the crucial year of 1972 approached, MACV and the Vietnamese Joint General Staff worked overtime to get the nation's defenses in a better state of readiness to meet the next NVA invasion. It was expected to come in January or February 1972 and to hit hardest in the northern provinces of South Vietnam.

An important element of the Vietnamization program entailed a large expansion of the regular South Vietnamese forces, which increased by almost one-third (from about 825,000 to over a million), while Saigon's paramilitary forces almost tripled in size (from 1.3 million to 4 million). (Most of the latter increase was in the People's Self-Defense Forces, which were armed with primitive weapons and had no organized units.)

The program for the regular forces (the Navy and Marine Corps doubled in size and the Air Force multiplied two and a half times) included a strenuous effort to build greater capabilities for air, naval, artillery, logistic, and other activities of a supporting nature. This effort involved training thousands of pilots, mechanics, navigators, engineers, and others requiring advanced skills, many of them in the United States, which in turn demanded a mastery of English as a prerequisite. Large numbers of U.S. aircraft, naval craft, armored vehicles, and artillery pieces were turned over to the South Vietnamese. Whether this program would give the South Vietnamese capabilities anywhere approaching U.S. standards was highly questionable. But given the limited time available to train the South Vietnamese in these long-term skills and to develop effective, modern forces, the program was probably the best that could have been achieved.

An encouraging development was the improvement in the combat performance of the 5th and 18th ARVN Divisions in III CTZ and the 7th ARVN Division in IV CTZ. On the negative side, ARVN divisions in II

CTZ had not significantly improved, and this was a worrisome factor for the allied high command, who were well aware of the importance of the Central Highlands in Hanoi's strategic thinking.[1]

The gravity of the situation in I and II CTZs was starkly heightened by the continuing withdrawal of U.S. combat troops. By mid-1971 almost two-thirds of American maneuver units had departed the theater, and by the end of 1971 there was less than a U.S. division equivalent total in the northern two corps tactical zones. Moreover, many of the so-called Free World forces had returned home. The South Korean government, however, agreed to retain its two-division force in II CTZ until the end of 1972, but operationally kept the force under wraps.

In addition to the withdrawal of American combat units, the senior American headquarters—MACV, USARV, 7th Air Force, and III Marine Amphibious Force—had been sharply reduced; the large U.S. headquarters in each CTZ that had controlled U.S. ground operations were replaced by small regional assistance groups; and most of the large, complex U.S. intelligence, communications, and logistics structures in Vietnam had been dismantled. Virtually all American-built bases had been turned over to the South Vietnamese, who lacked the means to secure and maintain them. In populated areas the result was widespread looting of supplies, dismemberment of buildings and facilities, and rapid deterioration, while in more remote areas the jungle took over.

The U.S. advisory structure was also being rapidly reduced during this 1971–72 period. By mid-1972 advisers were assigned only at ARVN corps, division, and province levels. But the advisory effort enjoyed the highest priority for quality personnel, a status it had not always enjoyed in the past.

To shore up the situation in the northern provinces, a new ARVN division, the 3rd, was organized in I CTZ in mid-1971. Although its major elements had cadres from experienced ARVN units in the corps, the bulk of its personnel, recruited from the northern provinces, were green and had received only minimal basic training. Moreover, there was little time left for small-unit training and combined arms training that would mold cohesive units ready for combat. The 3rd Division was deployed along the DMZ in the fire bases and other positions formerly occupied by American Marines. There was some logic to this decision because the new units could take over positions and some U.S. equipment and supplies in place, but it exposed an untested, relatively untrained division in an area that had been the scene of many hard-fought battles in the past and had long been the target of intense artillery and rocket fire from north of the DMZ. This turned out to be a costly mistake.

To make matters worse there was no overall South Vietnamese commander of all forces north of Hai Van Pass, which separates the two northernmost provinces of Quang Tri and Thua Thien from the rest of I

General Bruce Palmer, Deputy Commanding General, USARV, prepares to depart after an inspection in the Mekong River Delta, July 1967. On his left is MG George G. O'Connor. (#662700)

Except where otherwise indicated, all illustrations are U.S. Army photographs; photo numbers indicated in parentheses.

Above, LTC John Paul Vann (left) confers in the field with Major Nyugen Duy Bach (center), commander of the ARVN 11th Infantry, in February 1963. (#600276)

Below, General Maxwell D. Taylor (then U.S. Ambassador to Saigon) and General William C. Westmoreland are briefed on a February 1965 Viet Cong assault in Qui Nhon city that caused heavy casualties. (#031973)

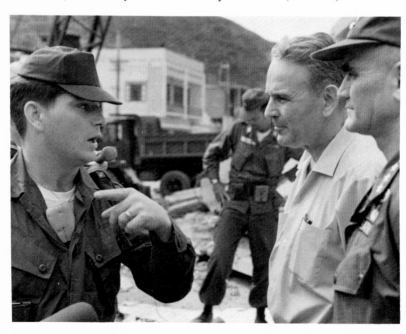

Above, Secretary of Defense Robert S. McNamara (right) is greeted by
Ambassador Ellsworth Bunker (left) and General Westmoreland on his
arrival in Saigon, 7 July 1967. (#041348)

Below, General Palmer briefs Ambassador Bunker and his deputy, Eugene
Locke, at Long Binh in May 1967. MG Frederick Weyand is at right.
Author's collection.

Above, Artillerymen of the U.S. 4th Infantry Division clean their 105 mm howitzer at a typical U.S. fire support base carved out of the jungle in the Central Highlands. (#SC 638669)

Below, a rifle company of the U.S. 1st Cavalry Division, on a reconnaissance mission, moves through a rice paddy in the coastal part of Binh Dinh Province on 15 October 1965. (#CC 32241)

A rifle company of the U.S. 9th Infantry Division moves across a stream in the Mekong River Delta in April 1967. Much of the Delta is under water, especially during the wet monsoon. (#SC 639067)

American riflemen of the U.S. 9th Infantry Division await artillery support in a swampy area of Dinh Tuong Province preparatory to a 4 April 1968 attack on an enemy machine gun bunker. (#CC 47770)

Above, as part of operation "Junction City," troopers of the U.S. 11th Armored Cavalry transport rice captured from the enemy in Binh Duong Province on 13 April 1967. (#SC 639312)

Below, a rifle company of the U.S. 1st Cavalry Division comes under enemy fire as it approaches a wooded area of Binh Dinh Province on 15 March 1967. (#SC 638547)

Above, a wrecked "Huey" helicopter lies on the edge of a CIDG-US Special Forces base in Tay Ninh Province near the Cambodian border after an enemy attack in April 1967. (#SC 639275)

Below, troops of the 7th ARVN Division prepare to board Vietnamese Air Force helicopters for an assault against NVA forces in Dinh Tuong Province in April 1970. (#SC 655138)

Above, General Cao Van Vien (second from left), Chairman of the South Vietnamese
Joint General Staff, arrives at Hue on 4 April 1969. With him are LTG Hoang
Xuan Lam (left), LTG Richard G. Stilwell, and MG Ngo Quang Truong. (#649680)

Below, South Korean Army troops ford a stream near Cam Ranh Bay in
November 1967. Two Korean Army divisions and one Korean Marine brigade fought
in South Vietnam. (#SC 643371)

A rifle company of the U.S. 1st Infantry Division moves out after a "Huey" assault in Tay Ninh Province during operation "Junction City," April 1967. (#SC 638865)

General Palmer visits the U.S. 3rd Brigade, 4th Infantry Division, commanded by Col. Eugene P. Forrester (right), in Binh Dinh Province in March 1968. Author's collection.

Above, General Westmoreland talks with George D. Jacobson and other military personnel in the embassy shortly after the attack. (#SC 644444 and #644454)

At left, Viet Cong dead lie near the main entrance of the American Embassy in Saigon after an early morning attack on 31 January 1968 at the start of the enemy's Tet offensive.

General Palmer leaves his headquarters at Long Binh on 1 January 1968 with General Harold K. Johnson, Army Chief of Staff, who spent the holidays visiting American troops in Vietnam.

Below, in a ceremony at the Pentagon, 29 July 1968, Bruce Palmer is sworn in as U.S. Army Vice Chief of Staff by MG Kenneth G. Wickham. General Westmoreland (center) looks on. Both photographs, author's collection.

Above, U.S. forces return the military base at Lai Khe to South Vietnamese forces, 25 February 1970. Left to right: LTG Do Cao Tri, MG Albert E. Milloy, MG Nguyen Van Hieu, and LTG Julian J. Ewell. (#064575)

Below, Secretary of Defense Melvin R. Laird presents the Defense Distinguished Service Medal to General Creighton W. Abrams, Army Chief of Staff, in a ceremony at the Pentagon, 16 October 1972. Secretary of the Army Robert F. Froehlke looks on at left. (#100850)

Secretary of Defense Laird poses with the Joint Chiefs of Staff in the Pentagon's Gold Room ("the tank") on 24 November 1972. Left to right: General Creighton W. Abrams, U.S. Army; Admiral Thomas H. Moorer, Chairman, JCS; Laird; General John D. Ryan, U.S. Air Force; Admiral Elmo R. Zumwalt, Jr., U.S. Navy; and General Robert E. Cushman, U.S. Marine Corps. (#088158)

CTZ. When U.S. troops held this area, a U.S. corps headquarters controlled all U.S. operations, but the Vietnamese Joint General Staff had not made similar arrangements. So the brave and experienced Major General Vu Van Giai, who commanded the 3rd ARVN Division, had no authority over the ARVN tank units and Vietnamese Marine brigade in the sector. This also was to prove costly.

The foregoing statements are not intended to be unduly critical of MACV. By the end of 1971 the headquarters was immersed in U.S. redeployment matters and could no longer devote as much attention to the operational side. The U.S. 7th Air Force constituted the only potent forces available to General Abrams, who continued to demonstrate a masterful use of air power in support of ARVN and still exercised considerable influence with President Thieu and his senior military leaders.

But time was getting very short for the South Vietnamese. ARVN needed greater armor, artillery, and logistic capabilities to replace support from the U.S. Army that was now no longer available. One of the most difficult capabilities to develop was the helicopter support provided by our Army—a system of dedicated support in which designated ARVN units were teamed up with specified U.S. Army aviation units. This task was made far more difficult by the MACV decision to assign this mission to the South Vietnamese Air Force rather than to ARVN. The decision was motivated by the fact that ARVN had no aviation element to build on, but it deprived South Vietnam of the U.S. Army's unique experience with helicopter airmobility, since the Vietnamese Air Force, advised by the USAF, had no knowledge, feel, or first-hand experience with such airmobility concepts.

While Vietnamization and U.S. disengagement were in train, the Nixon administration was also attempting to get serious negotiations underway with North Vietnam. Even before his inauguration, Nixon had written to Ho Chi Minh in late December 1968 on the subject as a gesture of goodwill from the newly elected U.S. government, but received a brutal, totally negative response on 31 December.[2] (Ho Chi Minh died in September of the following year, but the Hanoi regime continued its unrelenting and uncompromising outlook without a change in beat.) In February 1969 Henry Cabot Lodge replaced Cyrus Vance as the U.S. representative in the largely pro forma open talks in Paris, and in August 1969 Henry Kissinger tried to initiate meaningful secret talks with the North Vietnamese, but to no avail. Although serious secret negotiations were resumed between Kissinger and Le Duc Tho in February 1970, it was not until October 1972, when their Easter 1972 offensive ran out of steam, that the North Vietnamese finally indicated that they were ready to make a political settlement.[3]

In the meantime, President Nixon had sought to bring increasing pressure on the North Vietnamese to negotiate by seeking separate talks with the Soviet Union and China. The strategic arms limitations talks with the USSR, which began in mid-November 1969 and led eventually to SALT I, were initiated partly for this purpose. Likewise, the president's trip to China in February 1972, which reopened contact between the two countries, was also intended to put pressure on Hanoi.[4] It was the timing of this planned trip to China that led to the U.S. estimate that February 1972 might be a likely time for the next winter offensive by the NVA. Consequently, expecting the heaviest offensive of the war to come in early 1972, the president ordered that U.S. airpower in Southeast Asia be reinforced. Augmented levels now included six aircraft carriers on line and two hundred B-52s.

But the assault came considerably later. Under cover of a "crachin" drizzle and fog which hugged the ground, the enemy launched an allout offensive on 31 March 1972 across the DMZ—a campaign that was to become known as the Easter offensive. Coming directly through the DMZ with the most sophisticated weaponry yet seen in South Vietnam, the attack came as a surprise to HQ MACV, which had expected the enemy to invade I CTZ from the direction of Laos. Hundreds of medium tanks and armored personnel carriers poured across the DMZ, supported by heavy artillery, rockets, and modern mobile antiaircraft weapons, including some surface-to-air missiles—all supplied by the Soviet Union. The green 3rd ARVN Division was hit suddenly while units were being rotated on forward fire bases. One regiment deployed north of Dong Ha in the east was quickly driven back, while the regiment to the west at Camp Carroll surrendered without a fight.

On 4 April the enemy opened up a second front in III CTZ, surrounding Loc Ninh and An Loc near the Cambodian border with two NVA divisions, later reinforced with a third division. President Nixon responded to the grave threat by resuming U.S. bombing against NVN up to the 18th parallel, the first since President Johnson had stopped all bombing in the North on 31 October 1968. Then on 23 April the enemy invaded Kontum Province in II CTZ with two NVA divisions. In I CTZ by 28 April the 3rd ARVN Division had virtually disintegrated as the enemy overran Quang Tri Province and besieged its capital, Quang Tri City. The lack of an overall commander had been a major factor in the collapse. The enemy now seriously threatened the ancient capital of Hue to the south.

At this critical juncture President Thieu replaced Lieutenant General Lam, the I Corps commander, with Lieutenant General Ngo Quang Truong, a tough, seasoned, fighting leader, probably the best field commander in South Vietnam. Truong took personal command of all ARVN troops and South Vietnamese Marines in the area and, supported by stalwart American advisers such as Brigadier General Frederick Kroesen, U.S. Army, organized and fought a successful defense of Hue. With the help of massive close air support by tactical fighters of the U.S. Air Force, U.S. Navy, and U.S. Marine Corps, as well as U.S. Army attack helicopters, Truong's forces finally halted the enemy advance in I CTZ. Several hundred enemy tanks and other armored vehicles were destroyed, while the South Vietnamese lost most of their fledgling armored force. Later, in August, the South Vietnamese mounted a counterattack and retook Quang Tri City.

Meanwhile the legendary American civilian John Paul Vann, formerly the senior CORDS adviser in III CTZ, had become the senior American adviser in all of II CTZ. This was another first for Vann—as a civilian he formally commanded all U.S. advisory personnel in the region, both military and civilian. It was quite a tribute to his ability and strength of character. Vann had holed up in Kontum in late April with the ARVN corps commander and vowed to hold the city against a large NVA force. And they did. It was a bitter fight, but the enemy finally quit and withdrew his troops on 31 May. Vann was killed on 9 June in a helicopter crash in the same area. He had been convinced that he would die in Vietnam, probably violently, and some time before his death he left a detailed will with George Jacobson, the number two man in MACV's pacification organization. Vann's death was a devastating loss for South Vietnam. He had fought for over ten years in the most hotly contested areas of the Highlands, central III CTZ, and the Delta, and knew the enemy as well as any Vietnamese.

But the most prolonged and perhaps most celebrated fight was the defense of An Loc in III CTZ, where a few remnants from ARVN units and a handful of U.S. Army advisers held out against repeated attacks by elements of three enemy divisions. The battle was won on 9 June when the enemy withdrew from the area. Heavy, sustained, close air support by USAF fighter-bombers and U.S. Army attack helicopters were instrumental in this gallant stand. But the victory was only temporary, for the enemy thereafter effectively controlled Highway 13 (along which the battle had been fought) from the Cambodian border south to Lai Khe about halfway from the border to Saigon.

By late summer it was clear that Hanoi's country-wide offensive had failed to achieve a decisive victory. In the extreme north, however (in addition to permanent gains made in III CTZ), the enemy remained in strength inside South Vietnam. In effect, the boundary between North and South Vietnam had been moved about ten kilometers south of the DMZ. It had been a very costly ten kilometers for the North—NVA losses for the January–September 1972 period were conservatively estimated to be over 100,000 men killed.

While the North Vietnamese offensive was going on, U.S. forces continued to be withdrawn, the last American combat troops departing the country in August 1972, leaving only about 40,000 American support personnel in South Vietnam. The period had seen a significant demonstration of at least marginally successful Vietnamization. During the heavy fighting in 1972 General Abrams had stated emphatically that "By God, the South Vietnamese can hack it!" He remained confident of ARVN's ability to stop the NVA, albeit immeasurably helped by heavy U.S. air support and U.S. advisers on the ground.

On 8 October 1972 Hanoi dropped its demand that Thieu be replaced by an interim coalition, thus abandoning at the negotiation table what the North Vietnamese had fought to achieve for years, i.e., political sanction of their right to rule South Vietnam.[5] The United States and South Vietnam, however, had also made important concessions during the negotiations, the most significant one being not to call for mutual troop withdrawals, thus opening the way for North Vietnamese forces to remain in the South while the United States had to withdraw its forces. Hanoi, moreover, still had one very high card to play—the American POWs in the North.

Meanwhile, in May 1972, President Nixon had ordered the mining of Haiphong harbor, in effect a blockade of this important port through which passed most of Hanoi's warmaking arms, munitions, supplies, and equipment. On 8 May the U.S. 7th Fleet executed the mine-laying order in a well planned and beautifully conducted operation which took less than one hour.[6] Navy and Marine attack aircraft swarmed over the area laying enough various kinds of mines to make the approach to the port practically impassable. Some light antiaircraft fire was encountered, but there were no friendly casualties. The operation had been thoroughly discussed in advance and a decision to mine rather than blockade the harbor was made because it was operationally simpler, more decisive, and less provocative. Once done, there was little the North Vietnamese or their benefactors, the USSR or China, could do to reopen the port. However, there were ample overland rail and road links to North Vietnam from China to maintain the flow of supplies provided by the Soviet Union and China. Unfortunately, like the large cross-border operations, particularly the incursion into Laos, the bold action came years too late.

As the crunch period of the U.S. election in November 1972 approached, the pace of the secret talks with the North Vietnamese in Paris measurably picked up, as well as the frequency of U.S. discussions with Thieu in Saigon. General Haig as Kissinger's principal assistant played an increasingly direct and important role in the latter process. Beginning in September 1971 and accelerating in the summer of 1972, Haig made a series of trips to Saigon, with the dual purpose of assessing the situation and conferring with President Thieu, to get either his reaction or his agreement at a critical point in the Paris talks.

Thieu balked in the late fall of 1972, despite President Nixon's victory at the polls, which seemed to assure at the time some continuity in U.S. policy. It was not until 20 January 1973, after Nixon, Kissinger, and Haig brought enormous pressures to bear on him, that Thieu finally accepted the agreements drafted in Paris.[7] An unforgettable vignette told to me by Haig after one of his last visits to Saigon in late 1972 concerned a somewhat forlorn statement by President Thieu at the end of their meeting. Thieu said that he was not concerned about 1972 or even 1973, but about whether the United States would continue to stand behind South Vietnam thereafter, adding, prophetically, "in 1975."

During this period (June 1971–December 1972), Haig frequently visited my office in the Pentagon to discuss matters of particular interest to the U.S. Army, such as the situation in Vietnam, the Paris talks, and the post-Vietnam Army. Laird inevitably learned of these visits and informally made known his displeasure about such direct contacts made without his knowledge. This did not discourage Haig from those contacts, although when he had time he would usually make a brief protocol stop at Laird's office before returning to the White House. Although I regretted that such visits might exacerbate the less-than-cordial relationship between Laird's office and the White House, I found them invaluable, for they gave me insights into the Vietnam situation and how it was unfolding that could not be obtained in any other way. And so I was indebted to Haig for taking the time and trouble to come to the Pentagon.

I was also getting the benefit at this time of the views of F.G. ("Fritz") Kraemer, a special assistant to the Army's DCSOPS, whose specialty was interpreting important international developments and the foreign and defense policy implications for the United States. Kraemer and Kissinger, both German-born, had served together in the U.S. Army (Intelligence section, 84th Infantry Division) in Germany during World War II and were old, close friends. Kraemer had been instrumental in having Haig assigned to the NSC staff under Kissinger. Kraemer was much older and in many ways had been Kissinger's mentor. Indeed, during the enormous strains of the Vietnam War period Kraemer had become Kissinger's confidant. Complete with a haughty air, monocle, swagger stick, and authoritative voice and manner, Kraemer was an anachronism—a throwback to the days of the Prussian military autocracy. With his German-English accent (much less guttural than Kissinger's) and flowery, forceful oratorical style, Kraemer had become a great hit at the various American war colleges and service staff colleges. His main fault was his garrulousness, and when it came time for him to leave my office I had literally to push him out the door, still talking and wildly gesticulating.

From Kraemer, I gained an appreciation of the depth and complexity of Kissinger's personality. It was quite apparent that Kissinger was a deeply sensitive and emotional man, subject to wide and swift changes in mental outlook, and often immersed in a state of deep depression, almost despair, over the course and direction of the negotiations on the Vietnam War. Kraemer played a significant role in shoring up Kissinger at such times, dispelling doubts, restoring confidence, and generating a determination to negotiate the best possible deal for the United States and South Vietnam.

Significantly, I got the same impressions of Kissinger in this negotiating role from Haig. In fact, Haig had confided that there were times when he wondered whether Kissinger had the inner toughness and tenacity to stay the course. According to Haig, the president also harbored doubts about Kissinger, did not completely trust him on holding to the president's minimum position, and kept him on a short leash. In effect, the president and Haig teamed up to stiffen Kissinger's backbone at appropriate moments. This period during the last months of the negotiations no doubt laid the foundation for the president's increasing reliance on Haig, who ultimately served as his chief of staff in the dark hours of the Watergate hearings.

During 1972 the JCS lineup changed somewhat. General Westmoreland retired on 3 July at the end of his four-year tenure as Army chief of staff. Admiral Moorer's two-year term as chairman of the JCS also ended on 3 July. While he was chief of staff Westmoreland was an obvious and well qualified candidate for the CJCS position, and it was only natural that he had aspirations to succeed Moorer. But politically, there had been small likelihood of this happening. There had been some cloud over Moorer arising from the yeoman affair in the White House, as well as from irregularities in the conduct of U.S. air strikes against North Vietnam. President Nixon delayed extending Moorer for another two years until almost the last minute, finally ending the prolonged speculation.

On 3 July the Army Staff gave "Westy" and his wife, "Kitsy," a rousing sendoff from the Pentagon, and they departed for a much needed vacation in the North Carolina mountains. With great nostalgia we bade him farewell. It was the end of an era for the U.S. Army—a drama-packed and unhappy era.

It now seemed clear that the United States would have to settle for a less than satisfactory outcome in Vietnam. Although it was also evident that the U.S. military must inevitably share at least a part of the responsibility, it was patently unfair to pin the whole blame on one military leader—Westmoreland. Looking back I often recall what Hanson Baldwin said about Westmoreland: "This man has been as much sinned against as he has sinned."

Meanwhile, in late June 1972 General Abrams had turned over command of MACV to his deputy, General Weyand, and had departed Saigon for Washington, where the president had nominated him to succeed Westmoreland as Army chief of staff. This change of command occurred just after a scandal had broken in Southeast Asia, arising out of the conduct of U.S. air strikes in North Vietnam, and the Congress planned to hold hearings on the matter. Laird had personally selected Abrams for chief of staff and had succeeded in securing the president's approval despite strong opponents in the White House who wanted a younger man (and probably one more amenable to civilian control).

Secretary Laird instructed Abrams to stay away from the Pentagon, to avoid the press like the plague, and to stay out of sight until he was confirmed by the Senate. This turned out to be a break for Abrams, for he could unwind, catch up with his family, and visit friends and relatives at his leisure. It also allowed ample time to brief Abrams thoroughly on all the major problems and issues facing the Army at home and world-wide. When he was confirmed, he was probably the best prepared chief of staff the Army ever had.

Abrams was an outstanding choice because the Army needed a long rebuilding period and he possessed the high dedication and determination to get the job done. The Army was his first love, however, and he was never much enamored with his joint duties as a member of the JCS. He much preferred to work interservice problems directly with the other services without the benefit of any permanent joint mechanism.

The hearings of the Senate Armed Services Committee on U.S. air attacks against North Vietnam were extensive and difficult before the committee finally confirmed General Abrams on 12 October 1972. The problem stemmed from the rules of engagement imposed on U.S. fliers in Southeast Asia by the president, NSC staff, and the secretary of defense, all in the name of "civilian control." After the complete bombing halt of 31 October 1968 the United States, under the "informal agreements" reached with Hanoi, agreed to fly only reconnaissance missions over North Vietnam. Only a few weeks later, however, enemy surface-to-air missiles (SAMs) engaged our RF-4s over southern NVN and shot one down in late November 1968. This led to authority being given to the 7th Air Force not only to escort our reconnaissance aircraft over NVN but also to make "protective reaction strikes" to counter the increasing SAM and MIG fighter attacks against our reconnaissance missions. Later, as it became apparent that Hanoi was expanding and improving its communications network in the southern part of NVN and building up ammunition, fuel, and other supplies in the area, the 7th Air Force was given permission to expand "protective reaction strikes" to include limited attacks just north of the DMZ.[8]

The purpose of the U.S. restraints on the employment of U.S. airpower was, of course, a political one of maintaining the fiction of the 1968 informal agreements with Hanoi and furthering the Paris talks seeking a political settlement with North Vietnam. In the end, these limited strikes had little effect on the enemy buildup culminating in the massive Easter offensive across the DMZ in late March 1972. This buildup, incidentally, should have warned the allies of the strong probability of an attack launched directly from the DMZ.

Before President Nixon lifted the bombing halt and resumed attacks against the North in April 1972, a USAF sergeant publicly revealed that the 7th Air Force had been flying regularly scheduled strikes against various military targets in NVN and had directed the units and pilots conducting the operations to enter false reports attesting that the attacks were indeed "protective reaction strikes." Consequently, General Ryan, Air Force chief of staff, acting outside the operational chain of command (commander-in-chief—secretary of defense/CJCS—CINCPAC—CO-MUSMACV—CG 7th AF), relieved General Jack Lavelle, commander of the 7th Air Force, who had stoutly maintained that he was faithfully carrying out the intentions of his superiors. Lavelle was reduced to his permanent grade of major general and retired in disgrace. (In Washington, after Lavelle had retired, I asked Jack Ryan why he had fired Lavelle, and he simply replied, "He lied to me.") A short time later General Lavelle died, a brokenhearted and physically broken man. In his defense, it was well known that the commanders and pilots in the field continually complained about the restraints on airpower and had been advised informally by "higher headquarters" not to ask for a change in authority but to interpret their current authority broadly. Since this no doubt was a major factor contributing to the affair, the joint operational chain of command above the commanding general of the 7th Air Force clearly should bear some responsibility for what happened.

Obviously it was a complex, controversial issue. General Abrams, Admiral Moorer, and others in the responsible operational chain of command were in a very difficult position with respect to the Senate hearings. If they stated that they were unaware of the situation, they were vulnerable to a charge of incompetence or dereliction of duty. And if they admitted to knowledge, they were guilty of taking part in the duplicity. In my view, it was again a case, at least in part, of oversupervision by civilian officials and an unwillingness on their part to recognize the wartime realities of the military situation in Southeast Asia. Moreover, it is another demonstration of the wrongness of placing wartime military commanders in a position where their integrity is jeopardized for the sake of essentially political advantage.

During the period of more than three months from July to October 1972, between Westmoreland's retirement and Abrams's confirmation, I found myself acting as the U.S. Army's chief of staff, an unprecedented episode in the Army's history. This was the first, and to date the only, time that an individual was designated by formal Army General Order, issued by the secretary of the Army, as the acting Army chief of staff for an indefinite period of time. It was an extremely interesting period, and I was glad that I could take a heavy load off General Abrams, who very much needed a respite.

One of the more unpleasant events during this interim period was the

Senate hearings in July 1972 on SALT I, on which General Ryan, Air Force chief of staff, and I testified together. The strategic arms control negotiations had been concluded in almost a frenzy of last-minute negotiations during the summit meeting in Moscow between Nixon and Brezhnev in May 1972. The talks had been going on for almost three years. Washington knew that the Soviets were building up their offensive strategic nuclear weapon capabilities at an accelerating rate, and one major U.S. objective of the talks was to stop the momentum of this offensive buildup. A special channel (in addition to the regular negotiating teams) had been established from the start between the president and Brezhnev through Ambassador Dobrynin in Washington. The stated reason was that it had been made necessary by the pace and unpredictability of ongoing debates in the United States about Vietnam and other issues, such as the deployment of the antiballistic missile (ABM) and the defense budget. At any rate, agreement was reached at the very end of the Moscow summit, and the ABM Treaty and the interim agreement freezing offensive nuclear weapon levels (SALT I) were signed concurrently in Moscow on Sunday, 29 May 1972.[9]

Most of the details of the two agreements had subsequently become known and the Senate was debating their merits. At these particular hearings the subject was the role of the JCS during the negotiations, as well as their views on the outcome. Ryan and I tried to explain that the JCS role was basically advisory; that we had been kept informed of the situation through our JCS representative on the U.S. negotiating team at every step up until the May 1972 summit; that we had made known to all concerned on the U.S. side our views and recommendations at appropriate times; and that we had given our qualified support to the final agreements. We also told the senators that the gist of these final negotiations was gleaned piecemeal via JCS conference calls with the CJCS as he got them direct from Moscow. Furthermore, some of the so-called "details" of the final agreements were not revealed until much later.

The qualified support of the JCS hinged on specific safeguards with respect to accelerating ongoing, future U.S. offensive programs, and improving existing ones. (History records that these safeguards subsequently were not met.) But the senators, particularly Henry Jackson, Sam Ervin, and Stuart Symington, were not happy with our testimony and publicly castigated Ryan and myself for dereliction of duty as members of the JCS. The CJCS, Admiral Moorer, and the CNO, Admiral Zumwalt, got their come-uppance later at separate Senate hearings.

With respect to the ABM, the Army had fought a losing battle in the JCS and with the secretary of defense. To this day I do not accept the logic that defensive weapons are inherently destabilizing. Yet this was the basic argument, along with high cost and controversial performance potential, that killed the ABM. In SALT I we gave away our very substantial lead over the Soviets in ABM technology in exchange for a freeze on offensive weaponry. To make matters worse, the United States essentially dismantled its strategic air defenses, completely eliminating the U.S. Army Air Defense Command and its SAM defenses, and emasculating the U.S. Air Force's interceptor defenses. Today the United States has no strategic air defense of consequence, while the Soviets have deployed a massive one. As a military professional, the argument that a strong offense is the best defense makes little sense to me in an intercontinental nuclear weapons context where the numbers on both sides are large and where agreed limitations are only a cap with no provision for actual reductions.

Another incident, but a relatively minor one with a somewhat humorous side, occurred during this summer period of 1972, when the Army was awaiting its new chief of staff's confirmation. It was late summer and the chairman of the JCS, as well as the Navy and Air Force chiefs, were out of town. Since the commandant of the Marines was at that time precluded by statute from acting as the JCS chairman, I found myself, as the senior vice chief of staff, acting as chairman. An otherwise uneventful day was interrupted by a phone call from the White House in the person of an irate Henry Kissinger. He had just received word from Chinese authorities (the specific channel was not revealed) claiming that U.S. aircraft on a daylight combat mission over North Vietnam had violated Chinese air space and territory. The incident occurred during the famous LINEBACKER air offensive against North Vietnam culminating in the massive "Christmas bombing" in December 1972, which Kissinger later credited as finally compelling Hanoi's agreement to the January 1973 cease-fire.

Kissinger seemed to be very angry and upset, demanding that commanders concerned be roundly upbraided and threatening that "heads vould roll" amoung senior military leaders if it should happen again. He had implicitly accepted the Chinese allegation without waiting to get the U.S. side, which required debriefing pilots known to be in the air at the time and checking friendly data on U.S. aircraft positions against intercepted North Vietnamese and Chinese position data, all of which would take time. I assured him that we would make a careful check to verify or deny the allegation, but in the meantime would warn all concerned of the seriousness of the matter.

I then got on the secure voice phone with CINCPAC, Admiral "Chic" Clarey, and passed on the instructions from on high. Clarey had been through similar situations before and took it in good grace. He pointed out that our pilots flying at high speed and trying to carry out their missions and yet survive intercepting enemy jets and air defenses, had their hands full, and that during missions near the Chinese border under these circumstances, an inadvertent violation of the border could readily happen. I had tried to tell Kissinger that surely a pilot fighting to save his own life should not be faulted for an accidental violation, but the good doctor was not listening. He simply repeated the dire implications and unpleasant results of another such incident.

Our investigation of this particular incident produced ambiguous results. Intercepts of Chinese position plots indicated that the Chinese radar was probably out of calibration, for our radar plots showed no such violation. Several of our pilots had flown near the Chinese border but none felt that he had flown across the line.

In retrospect it has occurred to me that Kissinger's anger may have been more fore show than for effect. It had been eighteen months since the United States had reopened contact with China. Surely by this time our government knew first-hand that China had no intention of intervening with their own forces in the Vietnam War, and that China's interests lay in diminishing the Soviet influence in Southeast Asia and in preventing Hanoi from dominating the region.[10]

As 1972 wore on and the U.S. presidential election loomed, the pressure to reach an agreement with Hanoi became superheated. The North Vietnamese obviously had decided to wait out the American election but, even after Nixon's strong victory at the polls, continued to be intransigent. This led to the controversial, around-the-clock "Christmas bombing" of North Vietnam in late 1972, the heaviest of the war. It had the desired effect, for Hanoi finally agreed to a cease-fire on 29 January 1973. Our POWs in the North were to be freed at last.

7

1973-1975:
The Final War Years

Under the terms of the January 1973 cease-fire agreement, the United States and all other third countries agreed to remove their remaining forces from South Vietnam within sixty days. In addition, the United States agreed that it "would stop all its military activities against the territory of the Democratic Republic of Vietnam," that is, North Vietnam. Hanoi, on the other hand, was allowed to keep its forces in the South, supported from safe bases in the North and in Laos, while South Vietnamese military bases were vulnerable to attack. Neither North nor South Vietnam was allowed to accept the introduction of troops or military advisers into South Vietnam. The two Vietnams could replace material in the South, but only on a one-for-one basis of like items.[1] These restrictions did not apply to military assistance flowing into North Vietnam from the USSR and China, however. Thus the asymmetries of the agreement greatly favored Hanoi.

Although U.S. air forces remained in Thailand and U.S. naval forces continued to operate in the South China Sea, the United States was inhibited from attacking North Vietnam or supporting South Vietnam, not only by the proscriptions in the cease-fire agreement but also by the virtual disappearance of domestic support for any such moves. As time passed Hanoi grew even bolder in moving against the South, as the likelihood of U.S. reprisal diminished.

To replace MACV and to carry out the traditional functions of a U.S. defense attache and military advisory group for South Vietnam, as well as to monitor cease-fire activities, a small military headquarters called the Defense Attache Office (DAO), Saigon, was established in January 1973 under Major General John E. Murray, U.S. Army. The DAO was located in the old MACV headquarters at Tan Son Nhut Air Base and had small field offices in major cities in each military region. Ellsworth Bunker remained as the U.S. ambassador to Saigon until May 1973, when he was replaced by Graham Martin.

Ambassador Bunker served for over six years in Saigon during some of the most trying periods of the war. Well past the age when the strongest and most dedicated men would have retired, much less served as the ambassador to a nation at war, Bunker was resolute and steady, a leader of extraordinary capacity. Few Americans have served their country so faithfully and so well as this staunch patriot and superb diplomat.

The United States also established after the cease-fire a headquarters called the U.S. Support Activities Group and Seventh Air Force (USSAG/7th AF) located at Nakhon Phanom in northeast Thailand. This headquarters planned for the employment of air and naval power in Southeast Asia should the United States decide to take such actions. USSAG took over a USAF operational control site that previously had controlled and monitored all 7th Air Force combat and reconnaissance missions in Cambodia, Laos, and North Vietnam. After the cease-fire, U.S. bombing attacks against NVA and Khmer Rouge troops continued in Cambodia until the U.S. Congress in August 1973 prohibited any further air operations in that country. This marked the end of U.S. B-52 and fighter-bomber operations in the region. U.S. air reconnaissance operations continued over Laos until June 1974, when it was terminated primarily because of political pressures at home. Thereafter much of the timely and factual evidence of the large flow on enemy personnel, arms, and equipment into the South was now permanently lost to both U.S. and South Vietnamese intelligence.

When the cease-fire came in January 1973, the NVA had an estimated 150–160,000 troops inside the borders of South Vietnam and about another 100,000 regular troops in Laos and Cambodia. These forces were in poor shape as a result of the 1972 enemy offensive, which had gone on for almost six months and had cost Hanoi enormous losses of lives and materiel. South Vietnamese forces had likewise suffered heavy losses but were for the most part intact and still controlled the great bulk of the populated parts of South Vietnam. The NVA, on the other hand, controlled the extreme northern and northwestern part of I CTZ south of the DMZ and along the Laotian border; northwestern Kontum Province in the Central Highlands of II CTZ; and most of Phuoc Long Province and northern Binh Long Province in III CTZ along the Cambodian border.[2]

Unfortunately, Hanoi never intended to abide by the cease-fire agreements, explicit, implicit, or informally understood, and proceeded to violate them massively and repeatedly. It is true that the South Vietnamese also violated some of the terms of the 1973 cease-fire, but not nearly to the same extent as the North Vietnamese. The United States, on the other hand, closely abided by the terms of the agreement.

Although the NVA was "supposed to" withdraw from Laos and to stop using Laos and Cambodia as an infiltration corridor, the opposite occurred. Hanoi continued to move tens of thousands of replacements and large amounts of supplies down the Ho Chi Minh Trail. The Trail was converted into a complex of wide macadam roads, concrete bridges, and permanent drainage systems so that Hanoi was able to move major logistic units from Laos into South Vietnam and build up large supply dumps inside South Vietnam. To make matters worse, the International Commission of Control and Supervision set up under the cease-fire was completely frustrated by an uncrontrollable situation and after a few months ceased to function in any meaningful way.[3]

During the last years of the war there were many changes in the top military and civilian hierarchy of the U.S. national security establishment. Admiral Moorer retired as chairman of the JCS on 30 June 1974 and was succeeded by General George S. Brown, who had followed General Ryan as chief of staff, U.S. Air Force, on 1 August 1973. Brown had commanded the 7th Air Force in Vietnam and the Air Force Systems Command, and was an exceptionally well qualified and broadly experienced airman. He had an unfortunate penchant for putting his foot in his mouth, but no one ever questioned his integrity and candor, and on balance he made a solid chairman. Brown served two full two-year terms as CJCS despite a terminal illness which struck him while he was still on active duty. Retiring on 1 July 1978, this distinguished and greatly admired military professional died only a short time later.

General David C. Jones succeeded Brown as the Air Force chief on 1 July 1974. With a broad staff and administrative background, as distinguished from the more traditional one of combat command experience, Jones was not the sentimental choice of the Air Force. A shrewd, intelligent man, he knew his way around the Washington bureaucracy and so was at times susceptible to civilian influence.

On the naval side, Admiral James L. Holloway III, a descendant of a famous navy family, succeeded the controversial Admiral Zumwalt on 29 June 1974 and returned the CNO position to its more traditional stance. Holloway, a combat-blooded naval aviator, was well grounded and broadly experienced. He was far more open-minded and less parochial than the average senior naval officer and consequently not only got along well with the other chiefs, but also contributed much to the stature of the chiefs as a collegial body. As for the Marine Corps, General Robert E. Cushman, Jr., had succeeded General Chapman as commandant on 1 January 1972. Cushman, a big, no-nonsense man who looked like a Marine, thoroughly appreciated the special role and qualities of the Marine Corps, which, like the Army, needed a rebuilding period after the extraordinarily severe strain of the war. Cushman was not the intellectual type and never pretended to be.

The Army was much saddened by the untimely death on 4 September 1974, of its chief, General Creighton W. Abrams. Abrams was in the heroic mold of folklore and there will never be another quite like him in the U.S. Army. General Frederick C. Weyand succeeded him, serving until the summer of 1976. Homespun yet debonair, Weyand was deceptively shrewd and, when cast in the role, a superb diplomat. As chief of staff he chose to carry on Abrams's original design to rebuild the Army, and made substantial progress in carrying forward that mandate.

About a month before Abrams died I saw him briefly at Quarters One, Fort Myer, Virginia, where he was fighting to overcome a fatal malignancy. We talked a little about our cadet days at West Point, the situation in Southeast Asia, and how the Army was doing worldwide. I urged him to consider writing some memoirs, however brief, but his reply was vehement, "Never!" and when I asked why, he gave two reasons— because memoirs become larded with the "vertical pronoun," and because he would never reveal certain aspects of his service in Vietnam. And so he took those revelations to his grave.

By a quirk of fate, on the day he died I retired from active duty— we were the last two Army members of the West Point Class of 1936 on active duty. My last job was commanding the United States Readiness Command, with headquarters at MacDill Air Force Base, Florida, a unified command with operational control of the combat-ready Army troops and Air Force tactical squadrons based in the continental United States. General Brown, who had commanded the 7th Air Force under Abrams in Vietnam and was now CJCS, hosted my retirement ceremony at MacDill. We agreed to make the occasion also a memorial tribute to General Abrams. It was particularly appropriate because lined up in battle dress on MacDill's main runway were the colors and color guards of most of the Army divisions and Air Force combat units that had served under Abrams in Vietnam. None of us at the time realized that the fall of South Vietnam was so close at hand. Since that debacle, I have often reflected that General Abrams, who had worked so hard to make the South Vietnamese armed forces capable of defending their country, at least had been spared the agony of seeing the death of the Republic of Vietnam.

Westmoreland, on the other hand, was not spared that trauma, but seems over the years since the war to have become a national scapegoat, blamed for everything that went wrong in Vietnam, large or small, regardless of whether he had even a remote connection with the matter. It is a singularly unfair and unsupported judgment. Many scores of senior American officials, civilian and military, including the author, contributed to our Vietnam mistakes, most of which have been so judged in hindsight. The real "blame," of course, must be laid squarely on the Hanoi regime and the North Vietnamese people, who demonstrated to the world that they had the will to prevail. Although it is small comfort to

Westmoreland, history is replete with examples of one native son's being singled out, rightly or wrongly, as the person responsible for a national disaster.

Both Abrams and Westmoreland would have been judged as authentic military "heroes" at a different time in history. Both men were outstanding leaders in their own right and in their own way. They offered sharply contrasting examples of military leadership, something akin to the distinct differences between Robert E. Lee and Ulysses S. Grant of our Civil War period. They entered the United States Military Academy at the same time in 1932—Westmoreland from a distinguished South Carolina family, and Abrams from a simpler family background in Massachusetts—and graduated together with the Class of 1936. Whereas Westmoreland became the First Captain (the senior cadet in the corps) during their senior year, Abrams was a somewhat nondescript cadet whose major claim to fame was as a loud, boisterous guard on the second-string varsity football squad. Both rose to high rank through outstanding performance in combat command jobs in World War II and the Korean War, as well as through equally commendable work in various staff positions.

But as leaders they were vastly different. Abrams was the bold, flamboyant charger who wanted to cut to the heart of the matter quickly and decisively, while Westmoreland was more the shrewdly calculating, prudent commander who chose the more conservative course. Faultlessly attired, Westmoreland constantly worried about his public image and assiduously courted the press. Abrams, on the other hand, usually looked rumpled, as though he might have slept in his uniform, and was indifferent about his appearance, acting as though he could care less about the press. The sharply differing results were startling; Abrams rarely receiving a bad press report, Westmoreland struggling to get a favorable one.

Their relationships with people and their leadership styles were likewise quite different. Westmoreland worked hard to attract followers and win their willing loyalty, while with Abrams such things came more naturally. Westmoreland, for example, liked to stand on the hood of a jeep and gather a relatively large group of soldiers, preferably paratroopers, around him; he would then give them a pep-talk "by the numbers." Abrams liked to talk to soldiers or flyers man-to-man, or at the most in small groups, and to use earthy, Patton-like language. Abrams could talk to the "non-com's" of a tank outfit and speak their language perfectly, or belly up to a bar with the fighter pilots of a squadron and get along famously. But it would be difficult to imagine Westmoreland acting in a manner that was so natural for Abrams.

Correctly formal, with his emotions under tight control, Westmoreland was predictable in manner, while Abrams was not. When he wanted to show his displeasure, Abrams often used the silent treatment, chewing on his cigar and staring distantly into space, while his expression and whole body reflected an enormous disdain. Then when the silence had become unbearable, he would burst out with some pithy language that he obviously had thought out well in advance. He also had the knack of feigning anger—deliberately letting his blood pressure rise, growing red in the neck, and almost turning blue before exploding. One never knew, however, whether it was an act or whether he had in fact lost his temper, and most people did not want to find out—practically speaking, it made little difference.

Neither man could be accused of being overly endowed with intellect, but each, nevertheless, in his own way was shrewd and canny. Generally they were both good judges of people, and their choice of key commanders and staff officers was usually sound. But they also made mistakes and at times clung loyally to subordinates whom everyone else in the Army knew were well below par in ability. Still, in the final analysis, as different as they were, these men measure up as two of our great wartime leaders.

Early in 1972 when Westmoreland was the Army chief of staff, we began to get low-level reports to the effect that the president was considering the appointment of Haig, by now a wily, experienced bureaucratic infighter, as Westmoreland's successor. We put some credence in these reports when we read the annual letters submitted by the president and Kissinger on the newly promoted Major General Haig in lieu of the normal military fitness reports. The letters raised our eyebrows (and blood pressure) more than a little, for they portrayed Haig as the most outstanding officer serving on active duty in any service, including the incumbent Joint Chiefs of Staff. Although the letters ignored Haig's lack of any command or military staff experience of consequence and relative youth, they nonetheless were testimonials which could not be lightly dismissed. Westmoreland urged that Haig be given at least division (two stars) and corps (three stars) command experience before being considered for a very senior four-star position. This was not only the traditional route to high rank, but, far more importantly, would have given Haig the experience he sorely needed and made him significantly better qualified and more acceptable in the eyes of all ranks of the Army. Moreover, it would have been much fairer to Haig himself. It does a military man no favor to promote him before he is ready to take on increased responsibilities. I am certain that Haig himself would have preferred the more conventional road to the top, but at this juncture his future was not even remotely in his hands. President Nixon was determined to reward Haig, and, having selected Abrams, at Secretary Laird's insistence, as the Army's chief, nominated Haig to succeed me as the vice chief of staff in late January 1973. Privately Abrams was most unhappy about this choice for his deputy, but characteristically accepted it with aplomb.

Secretary of the Army Froehlke was puzzled about the Army's obvious disapproval of the Haig appointment as nothing more than a four-star example of presidential patronage, and was taken aback by the numerous senior army officers, active and retired, who made no secret of their disapproval. I tried to explain to him that promotion in the military service is based on demonstrated professional ability, that there is no short-cut to the knowledge and judgment gained from experience, and that five years of chair-borne duty in the White House was no substitute for the real thing. When the secretary opined that such rapid promotions were common in the private sector, I pointed out that the stakes involved were vastly different and that the cost of failure in a high military post could not be measured by a profit and loss sheet. Bob Froehlke is a reasonable and intelligent man, and I believe he appreciated hearing the other side of the issue.

Fate intervened very soon after Haig moved into the Army vice chief of staff's office in late January 1973. The president phoned Haig the next day and when he discovered that it was not on a secure voice circuit, directed that one be installed immediately. This was done promptly by White House communications people, the equipment completely filling a large closet situated behind my old desk. Thereafter Haig was deeply involved daily on White House business. Since such secure voice communications with the White House were not available to either the secretary of defense or the Joint Chiefs of Staff, one can readily imagine the resentment in those quarters, not to mention the heartburn caused by the direct channel between the commander-in-chief and a subordinate of the secretary of defense.

It was Watergate, however, that administered the coup de grace to Haig's short-lived Pentagon tour. The "Plumbers" break-in at the Watergate office complex in Washington, which had occurred in June 1972, was rapidly building to a major national crisis. The president's top aides resigned on 20 April 1973, and it was apparent that presidential counsel John W. Dean III would bare his breast during the imminent Watergate congressional hearings. It was no surprise, then, when President Nixon early in May 1973 recalled the versatile general to the White House to become his chief of staff. Haig's military career thus came to an abrupt, even though temporary, end. President Ford assigned Haig as supreme allied commander in Europe in the fall of 1974. To his credit, Haig was highly effective in this largely political-military, but very sensitive and important, position. By the end of his roughly five-year tour he was a respected and admired military leader and statesman.

Although I thought at the time that my Army career was nearing an end, Laird and Froehlke persuaded me to take over the unified command known as U.S. Readiness Command, whose headquarters was at MacDill Air Force Base on the outskirts of Tampa, Florida. I did so on 1 February 1973, succeeding General John Throckmorton, U.S. Army, who retired.

The U.S. Readiness Command (REDCOM) controls the unassigned U.S. land-based strategic reserves in the continental United States, a very sizable proportion of the ground combat and tactical air forces of the nation. Secretary of Defense McNamara had established the command, originally called the U.S. Strike Command (STRICOM) in 1961 in order to create a strategic reserve force of all services under one unified commander. The Navy and Marine Corps, however, had successfully circumvented the intent of the secretary of defense by keeping all naval and marine combat units under either CINCPAC or CINCLANT (CINCPAC's Atlantic counterpart). These were both unified commands, but predominantly naval and marine in CINCPAC's case, and all naval and marine with respect to CINCLANT. Inasmuch as these two commands have always been under a naval officer, the sea-based services have thus managed to keep their forces away from the "landlubbers," the Army and the Air Force.

For awhile (from 1963 to 1971) STRICOM also had a geographic area of responsibility, the Middle East, Africa south of the Sahara, and South Asia (MEAFSA), a vast area, parts of which are of critical strategic importance. STRICOM's area unified command responsibilities mainly consisted of strategic overwatch, contingency planning, and military assistance programs. When the Navy took over the CJCS position in 1970 (Admiral Moorer), the Navy-Marine combination was in a position to dominate the JCS, which they did. One result was the disestablishment of MEAFSA in 1971 and the dissolution of the very substantial area expertise acquired by the STRICOM/MEAFSA staff. In the process STRICOM was redesignated REDCOM and divested of any overseas responsibilities.

The action was taken at precisely the wrong moment in history, as subsequent events in the Middle East, the Horn of Africa, Angola, southern Africa, and the subcontinent of Asia have dramatically demonstrated. To date, completely satisfactory unified command arrangements covering operational and planning responsibilities for these critical areas have yet to be made. It is a parlous situation which holds considerable potential for failure in an emergency or in wartime. In my judgment, the ill-fated Iranian hostage rescue mission in the spring of 1980 would *not* have been botched under the old STRICOM/MEAFSA arrangement. The command arrangements and plan would have been far simpler and more practical; there would have been more effective joint training and adequate full-dress rehearsals; and the assured professional execution of the operation would have justified a high likelihood of success.

My REDCOM staff was an excellent one, composed of roughly half Army, half Air Force, and a sprinkling of Navy and Marine personnel; most had joint staff experience. I felt, however, that the key to REDCOM's effectiveness lay in the person of the deputy commander, specified to be a lieutenant general, U.S. Air Force, for it was he who had to break down the natural barriers between the Air Force and an Army unified commander. I was blessed with outstanding deputies, in particular Lieutenant Generals Timothy O'Keefe and Ernest C. Hardin, Jr. O'Keefe was a small, feisty fighter pilot with a hot temper but much good sense and leadership ability. Hardin was a big, cigar-chewing Kentuckian (his nickname was "Moose") with a big heart, a lot of savvy, and broad experience in the Air Force and the Department of Defense. Universally admired, he was almost as well known in the Army as in the Air Force.

At REDCOM we got along well with our component commanders, the CG, Tactical Air Command (initially General William "Spike" Momyer and Later General Robert Dixon), with headquarters at Langley Air Force Base, Virginia; and the CG, Continental Army Command (CONARC) (General Walter Kerwin), with headquarters at Fort Monroe, Virginia. In mid-1973, in a major Army reorganization, CONARC was split into two separate commands—the Training and Doctrine Command (TRADOC), whose headquarters remained at Fort Monroe, and the Forces Command (FORSCOM), with headquarters at Ft. McPherson, Georgia. General Kerwin became the CG of FORSCOM, which contained all the Army operational units in the United States and became the Army component command of REDCOM, while General William De Puy took command of TRADOC, taking over all the Army's schools and training centers and assuming the missions of the Army's Combat Developments Command, which was eliminated.

The first such basic structural change in the Army's organization at home since the Revolutionary War, it was a bold, innovative move that not surprisingly was quite controversial among Army old-timers and came under heavy attack from military traditionalists and entrenched civilian bureaucrats. But the Army's command structure in the continental United States was antiquated and incapable of exploiting modern communications and computer technology that could streamline Army functions. While I was the Army's vice chief of staff I became convinced of the urgent necessity for such a drastic change and encouraged my assistant, then Lieutenant General De Puy, to develop the conceptual basis, followed by the detailed plans, to carry it out. One of the truly brilliant brains in the Army at the time, De Puy was not merely the architect of the reorganization; he also became the articulate proponent who obtained the approval of the army chief of staff (Westmoreland initially and later Abrams) and secretary (Froehlke), as well as that of the secretary of defense (Laird). And finally he was the hard-driving sparkplug who carried the plan to fruition. Then Major General Donn R. Pepke, chief of staff of CONARC during the planning and initial planning period, was the indispensable key to making the plan sound, workable, and acceptable to affected commanders in the field. Pepke, promoted to lieutenant general, later became the first deputy of FORSCOM. To their credit, Secretaries Froehlke and Laird recognized the need for reorganization and the straightforward nature of the Army proposal, and gave it their allout support.

As a unified commander I had an unusual opportunity to work directly with both the secretary of defense and the JCS, in particular the chairman, as well as with the Joint Staff. Elliot L. Richardson succeeded Laird as secretary of defense on 30 January 1973, almost the same date I went to REDCOM. In his very short tour (slightly less than four months) Richardson was impressive, and I thought that, given the opportunity, he would have become one of our better secretaries of defense. I especially liked his open-minded approach to the job and his willingness to try something different. He showed a strong interest in the unified commands and wanted to integrate them considerably more deeply in force structure planning and programming, which traditionally are service prerogatives.

Richardson was at Fort Hood, Texas, in mid-May 1973 observing a large REDCOM joint field training exercise when President Nixon telephoned him. We had been out in the field together all day and had just completed a press conference at Grey Army Air Field when the call came. I left him alone in a small, austere, almost bare waiting room in the airfield operations center to talk to the president. His face was ashen when he emerged and I knew at once that something serious was wrong. He took off in a special air mission Lockheed jet shortly thereafter, very tight-lipped and grim, but not before confiding to me that he would be leaving his job just as he was beginning to learn something about defense and to enjoy the work. Not long afterward the news broke that he had agreed to become attorney general just as the Watergate affair was beginning to break wide open. From my parochial point of view it was a real loss to see him leave the Department of Defense.

James R. Schlesinger succeeded Richardson on 2 July 1973 and served until 30 October 1975, working for both Presidents Nixon and Ford. Schlesinger was easily the most intellectual of all our secretaries of defense. I personally found him not only brilliant but quite down-to-earth and practical in his usually very direct approach to a problem. He did not suffer fools easily, however, and I felt sorry for those unfortunates who unwittingly gave him such an impression. He had a reputation for being unsociable and irascible, but I found him quite the opposite. He was easy to talk to, an alert, intelligent, and courteous visitor when he attended exercises, demonstrations, and the like, and a delightful guest on social occasions.

The first major crisis in his tenure was the October 1973 "Yom Kippur" war in the Middle East. REDCOM played a modest but important role during the crisis, which I thought Schlesinger and Moorer handled rather well. At headquarters REDCOM we were a little smug about the striking similarities between the Israeli-Egyptian conflict in the Sinai and a large U.S. joint field exercise that REDCOM had held in the Hueco Tanks desert area near Fort Bliss, Texas, a few months earlier. We had widely disseminated the lessons learned in that exercise within the Army, Air Force, and the Joint Staff, as well as to selected military schools and colleges.

Vietnam, of course, was a continuing crisis up to the bitter end. The only other crisis of note was a domestic one, Watergate, climaxed by President Nixon's resignation in August 1974. Schlesinger sent two rather strange messages to unified commands worldwide at the time, the earlier message admonishing us to be alert and to keep our powder dry in case any unfriendly people tried to take advantage of the situation. The second message, however, irritated me. It seemed to call for our steadfast loyalty at this moment of great domestic strain and I frankly resented it. Apparently, someone felt that some elements of the armed forces might be tempted to side with President Nixon; hence the cautionary message to the effect that U.S. forces were expected to support the succeeding president, Gerald R. Ford. I thought it not only unnecessary but insulting to our uniformed men and women. But it went by largely unnoticed outside the Department of Defense and eventually I chalked it up to an overly active imagination on the part of some staff assistants caught up in the paranoia of the times in Washington.

There had been other changes in the councils of government. Henry Kissinger became Nixon's secretary of state in September 1973, retaining the NSC advisory hat until President Ford appointed Lieutenant General Brent Skowcroft, USAF, as his national security adviser in November 1975. Howard H. Callaway succeeded Froehlke as secretary of the Army, serving from 15 May 1973 to 3 July 1975. Warner was replaced as secretary of the Navy in June 1974 by J. William Middendorf, who served until February 1977. John L. McLucas, another distinguished scientist, followed Seamans as secretary of the Air Force, serving from July 1973 until early 1977.

During the final years of the Republic of Vietnam, few if any of our national level civilian leaders were inclined to take much interest in the fate of South Vietnam. Even in the Department of Defense it had become a lost cause. The attitude was one of "It did not happen on my watch" as well as one of "We did our best and now there's nothing more that we can do."

The third and final turning point in the war was, of course, Watergate. Once the hearings started in the summer of 1973, the president was fighting for his political life and could no longer meaningfully influence the outcome. Had Watergate not occurred, there was at least a slim chance for South Vietnam to obtain adequate U.S. aid and to hold its own despite the grave disadvantages of the cease-fire agreement, although my own personal judgment was that, without the presence of American advisers,

the odds for South Vietnam's survival fell below 50-50. Even more bind-
ing were the multiple roadblocks put up by the U.S. Congress in such
forms as the Congressional War Powers Act of November 1973.

After using much of 1973 to recoup their losses of 1972, the North
Vietnamese decided to step up the pressure against the South during 1974
in what amounted to a series of strong "strategic raids" in key localities
country-wide. Skillful and daring counterattacks by the ARVN in early
1974, however, thwarted NVA efforts to isolate Saigon from the Delta,
and in III CTZ, the ARVN held its own, although in the northeastern
sector the NVA gained several base positions closer to Saigon.

But the situation was grim in II and I CTZs. In the Central Highlands
of II CTZ and in western I CTZ, the NVA overran important ARVN
outposts, while simultaneously moving ever closer to the populated coastal
lowlands. By the end of the year the ARVN held only the major cities
in the Highlands, with but tenuous lines of communications to the coastal
areas of II CTZ. In I CTZ there were simply not enough South Vietnamese forces to protect the Danang-Chu Lai-Quang Ngai coastal areas south
of Hai Van Pass as well as the important Hue-Phu Bai area north of the
pass. By year's end the 2nd ARVN Division was exhausted, the 3rd ARVN
Division was almost ineffective, while the famed 1st ARVN Division was
low in strength. Ranger battalions had fought gallantly throughout the
area but could not hold their exposed positions against overwhelming con-
centrations of enemy troops. Airborne battalions likewise had borne the
brunt of much sustained fighting and many were in poor condition. At
the end of 1974, I Corps forces in the north were regrouping with the
certain knowledge that the worst was yet to come, while II Corps braced
for the expected enemy onslaught against Kontum and Pleiku in the Central Highlands, as well as along Highway 19, the South Vietnamese lifeline to the coastal plains.[4]

Meanwhile, earlier in 1973, while the Watergate hearings were going
on, drastic reductions were made by the Congress in U.S. aid to South
Vietnam. This caused a situation, beginning in early 1974, in which military assistance levels were well below minimum operational requirements for such crucial items as ammunition, fuel, and medical supplies.

During 1974, both sides suffered heavy casualties, particularly the
NVA in I and II CTZs. But whereas the NVA received trained replacements and ample resupply from a secure homeland via a safe, all-weather
logistic structure immune from attack, South Vietnam's replacement and
supply system was subject to constant enemy disruption and attack. Understandably, morale in South Vietnam dropped lower.

The late Warren G. Nutter, former assistant secretary of defense for
international security affairs under Laird, told me after a visit to Saigon
in the early fall of 1974 that South Vietnamese morale was shattered and
that President Thieu felt betrayed and abandoned. In Nutter's words, the

declared American policy of building a viable South Vietnam was only a sham; the real policy was to cut American losses and get out of Vietnam. The word in Washington was that, after all, the South Vietnamese had been given ample time to get on their own feet. Nutter was quite bitter and expressed the opinion that the United States might well have great difficulty in finding allies in the Pacific in the future.

Despite heroic efforts on the part of Ambassador Martin and General Murray, who headed up the DAO in Saigon, military assistance funds were not restored to even austere levels. Draconian measures were applied in South Vietnam, where the number of deadlined tanks, armed personnel carriers, and helicopters steadily rose; and battles were lost because of inadequate air and artillery support, or insufficient airmobility to bring in reinforcements, all arising out of shortages in spare parts, ammunition, and fuel. Tactical shifts of ARVN units were sharply reduced, medical supplies were cut to the bone, combat aircraft and vehicles were cannibalized or grounded, and many Vietnamese Air Force and naval units were simply disbanded for lack of aircraft or ships.[5]

Allied intelligence had solid data on the ominous buildup of NVA forces two years after the cease-fire. In January 1975 the enemy's combat forces in South Vietnam were estimated at roughly 200,000 troops, with an additional 100,000 in combat support and logistic units, about a 100 percent increase since the January 1973 cease-fire. (Viet Cong strengths are not included.) Enemy armored vehicles, mostly tanks, in the South had increased from about 100 to over 700, while medium artillery pieces numbered over 400, up from about 100. The NVA now had twice as many tanks as did the ARVN. Hanoi had built its strategic reserve in the North from two to seven divisions, and with its new road net to the South and in the absence of U.S. air interdiction, could move a division from North to South in a fraction of the time it formerly took.[6]

Meanwhile, in mid-1973, my deputy at REDCOM, Tim O'Keefe, was promoted to four stars in the U.S. Air Force and ordered to Southeast Asia, where he took command of USSAG/7th Air Force, with headquarters at Nakhon Phanom in northeast Thailand, the senior U.S. operational headquarters in the region. For about a year (until the United States terminated all air reconnaissance operations over Laos) O'Keefe's command sent to CINCPAC and the JCS a steady stream of photographic and visual reconnaissance evidence of enemy troop and logistic buildup in the Laotian panhandle and the NVA entry points into South Vietnam along the Laotian border. As a unified command with direct interest in the region, REDCOM received copies of this traffic as well as copies of O'Keefe's personal back channel reports to Washington. It was particularly galling for General O'Keefe, a combat fighter pilot himself, who had lost a son (also a USAF fighter pilot) in air action over Vietnam, to observe first-hand the massive military movements of NVA forces and supplies from the North into the South, yet to be helpless to do anything about it.

With a mature logistic system in place, the NVA was ready to support a sustained major offensive at any time. Possessing the decisive advantages accruing to the attacker, the enemy could more readily gain surprise and mass overwhelming force where he chose to attack. The defending South Vietnamese forces, on the other hand, even when they were able to detect the enemy's offensive intent in advance, often lacked the troop reserves or the means to move reinforcements rapidly, or both. Thus they were subject to defeat in detail. It seemed clear that South Vietnam was now in an inferior military position.

The prelude to Hanoi's final offensive against South Vietnam in 1975 came in mid-December 1974 and occurred in Phuoc Long Province in northeastern III CTZ. Partially screened by diversionary but strong attacks in other sectors of III CTZ, the NVA launched a two-division attack supported by tanks and artillery, placing Song Be, the provincial capital, under siege. The town finally fell on 6 January 1975 after a gallant fight by its defenders, mostly territorial (RF and PF) forces. Captured province, district, and hamlet officials were summarily executed. Friendly military losses were heavy, only 20 percent of the forces committed in the province surviving. the loss of the first provincial capital since the cease-fire was a particularly severe psychological blow.[7]

The U.S. State Department immediately protested officially to Hanoi, but significantly President Ford made no mention of Vietnam in his State of the Union message delivered to the Congress on 15 January. A few days later at a press conference the president stated that he could not foresee the circumstances in which the United States might actively intervene again in the Vietnam War. The lack of any effective American reaction was not lost on the North Vietnamese, who concluded that the time to strike for the kill had come.

The final NVA offensive began in early March 1975 in II CTZ with diversionary attacks in the Kontum and Pleiku city areas, as well as along Highway 19 leading from the Central Highlands to the coast, all designed to conceal the main effort, a three-division assault against Ban Me Thuot, the traditional capital of the Montagnard country. After a stiff defense by the 23rd ARVN Division and local forces, the city was overrun on 11 March.

At this juncture President Thieu decided to abandon his general policy of trying to hold all of South Vietnam and ordered the CG of II Corps, the courageous and combat-experienced Lieutenant General Phan Van Phu, to retake Ban Me Thuot even though Kontum and Pleiku might have to be sacrificed. As a result, Phu decided to abandon these two provinces immediately and to withdraw his remaining forces via the "Jungle" Route 7B (a logging trail used only intermittently) toward Tuy Hoa on the coast.

All the while the 22nd Division held An Khe Pass, the gateway on Highway 19 to Qui Nhon on the coast, despite repeated NVA assaults. Phu issued the withdrawal orders hastily, without benefit of any planning. The very forward location of Headquarters II Corps in Pleiku (maintained there so that the South Vietnamese government could keep a close eye on the Montagnards who populate the region) added to the confusion because communications between the corps commander and his units became almost impossible as soon as the withdrawal began. In an effort to conceal the move from the enemy, Phu kept the word from the province chiefs concerned, and *no* Americans—not even the ambassador—were informed. Ambassador Martin was not in Vietnam at the time, but was on leave in the United States.

The net result was disaster, as troops, their families, and civilian refugees withdrew from the highlands to the coast, harassed, ambushed, and pursued by the enemy. Now isolated in Binh Dinh Province, the 22nd Division fought its way to Qui Nhon, where most of the division was evacuated by sea to Vung Tau in III CTZ. Remnants of the 23rd Division were likewise evacuated later out of Cam Ranh Bay. Paratroopers from the ARVN Airborne Division, along with very stubborn and brave local regional troops, tried vainly to hold Nha Trang on the coast, but finally had to be rescued by sea. By mid-April, organized South Vietnamese resistance had ended in II CTZ.[8]

Meantime, in early March, Hanoi launched another multidivisional offensive in I CTZ, advancing from the foothills on key positions protecting Hue and Danang farther south. At this crucial time President Thieu ordered that the elite ARVN Airborne Division be moved from the Danang area of I CTZ to III CTZ for the defense of Saigon. Later one brigade of the Airborne Division was diverted to take part in a futile counterattack to recapture Ban Me Thuot, only to be caught in the tide of the disorganized retreat along Highway 21 running east from the Montagnard capital to the coast.

To replace the paratroopers, General Truong, the valiant veteran of countless battles and campaigns who commanded I Corps, shifted most of the Marine Division from Quang Tri City in the extreme north to the Danang area, leaving Truong's old reliable 1st ARVN Division and one Marine brigade to cover Hue. Truong, anticipating a civilian exodus from Quang Tri City as the Marines pulled out, ordered his staff to assist the refugee movement, which soon became a flood heading south.[9]

At this moment President Thieu again intervened in the tactical plans and operations of his major commanders. Having initially told Truong that the Danang area was the most important part of I CTZ and that the rest of I CTZ could be sacrificed if necessary, Thieu one week later changed his instructions and directed that *both* Hue and Danang be held at all costs. But the exodus from Hue south had already started and Danang was now massively swollen with refugees. When the territorial forces holding north of Hue withdrew without orders, fearing for their families in the Hue area, a general rout developed. Truong, realizing that Hue could no longer be defended, ordered the troops to evacuate the area on foot along the beach toward Hai Van Pass and Danang. Tanks, guns, trucks, and the like had to be destroyed in place.[10]

Meantime in the southern part of I CTZ, the 2nd Division and other forces in Quang Ngai Province were being concentrated for the defense of Chu Lai. Once again, however, Saigon intervened and Truong was ordered to release the Marine Division for redeployment to III CTZ for the defense of Saigon, to give up Chu Lai, and to use the 2nd ARVN Division in the final defense of Danang.

Thereafter it was all downhill for the South Vietnamese. The 1st and 2nd ARVN Divisions and the Marine Division all tried desperately to reach the Danang area, but NVA units controlled Highway 1, the main coastal road, north and south of Danang. Soldiers of the 3rd Division originally responsible for the defense of Danang, becoming more and more concerned for their families (large numbers of whom had been wounded in the heavy rocket and artillery shelling of the Danang Air Base and other outlying parts of the city), began to melt away. With total defeat imminent, Truong shipped all organized forces, mostly Marines, out of Danang for movement to III CTZ. Danang, the last enclave held by the South Vietnamese in I CTZ, belonged to Hanoi by the end of daylight on 30 March.[11]

General Truong had fought a tremendous fight against insuperable odds. At the end he and the remnants of his corps staff swam through the surf to the rescuing fleet of South Vietnamese boats of every description. (President Ford committed substantial U.S. naval forces in support of the South Vietnamese evacuation from the Danang area. American ships, however, were held outside the three-mile limit.) This fine soldier, who was brokenhearted over the loss of practically all of his beloved 1st ARVN Division, deserved a better fate.

The country-wide coordinated enemy offensive struck in III CTZ at about the same time (early March) as it did in the northern military regions. The large-unit attacks began on 11 March in Tay Ninh Province northwest of Saigon, followed shortly by multiple-pronged attacks launched from Cambodian bases only a few kilometers west of Saigon. In all, three NVA divisions were involved and roughly half of the ARVN III Corps's regular forces, elements of the 5th, 25th, and 18th ARVN divisions, plus the 3rd Armored Brigade, were employed to blunt the attacks.

At about the same time, a one-division NVA attack also developed astride Highway 13, running south from Cambodia to Saigon; South Vietnamese troops fought well but were driven back toward Saigon. Earlier in Long An Province, through which passes the critical Highway 4, Saigon's vital link to the Delta, territorial forces had fought well against local main force battalions seeking to cut the highway south of Saigon.

In mid-March another major front was opened when a three-division NVA force struck the Xuan Loc area due east of Saigon. Elements of the 18th ARVN Division and regional forces, after days of bloody fighting, repulsed the enemy forces, which then pulled back to regroup.[12]

As the end of March approached, the proportions of the disastrous chain of events in South Vietnam began to penetrate the highest levels of Washington officialdom. Even as the ring of enemy forces was tightening around Saigon, President Ford decided to send General Weyand to Saigon for a personal assessment on the scene. Weyand, the last commander of MACV and now the chief of staff, U.S. Army, was obviously the best qualified man for such a mission. Ambassador Martin, who had been in the United States for several weeks, accompanied Weyand on the same special mission military aircraft, arriving in Saigon on 27 March 1975.

Although Defense and State were receiving reasonably accurate information from Saigon, media reporters in Vietnam had mainly only fragmentary and often highly colored and inaccurate reports, sometimes based on rumors, to go on; the results were unfortunate, and badly hurt South Vietnam in the eyes of its detractors. The old, unfair refrain of "their lions and our rabbits" reappeared in comparisons of North and South Vietnamese forces, and the whole world consequently got the false impression that the South Vietnamese universally had performed poorly and lacked the will to fight. Even high American officials, including Secretary of Defense Schlesinger, had the erroneous notion that relatively little large-scale fighting had gone on since the early battle of Ban Me Thuot in II CTZ. Major General Homer D. Smith, U.S. Army, who had replaced Murray as DAO, Saigon, in August 1974, tried unsuccessfully to change this false image, but the effort was too late in the day. Upon Smith's arrival in Saigon, Murray returned to the United States, bitter about the indifferent attitude toward the fate of South Vietnam that he found in U.S. officialdom. Retiring shortly after his return, he was outspoken in his critical assessment of U.S. performance in the last months before the fall of Saigon.

Although some units did perform poorly in combat, there were numerous instances of great tenacity and uncommon valor, as well as battles in which the South Vietnamese outfought numerically far superior enemy forces. On the other hand, there was no question that severe cuts in U.S. military assistance, as well as American unwillingness to intervene militarily in the face of Hanoi's brutal disregard of the cease-fire agreements, had undermined the morale of the South Vietnamese people. Inevitably this had to affect the combat effectiveness of their forces.

President Thieu once told Ambassador Bunker that the Vietnamese placed the safety and welfare of their families ahead of the security of their country, and that this factor could critically influence how well South Vietnamese troops would fight. Indeed, this had proved to be a decisive factor in I and II CTZs, where South Vietnamese forces became intermingled with their own families in the battle area, as well as in III CTZ where, conversely, the 18th Division and other ARVN units whose families were relatively secure in areas to the rear fought tenaciously and bravely.

Upon reflection, I conclude that South Vietnamese troops are probably not much different in this respect from the soldiers of any other country. During the American Civil War, for example, Confederate soldiers often left their units because they were needed at home for spring planting. Southern leaders tried to discourage the tendency, but it worsened as the war grew longer; unit commanders wisely considered the offense to be simply taking a temporary, unauthorized leave of absence, rather than desertion. Only a nation engaged in a war on its own soil, rather than in the enemy's homeland, can appreciate what this means. The American South knew full well what it meant, as did the South Vietnamese. Today the U.S. Seventh Army in Germany faces a somewhat similar situation in that the military families live on the potential battlegrounds. More than one American on duty in Germany has asked himself the question, "What would I do if war broke out suddenly and my wife and children were in danger?"

General Weyand's presidential instructions were to assess the situation in Vietnam and deliver a personal message to President Thieu from President Ford that although the U.S. government would support South Vietnam to the best of its ability, the United States would not fight again in Vietnam.[13] Implicit in the message was the reality that the Ford administration's ability was effectively hamstrung by congressional actions and domestic opposition.

Weyand and his team stayed for about a week, leaving Saigon on 4 April to report back to the president. In Saigon the visitors held numerous staff meetings with U.S. and Vietnamese officials, civilian and military, as well as several high-level meetings with President Thieu and General Vien. The Weyand group were soon seized by the extremely precarious military situation in the Republic of Vietnam, where the prospects for survival were indeed bleak.

With the loss of I CTZ and the imminent loss of most of II CTZ, Thieu's strategy now called for the last-ditch defense of what remained of III and IV CTZs. For this defense the following organized forces were available:

In III CTZ: three understrength ARVN divisions (5th, 25th, and 18th)

Airborne Division (at about one-third strength)

Marine Division (at about one-third strength)

22nd ARVN Division (at about half strength)

four ranger groups (equivalent to about six light infantry battalions)

3rd Armored Brigade (understrength and short of tanks)

four armored cavalry squadrons (understrength)

In IV CTZ: three understrength ARVN divisions (7th, 21st, and 9th)

Total: nine-plus divisions in a degraded condition

In addition, the remnants of four other ARVN divisions (the 1st, 2nd, 3rd, and 23rd) from I and II CTZs were straggling into III CTZ. Provided they received replacements and new equipment and underwent minimal unit training, they could be ready for action in about two to four months. For the moment, however, since the ARVN divisions in IV CTZ could not be redeployed without uncovering the Delta and risking its loss to the enemy, only six-plus very understrength divisions, all of which had been fighting for weeks, were available for the final defense of Saigon.

Against these forces the NVA now had sixteen divisions deployed in III CTZ:

In Tay Ninh Province (northwest of Saigon):	three NVA divisions
In Hau Nghia Province (west of Saigon):	three NVA divisions
In Binh Duong and Binh Long provinces (north of Saigon):	two NVA divisions
In Long Khanh and Bien Hoa provinces (east of Saigon):	three NVA divisions
In Long An Province (south and southwest of Saigon):	one NVA division
In Phuoc Long Province (northeast of Saigon):	I NVA Corps of four divisions (recently arrived from NVN)
Total:	sixteen NVA divisions

About half of these NVA divisions had also been fighting for weeks, but the others were up to strength and were fresh.

In early April 1975 the DAO estimated that the enemy very probably would not give Saigon any chance to recover from the disaster in the north, but would go all out to seize Saigon and end the war. The DAO concluded that a renewed U.S. commitment of aid and emergency air resupply would help, but that it was extremely doubtful that the South Vietnamese could hold without, as a minimum, U.S. airpower directed against NVA troops, bases, and lines of communications in South Vietnam.[14] This was a gloomy but realistic and, as history records, accurate estimate.

Weyand agreed with this assessment, namely, that the military situation could not be retrieved without direct U.S. intervention, and he so reported to President Ford upon returning to Washington in early April. He also urged a massive military aid program, even though recognizing that it was a forlorn hope. Despite the military situation, however, Ambassador Martin, apparently encouraged by belated French political initiatives and by Secretary of State Kissinger, still clung to the hope of a negotiated settlement which would leave a new Saigon government, possibly without Thieu, in control of the southern half of the Republic. As it turned out, these hopes were totally unfounded and false.

As anticipated, Hanoi continued on the attack. In the Xuan Loc area, after a short breather, the enemy resumed operations on 9 April but now with a total of five NVA divisions, having deployed two more divisions in the area from the I NVA Corps located in Phuoc Long Province. An airborne brigade tried desperately to counterattack Xuan Loc from the south but could make no headway. Frustrated, the paratroopers retired through the jungle to Ba Ria in the Vung Tau area south of Saigon. The 18th Division, now reinforced with an armored task force, again repulsed the massive enemy assault, but by 20 April was finally driven back with heavy losses to the Long Binh-Bien Hoa Air Base area only about twenty kilometers east of Saigon. A Marine brigade joined the force at Long Binh. It was now obvious that this onslaught was the major effort in the enemy's final drive.

Meanwhile in Long An Province, where the 22nd ARVN Division had been sent to bolster the 7th ARVN Division and territorial forces along Highway 4, there had been heavy enemy attacks that had been finally blunted by 15 April. But the future looked ominous, for it was now known that more fresh NVA troops were on the move from Cambodia and the Delta toward the Tan An area along Highway 4.

An unnatural quiet descended on all fronts around Saigon on 20 April and lasted for about six days. (Some speculate that Hanoi wanted to give the United States a "decent interval" to evacuate the remaining Americans from the country.) President Thieu resigned on 21 April and was succeeded by Vice President Tran Van Huong in a futile effort to form a government with which the enemy would negotiate. The NVA gave Hanoi's response to this hopeless act of desperation by resuming the offensive on 26 April, with the main effort focused on Bien Hoa Air Base but with secondary efforts against Saigon's outer defenses to the south and west in Long An and Hau Nghia provinces, where the defenders held. On 29 April Tan Son Nhut Air Base on the edge of Saigon (and earlier the site of MACV and 7th Air Force headquarters) was heavily shelled, and Cu Chi, only twenty-five kilometers northwest of Saigon, came under attack.[15]

Full-scale American evacuation meanwhile had begun on 20 April, initially by air and at the end by helicopter to a large armada from the U.S. Pacific Fleet which lay off the coast nearby, covering the final pullout from Saigon. By dawn on 30 April the last Americans, other selected foreign nationals, and many thousands of South Vietnamese had departed Saigon for good. An estimated 52,000 South Vietnamese nationals were taken out by U.S. military aircraft, and roughly another 6,000 South Vietnamese flew out by commercial aircraft. Several thousand more were flown out by helicopter to U.S. naval ships in the South China Sea off Saigon.[16]

That morning, Duong Van "Big" Minh, who had succeeded Huong as president on 27 April, surrendered the country to the North Vietnamese Army. When the war ended, loyal South Vietnamese troops were still fighting on the outskirts of Saigon and almost all of the main district towns and provincial capitals in the Delta. They were prepared to fight on until "Big" Minh told them to lay down their arms on 30 April.

Although the decline of American support was the crucial factor in the collapse of the South Vietnamese, the proximate cause in a tactical sense was the debacle in the Central Highlands of II CTZ. An unlucky II Corps commander, Lieutenant General Phu, was directly responsible for the calamity, but President Thieu and the Joint General Staff in Saigon must also share the blame. Before Saigon fell, Phu, after arranging for the evacuation from South Vietnam of his wife and some other family members, put his own pistol to his head. The suicide took place inside the Joint General Staff compound at Tan Son Nhut.[17]

Thieu's commendable desire to defend all South Vietnamese territory is understandable. He understood all too well not only the political and military risks of willingly giving up South Vietnamese soil, but also the even greater psychological risks entailed. In hindsight, however, one can argue that had he earlier made the decision to give up the northern two provinces in I CTZ (the area north of Danang and Hai Van Pass), where he had deployed four divisions, including his three best—the 1st ARVN, the Airborne Division, and the Marine Division—he might have fared better. Surely he was aware that he did not have sufficient forces to defend the whole country, that he had only meager strategic troop reserves, and that his ground forces could not be readily moved from one area to another. As it was, the decision to evacuate the Central Highlands, particularly at the critical time when the decision was made, was inexcusably poor. It led to the uncovering of the critical Highway 19 from the Highlands to the coast and ultimately the complete loss of both I and II CTZs.

In this connection, I have often wondered what might have happened had a senior, well-known, combat-experienced four-star U.S. Army officer headed up the DAO in Saigon. Could such a person—a Fred Weyand, a Dick Stilwell, or a Mel Zais—have made any difference? Could such an American have been able to keep President Thieu from making such fatal errors? This question is not intended to detract from Generals Murray or Smith. Although they were fine soldiers and outstanding logisticians, they were relatively unknown to Thieu and had little influence on him with respect to nonlogistic matters.

Notwithstanding the foregoing, the fact remains that the United States did not do well by its hapless ally. We left South Vietnam with the legacy of a fatally flawed strategy that gave the strategic and offensive initiative to Hanoi, as well as a cease-fire agreement that allowed a large NVA force to remain in place in key locations in South Vietnam, granted Hanoi secure sanctuary bases in Laos and Cambodia and secure lines of communications from the North to the South, and gave North Vietnam a secure logistic pipeline from the USSR and China for the wherewithal to continue a protracted war strategy. Moreover, we did not maintain an adequate flow of military aid to the South, nor did we give the country the necessary military capability to survive. This was particularly evident with respect to Saigon's air forces. They were simply too weak to make up for the loss of the critically needed heavy firepower available from U.S. air and naval forces.

Likewise, the hard truth lingers on that when South Vietnam in its dying hours turned to us in despair, the United States looked the other way. Although we Americans can rationalize our actions in light of the realities of the military situation in Vietnam and the domestic situation at home, our South Vietnamese friends can never forget the tragic nightmare of those last scenes in Saigon.

I have often speculated also on what might have been the outcome had General Abrams lived. Would he have been able to persuade the Congress and the American people to go to the rescue of a nation whose only sin was to look to us for their survival? Abrams had a "father-savior-hero" image in Vietnam somewhat akin to General James Van Fleet's image in Greece during the Greek civil war right after World War II, and later in Korea during and after the Korean War. But because of the Watergate affair and its calamitous effect on the U.S. presidency, my answer is that it would probably have made no difference in the outcome. Even a Van Fleet or an Abrams could not have overcome such obstacles. After Watergate the presidency was paralyzed insofar as Vietnam was concerned. It was not so much that the American people were disinterested as that they would support neither a reengagement of U.S. power nor an indefinite commitment to provide military aid to South Vietnam. The war had gone on too long and there was no convincing evidence to show that continued U.S. support would not be throwing good money after bad.

PART II

Assessment

8

American Operational
Performance

So far, this examination has dwelt somewhat more on the negative aspects of U.S. involvement in Vietnam than on the positive side—things the United States did well. This is a natural outcome because the analysis to this point has been largely problem and issue oriented. This chapter will bring out some of the strengths, as well as the weaknesses, of American performance. U.S. Army activities will be the focus.

American direction and conduct of the war and the operational performance of our armed forces, particularly during the 1962–69 period, generally were professional and commendable. Performance continued to be of a high quality until the 1969–70 period, when dissent at home began to be reflected in troop attitudes and conduct in Vietnam. From 1969 until the last U.S. combat troops left in August 1972, a decline in performance set in; the discovery of widespread drug use in Vietnam in the spring of 1970 signalled that more morale and disciplinary troubles lay ahead. The so-called "fraggings" of leaders that began in 1969–70 were literally murderous indicators of poor morale and became a matter of deep concern.

Extremely adverse environmental conditions and very trying circumstances contributed to this decline in performance. Particularly galling to our forces in the field were the widely publicized statements of highly placed U.S. officials, including senators, against American involvement. Such statements were perceived to support the enemy and badly damaged the morale of our troops. The deteriorating climate at home also affected the conduct of American prisoners of war (mostly airmen) held in North Vietnamese POW camps; this was reflected in the increasing number of men who were accused of collaborating with the enemy in the 1969–71 period, as compared to the very few during the earlier years of the war.

For the ground combat troops, Vietnam was a light infantry war of small units, mostly rifle platoons and companies, rarely of formations larger than a battalion. The Army tailored its basic fighting units of infantry and direct support artillery to the terrain and the peculiar nature of combat in Vietnam. Rifle companies, for example, were reduced in strength and lightened up by eliminating some of the heavier supporting weapons and equipment found in the normal organization. As a result, American infantry could move more swiftly and easily over the ground, and the tactical airmobility of the modern assault helicopter could be fully exploited.

Before Vietnam, the Army was primarily geared to fighting a highly sophisticated, mechanized war in Europe. Although a few relatively light divisions existed, most of the Army divisions were heavy armor or mechanized divisions either already deployed in Germany or earmarked for service in Europe. Thus the Army's problem of adjusting to a much different kind of warfare in Vietnam on terrain far different from the European scene was a complex one. The Army had to maintain a ready capability to fight in Europe even while conducting a major war in Vietnam. The questions of priorities between the two theaters were never answered satisfactorily.

The military helicopter truly came of age in Vietnam, where the Army, at times opposed by its sister services, never lost its faith in this remarkable instrument. Clearly the single most outstanding military innovation in the Vietnam War was the development and introduction into combat of the "chopper" in various forms—the troop-carrying assault helicopter, the helicopter gunship for escort and close fire support missions, the attack helicopter with a tank-killing capability, and the scout helicopter for performing classic but still essential cavalry missions.

The contribution of the Army's organic aviation arm, rotary and fixed wing, cannot be overstated. These aircraft were involved in practically every military function—command and control, reconnaissance, firepower, mobility, medical evacuation, and supply, as well as utility missions of every conceivable description. But it was the airmobile divisions (1st Cavalry and 101st Airborne) and air cavalry squadrons that brought the airmobile concept to the pinnacle of its potential. In these units the helicopter literally substituted for ground vehicles of every kind and totally freed the fighting elements from the tyranny of surface obstacles to movement. "Owning" their own helicopters and possessing a field maintenance capability that could accompany the forward assault forces, these units gave the theater commander a "Sunday punch" of unequalled flexibility and versatility.

Army aviators were committed in combat in the early 1960s, providing aviation support to South Vietnamese troops and developing battle-tested airmobility tactics and techniques long before the first Army ground combat forces arrived on the scene. In Vietnam these pioneer flying men earned a permanent place among the Army's elite—the combat arms. These men and their wondrous flying machines are here to stay in the Army—they will more than pay their way on future battlefields.

Although it was essentially a light infantry war, armor played a valuable role and did it well. The 11th Armored Cavalry Regiment was the largest armor unit in Vietnam and performed a variety of important reconnaissance, security, and offensive combat missions. The regiment was often employed on independent missions with decisive results. Each Army division had its own organic armored cavalry squadron, and at least one of its infantry battalions was mechanized; that is, its infantry was normally transported in armored personnel carriers. Armored units fought numerous key battles in every corps tactical zone; their heavy firepower and high ground mobility were well known to and respected by the enemy. In the dry monsoon they could operate almost anywhere, penetrating some of the most rugged and densely covered enemy war zones and base areas in Vietnam and Cambodia.

Army field artillery performed extremely well in Vietnam. In the American artillery system the ubiquitous forward observer, accompanying his supported infantry rifle company wherever it moves, is the key to the optimum functioning of the entire system. Despite the unusual terrain encountered—thick jungle foliage, rugged mountains, and land like the Mekong Delta, so flat and unvarying that determining troop positions was especially difficult—our forward observers performed effectively. Quick response was often a problem when operating near populated areas because of the necessity to make checks and even double checks to insure safety and accuracy. On the other hand, in a situation such as the defense of Khe Sanh, rounds were on the way in forty seconds after fire was requested.

Vietnam also brought out the need for fire support coordinators in modern battle, even in counterinsurgency situations, because of the proliferation of weapons systems available to support ground troops. The high density of aircraft in the battle area—Air Force, Marine, and Army—further complicated fire coordination. Overlapping control of airspace brought on by the legitimate claims of each service to control the use of airspace required by its forces, was often a potential problem. Nevertheless overall fire support coordinators in Vietnam performed generally in an outstanding manner.

At Khe Sanh, the Air Force (that is, MACV's component air command, the 7th Air Force) was designated as the overall manager of airspace, and although the Marine Corps objected vehemently to the arrangement, it worked well. Indeed, the close and skillfull coordination of Marine light artillery fires, Army long-range (175 mm) artillery fires, Air Force B-52 strikes, and Air Force and Marine tactical air strikes resulted in devastating casualties among attacking enemy troops.

The most common military term, and certainly one of the major tactical innovations, to come out of the Vietnam War was the "fire support base," or simply "fire base." The fire base was not just a defensive position but also the firepower element integral to any offensive effort. The concept developed partly because of the vulnerability of artillery firing batteries in unsecured areas to close-in mass enemy assault and hence the need to protect them with infantry. Thus a position jointly occupied by supporting artillery and defending infantry became known as a fire base. Normally the fire base was also the location of the forward command post of the infantry battalion conducting operations in the area and providing for the defense of the base. This arrangement insured that the artillery firing units would always be effective, day or night, when called upon to support offensive operations with indirect fire. Infantry and artillery units located on a fire base came in close, intimate contact with each other, and when the fire base was attacked infantrymen and artillerymen soon learned to value highly the mutual support they could give each other. There were many variations of fire bases according to their location, the ground available for defense, the units and weapons involved, and the like. In short, the organization of a fire base reflected the flexibility and ingenuity of the American soldier and his leaders.

Battalion, brigade, and division commanders generally showed considerable professional skill in maneuvering their units and employing their combined arms. The 4th Infantry Division, for example, operating in the vast Kontum-Pleiku plateau region of the Highlands, time and again outwitted, outmaneuvered, and outfought its NVA foes despite the latter's inherent advantages—the enemy's ability to decide when to leave the sanctuary of Cambodia, where to cross the border, and what objectives to attack in South Vietnam.

Having addressed the performance of U.S. troops in action, I would be very remiss if I did not include at least a brief word about the selfless service of our advisers. Their performance—Army, Navy, Air Force, and Marine—generally was outstanding throughout the war, from the earliest days in the 1950s to the end. The great majority were U.S. Army officers and NCOs who served from the palace level to the ARVN battalion and the district/subdistrict level in the field. As ARVN advisers, they shared the hardships and dangers of infantry combat; as CORDS advisers, the equally risky and austere environment of a South Vietnamese district chief in a Viet Cong-infested area; and as Special Forces advisers, the lonely, perilous life in a CIDG camp on the border. In the vast majority of cases they never complained, asked for very little, and literally gave their all for their South Vietnamese counterparts. The American people should be very proud of them.

These comments on the performance of our ground forces have been made basically with the U.S. Army in mind. Marine and Army ground combat elements, because of the commonality of their primary task—combat on the ground—have many similar interests, characteristics, organizational patterns, and operational modes. Recognizing that comparisons can be odious, and usually are, I hesitate to make any. Nevertheless, having had some close experience with U.S. Marines in various operational theaters in the past, I will venture one major observation, a difference between the Marine Corps and the Army that I have found striking. Marines traditionally place far more responsibility and authority on their noncommissioned officer corps. Inherently this is a sound principle, and I fault the Army for the converse—not giving NCOs sufficient authority and responsibility, and instead putting too great a load on company grade officers. But as a result of this Marine emphasis on NCOs, I have repeatedly noted two general shortcomings—inadequate supervision of NCOs by the Marine officer corps, and marine officers, especially the more senior ones, not always knowing what is going on at the troop level and consequently not taking adequate care of their men.

The offensive air war, controlled by CINCPAC more or less independently of the war in South Vietnam conducted by COMUSMACV, was conducted by and large in a very commendable manner. These air operations consisted of two different but concurrent campaigns—the offensive against North Vietnam itself, and the interdiction campaign along inland and coastal routes in North Vietnam and inland routes through the panhandle of Laos.

The two air campaigns, frequently overlapping in a geographical sense, were conducted primarily by the land-based aircraft of the 7th U.S. Air Force located in South Vietnam and Thailand, and by U.S. Navy carrier-based aircraft located in the South China Sea. CINCPAC assigned to MACV the responsibility for air operations in Laos, basically an interdiction mission; MACV in turn delegated control of these operations to MACV's air component, 7th Air Force. But for air strikes against North Vietnam, CINCPAC decentralized operations to the Pacific Air Forces and the Pacific Fleet, coordinating their operations principally by geographic assignment of targets, the Navy taking targets generally more accessible by attack from the sea, and the Air Force taking targets further inland. But true unity of air operations against North Vietnam was never fully achieved; B-52 operations in the region, for example, remained under the control of SAC throughout the war.

CINCPAC's geographic assignment of targets nevertheless worked well primarily because it avoided the inherently far more difficult task of coordinating the operations of aircraft from two different services. Such coordination would have been quite difficult because the Navy and the Air Force have different doctrine and operating procedures, their communications systems and equipment are different, and they do not normally train and operate together. These are basic facts of life which are all too often overlooked by ardent proponents of joint operations.

Combat aircraft pilots and crews performed exceptionally well under very tough conditions. As I have already observed, enemy air defenses were the heaviest and most formidable ever encountered by our air and naval forces in history. The advent of the "smart bomb" in later stages of the war was a great boon, but the losses of U.S. aircraft and crews continued to be heavy. Adverse weather and rugged terrain were also major handicaps. Finally, our incredibly complicated rules of engagement, which varied from country to country and even from area to area were often too much for pilots to handle. These rules, imposed by the U.S. government, were simply unreasonable for men flying at 500 knots, trying to stay alive and yet close on their targets. Near the end of American involvement, when Chinese territory was unintentionally violated by our aircraft, the Chinese seemed to understand the problem better than our own statesmen.

One lesson that seems rather apparent has emerged from these operations. Sustained air operations during a long, difficult war are more readily conducted by land-based aircraft with their land-based support, a system designed for the long haul. Carrier-based aircraft and their carriers, on the other hand, are not designed to remain on station for prolonged periods. As a result, our carrier task groups took a terrific beating and fell far behind in their ship overhaul schedules. The impact of this extraordinary strain is felt even today in the Navy.

In terms of tactical air support in South Vietnam, Army-Air Force relations were close, cordial, and mutually satisfying, and the Air Force's performance was generally outstanding. Emergency tactical air support was available on short notice, day or night, in almost any kind of weather. B-52 support was more than impressive—when a B-52 saturation attack occurred, the ground nearby literally shook and our own troops well understood why the enemy was terrified. Aerial resupply reached new levels of reliability, accuracy, and volume in Vietnam. Various parachute drop techniques, including low-level parachute extraction, were extensively used and successfully demonstrated. Medical air evacuation was also well executed.

Organic Marine aviation support of their own Marine forces on the ground was likewise outstanding. The Marine system, whereby the Marine division commander has full control of the Marine Air Wing associated with his division, works well for their purposes. The only area where the Marines seemed to come up short lay in airmobility, that is, the exploitation of the helicopter's unique capabilities. Because of the relatively larger size of their assault helicopters (compared to the Army's squad-carrying-sized "Huey") and their centralized control of helicopters under the Air Wing commander, the Marines, in my opinion, did not fully achieve the tactical advantages of integrated airmobility.

The overall control of air operations involving more than one service caused a major problem only once in South Vietnam—during the siege of Khe Sanh in western I CTZ in the winter of 1968. General William Momyer, commanding the 7th Air Force, insisted that his headquarters, under the overall command of General Westmoreland, be assigned the responsibility, with commensurate authority, for controlling all air operations, regardless of the services involved, in support of the besieged Marines at Khe Sanh. The Marines strongly objected and carried their case through Marine channels all the way to the JCS. Westmoreland agreed with and supported Momyer's position, which the JCS carefully considered and finally approved.[1] But the matter left some bitterness in the Marines, who understandably resist any attempt to interpose external control between their ground and supporting air elements.

Very few joint Army-Air Force operations, other than normal tactical air support missions, were undertaken in Vietnam. Only one sizable airborne (parachute assault) operation was conducted, but it was not of major consequence. Nevertheless, countless American paratroopers served with distinction in practically every combat unit in Vietnam, although the nature of the war was not conducive to airborne operations.

But there was one major joint operation, the Son Tay POW camp raid of November 1970. The main effort of this raid was made by a joint Army-Air Force task force, with the Air Force providing large troop-carrying helicopters, air cover, and air support, and the Army providing the assault ground force. The Navy and Marines flew major air attacks in other areas of North Vietnam as diversionary efforts designed to deceive the enemy as to the true location, direction, and nature of the main attack. The plan worked well, the enemy was confused, and surprise was achieved. Unfortunately, our POWs had been removed from the camp before the operation was launched and the mission was unsuccessful— an intelligence failure but an operational success.[2]

This raid also raised the morale of the families of our prisoners of war and of our men missing in action. These gallant relatives never gave up hope and very properly kept the pressure on the State and Defense departments to do everything humanly possible to determine the status of their men. Fortunately, too, the raid resulted in noticeably improved treatment of our POWs in North Vietnam. Unfortunately, the situation of many of our men lost, missing, or captured in Laos, Cambodia, and South Vietnam has never been satisfactorily established, and the agony of uncertainty about the fate of their loved ones continues in some American families to this day.

But even sustained, outstanding operational performance can go for naught if the intelligence that guides operations and generates the thrust of operational efforts is lacking in quality. Accordingly, let us turn to a brief examination of the performance of American intelligence at the national level as well as in the theater of operations.

For the president and other U.S. policymakers in Washington, there was a plethora of intelligence studies and estimates about the Vietnam War originating from a wide variety of official organizations, ranging from the U.S. Embassy, the CIA station chief, and HQ MACV in Saigon, as well as HQ CINCPAC in Honolulu, to the proliferation of intelligence agencies in Washington. Most of the Washington-level wartime studies were produced by a single agency, some by two agencies working together, and only relatively few by the whole intelligence community.

The Washington players making up the community were: (1) The director of Central Intelligence (DCI), his Central Intelligence Agency, and the now-defunct Board of National Estimates, reporting through the DCI to the president and the National Security Council. (2) From the Pentagon, the Defense Intelligence Agency (DIA), responsible to the secretary of defense and the JCS; and the intelligence organizations of the services, each reporting to its own service chief. (3) From the Department of State, the Bureau of Intelligence and Research (INR), responsible to the secretary of state. And (4) The cryptological community, consisting of the National Security Agency (NSA), responsible to the secretary of defense; and the service security agencies each reporting to its service chief.

The DCI presided over this basically loose confederation and chaired the U.S. Intelligence Board, now known as the National Foreign Intelligence Board, whose principal members are the heads of the CIA, DIA, INR, and NSA. Obviously, the DCI's authority over this board is somewhat attenuated, inasmuch as three of the four other principals are responsible to a cabinet member.

In wartime the theater commander, usually a unified commander, normally assumes control of all intelligence assets, including the CIA's, in his area of responsibility. The Vietnam War was a unique case, however, and this wartime takeover was not invoked. So the CIA station chief in Saigon continued his regular peacetime function as the senior intelligence adviser to the U.S. ambassador. As a consequence, unity of U.S. intelligence effort was not achieved in Vietnam and, despite coordination and cooperation between the CIA and the MACV J-2, undesirable duplication and competition did take place. Unfortunately, this jurisdictional problem spilled over into combined U.S.-South Vietnamese intelligence activities, resulting in such unhelpful consequences as having separate CIA-South Vietnamese and MACV J-2-South Vietnamese interrogation centers operating in the same provincial and district capitals.

While the CIA station chief in Saigon, MACV, and CINCPAC naturally concentrated on the more immediate aspects of the conflict, the national-level intelligence organs focused on the longer-term strategic aspects. The latter included such matters as the assessment of opposing U.S./allied and North Vietnamese strategies; North Vietnamese perceptions of the U.S. war effort; the effectiveness of the U.S. air war against

North Vietnam; North Vietnamese capacity to wage a prolonged war and their dependence on the Soviet Union and China; and the prospects for survival over the longer term of a free and independent South Vietnam.

During the earlier years of the direct American military involvement in Vietnam, up until the time of the enemy's Tet offensive of 1968, the military held the center of the intelligence stage. MACV, CINCPAC, and DIA were the dominant intelligence voices and had the ear of the president and his NSC staff. But beginning a few months after the start of the sustained American air offensive in March 1965, the CIA, at the request of Defense Secretary McNamara, played an active intelligence role, initially evaluating the effectiveness of U.S. air attacks against North Vietnam and later judging the progress of the war and the prospects of allied success. After Tet 1968 and the turn-about in the Johnson administration's attitude toward the war, the intelligence clout in Washington shifted more in favor of the CIA.

On balance, the Agency did a good job in assessing the situation in Southeast Asia during the 1965–74 period. Its overall intelligence judgments were generally sound and its estimates were mostly on the mark.[3] Several facts illustrate the truth of this statement. First, the Agency, in evaluating the effectiveness of U.S. air attacks, consistently concluded that the attacks did not reduce North Vietnamese logistic capabilities to sustain the war, that North Vietnam could afford to take the punishment, that Hanoi's will was not shaken, and that the material cost of the resulting damage to North Vietnam was simply passed on to the USSR and China, while Hanoi's constantly improving air defense system (provided by the USSR and China) inflicted rising air losses on the United States.

Second, with respect to North Vietnam's ability to wage a prolonged war, the Agency consistently estimated that Hanoi would continue to base its strategy on a war of attrition, since North Vietnam had the manpower base as well as an assured source of adequate arms and supplies to continue such a grinding war indefinitely, and that Hanoi's leaders believed they possessed more staying power than the United States and South Vietnam, and would ultimately prevail. Because of redundant land routes linking North Vietnam to China and the Soviet Union, the Agency did not judge North Vietnam to be vulnerable to a U.S. naval blockade.

Finally, as South Vietnam's fortunes waned and U.S. support faltered in late 1973 and in 1974, the Agency consistently warned that the South Vietnamese situation was becoming parlous and that the North Vietnamese would exploit their military advantage to gain their long-sought final victory. The Agency did not, however, anticipate that this victory would come as early as the spring of 1975. As South Vietnam's security posture deteriorated in 1975, especially after Hanoi's final offensive was launched early that year, the military situation on the ground became the preeminent factor in deciding the country's fate. Thereafter, overall strategic-political assessments of South Vietnam's longer-term viability were simply not possible.

As I indicated in an earlier chapter, one particularly complex and contentious problem plagued the intelligence community throughout the war—estimating enemy troop strength and determining the composition of his major units, the so-called order of battle. These are among the most difficult military intelligence judgments of all to make in wartime, especially in a people's war like Vietnam in which regular troops (so-called main force and local force units), their administrative and logistic support forces, part-time guerrillas and militia, and political cadres are often intermingled. Enemy ground combat casualties are particularly difficult to estimate as a result of battles involving civilians, regular soldiers, and local guerrillas and militiamen.

But I also implied earlier that in the MACV-CIA order-of-battle controversy, the CIA's estimates were probably more accurate overall than MACV's. As time went by, CIA and MACV estimates moved much closer together in the category of regular combat units but were never fully reconciled with respect to guerrilla strengths. In this latter category, the differences were partly conceptual, partly philosophical, and partly methodological. Basically, MACV held to a conservative approach in recognizing military capabilities that resulted in an underestimation of guerrilla forces. Likewise, MACV's conservative approach to estimates of enemy units and personnel infiltrating from the North led to a time lag in MACV's acceptance of new infiltrators, and hence higher total infiltration figures.

Estimating enemy casualties—the "body count" syndrome—is not a new problem; it has been a complicating factor in past wars. More than one example of highly exaggerated body counts resulting in inflated enemy loss estimates can be found in the American campaign records of World War II and the Korean War. In both Korea and Vietnam, the United States was faced with the very different and complex problems of fighting a major war but in a limited manner—limited in terms of objectives, geography, means employed, and resources committed. In both wars there was no territorial objective other than to defend the status quo ante; thus it was not possible to demonstrate or assess progress in terms of territory gained and held. Leaders quite naturally turned to other indicators of how the war was going, among them the number of enemy battle casualties. At one point in the Korean War, the explicit, if crudely stated, military objective was to kill as many Chinese ("Chinks") as possible. In Vietnam a similar objective of attriting enemy forces was present. Moreover, the difficulty of distinguishing regular and irregular forces from noncombatants tended to break down normal inhibitions against causing civilian casualties. Such incentives were invitations for fighting units to exaggerate claims of "enemy" killed. Unfortunately, a few small-unit commanders condoned or even encouraged padded reports, further exacerbating the "body count" syndrome.

Higher headquarters, nonetheless, have ways to judge the validity of unit claims; for example, by weighing the intensity of the fighting by comparing friendly and enemy casualties and by noting the number of weapons captured in comparison with the number of enemy reported killed. Comparatively low friendly casualties and few enemy weapons captured should arouse the suspicions of the higher headquarters and call for a check on the intensity of fighting when a high "body count" is reported.

In Vietnam, especially in the Delta, some units were inclined to exaggerate claims of enemy killed and were careless about avoiding civilian casualties. But by and large the great majority of American units tried to submit factual reports based on actual evidence rather than estimations, and conscientiously sought to limit casualties among noncombatants. In addition, field force headquarters and HQ MACV, whenever feasible, checked the overall circumstances of the battle reported before accepting the enemy casualty figures submitted.

Even when heavy enemy battle losses are substantiated, one must be careful not to judge their psychological effect on the enemy on the basis of occidental values. Indeed, American military professionals who fought in the Pacific in World War II or in Korea became acutely aware of differing oriental values with respect to human life, and knew the pitfalls of putting too much store in the impact of heavy casualties on the morale of a determined foe or on the will of a ruthless totalitarian government.

In Vietnam, the factual evidence concerning the enemy's manpower capacity seemed pretty clear to our leaders in the field. We realized that the enemy decided where and when he would do battle and could therefore control his casualty rate. We repeatedly saw specific, identified enemy fighting units decimated in combat only to return a few months later from their base sanctuaries at full strength, ready to fight again. These facts, coupled with what theater intelligence told us about the rate of infiltration of enemy troop units and replacements down the Ho Chi Minh Trail, timed with planned enemy "high points" (offensives), constituted positive indications that the enemy could fight this kind of war indefinitely. Raw manpower did not seem to be a limitation. Moreover, frightful enemy casualties, which, had they been American would have had major repercussions in our society, seemed to have no effect on the leadership in Hanoi or on the North Vietnamese people. Thus one might conclude with some reason that U.S. officials should not have been misled by faulty estimates of enemy losses and of the enemy's effective troop strength.

One might well ask why senior U.S. policymakers in Washington, with the exception of Defense Secretary McNamara, did not pay more attention to CIA views and to the disagreements within the intelligence community. There is no simple answer to this complex question. As already indicated, given the nature of the intelligence community it would be unreasonable to expect unanimous views, especially when matters of great import are involved. Moreover, the exposure of differing views, particularly on major issues, can be considered a strength rather than a weakness, because to paper over or submerge them runs the risk of badly misleading policymakers. International relations are difficult to judge even in normal times, but when examining them through the fog of war, policymakers are entitled to know what honest differences of opinion may exist before making judgments. With respect to Vietnam, the head of the CIA was up against a formidable array of senior policymakers, including the president, the secretary of state, the secretary of defense, the chairman of the JCS, and the national security adviser to the president—all strong personalities who knew how to exercise the clout of their respective offices. It is not surprising then that the director of Central Intelligence, Richard Helms (from 30 June 1966 to 2 February 1973), who served under both Presidents Johnson and Nixon, was reportedly content to let the responsible policy officials make up their own minds.[4] No doubt Helms was also determined to protect and preserve the traditional objectivity of intelligence vis-a-vis policy. But, as alluded to above, McNamara was not entirely satisfied with his intelligence from the Defense Department and beginning in late 1965 relied more and more on the CIA for what he believed were more objective and accurate intelligence judgments.

Having made the case for a reasonably good record of consistency and accuracy on the part of the CIA during the war, however, I should mention one exception, one which at the time caused much heartburn at high policy levels. It had to do with North Vietnam's use of a sea line of communications to South Vietnam via Cambodia. In this instance, the CIA and the DIA held similar views which turned out to be wrong, while MACV was shown to be mostly right. During the 1966–70 period, the CIA and the DIA greatly underestimated the volume of supplies entering Sihanoukville by sea and transported overland through Cambodia to VC/NVA forces operating in II, III and IV CTZs of South Vietnam, while MACV insisted that this was at least a major enemy supply route.

The question was settled after the invasion of Cambodia in May 1970, when abundant evidence was obtained that proved without a doubt that the great bulk of the arms, ammunition, and supplies for enemy forces operating in South Vietnam from the Central Highlands to the Delta arrived by this route. In the CIA's defense it should be noted that they were misled by the statements of high-level Cambodian officials, not to mention the official denials of some of our close allied friends, who knew full well the truth of the situation.

At this point, several comments in the realm of tactics and techniques should be underscored. First, let us look at the matter of surprise. Whether the North Vietnamese achieved truly strategic surprise in an overall political-military sense during the Vietnam War is arguable. But unquestionably they achieved surprise in a tactical sense in two notable cases before the January 1973 cease-fire. These were their Tet offensive of 1968 and their March 1972 "Easter" offensive across the eastern part of the DMZ. The NVA also achieved major tactical surprise after the cease-fire when it attacked Ban Me Thuot in II CTZ in March 1975 at the beginning of the final offensive against South Vietnam.

Examining the question of why this came about, one must conclude that a major factor was our overreliance on signal intelligence, from which we derived most of our strategic and tactical information pertaining to Southeast Asia. This kind of intelligence can be very misleading and is also subject to manipulation by the enemy. It is more suitable for judgments of a longer-term strategic nature, and is not always reliable or appropriate for short-term tactical purposes. Identifying and, by direction-finding techniques, locating a radio transmitter belonging to a specific NVA regiment, for example, does not necessarily mean that the regiment is there too, although it is a good indication that elements of the regiment are in the vicinity. But in actuality, a small forward communications detachment might be the only element of the regiment present. One obvious conclusion is that we did not put enough emphasis on direct human sources of intelligence, as opposed to those of the electronic variety.

We were also weak in counterintelligence, that is, an organized, disciplined effort to deny information about our own plans, operations, and other military matters to the enemy. U.S. communications security, for example, was not satisfactory in Southeast Asia; we never achieved even a reasonably good posture. Because of our careless habits, talking in clear (uncoded) text over insecure phone or voice radio, and our frequent failure to use truly secure codes, the enemy all too often knew our planned moves well in advance, even strikes by the Strategic Air Command, and took action to alert their units and people. As a consequence we deprived ourselves of numerous opportunities to surprise the enemy, a prized advantage.

At times we used more military force than was called for by the situation, especially when fighting near or in populated areas. Since heavy firepower and area-type weapons, such as tactical air support, artillery, and mortars, are not discriminating enough, their use risks civilian casualties and material damage which can be self-defeating in pacification efforts. Unobserved "H&I" (harassing and interdiction) artillery fire and air strikes, often based on dubious intelligence reports, were at times directed into areas (sometimes designated by South Vietnamese officials as "free fire zones") believed to be occupied only by enemy forces. This practice was not really effective militarily and was generally a waste of ammunition. Moreover, it ran the unnecessary risk of inflicting casualties on civilians and being counterproductive politically and psychologically, whether the people concerned were helping the enemy or not.

Related to the foregoing, American and South Vietnamese troops during the period when U.S. troops were still present in strength (1966–71) often became too accustomed to an abundance of externally provided heavy firepower and neglected their own organic capabilities that were more discriminating. This habit can also result in less capable infantry troops who come to rely on massive externally provided firepower rather than on the skillful use of fire and maneuver on their own.

In later years (1971–75), however, after most U.S. ground forces had been withdrawn, massive U.S. airpower was needed to make up for South Vietnam's principal shortcomings: the lack of enough forces overall (in particular armor and artillery), an inadequate strategic reserve, and an inability to shift forces from one region to another. After the cease-fire in January 1973, when U.S. airpower was no longer available, a new situation existed wherein the South Vietnamese simply lacked enough airpower, armor, and larger caliber artillery of their own to handle the numerous large, modern NVA formations arrayed against them.

The helicopter can be both an asset and liability. This is a costly resource requiring considerable logistic and maintenance support that must be used wisely. Airmobile operations require tactical skill and intensive training by both aviation and infantry elements; a poorly conducted operation can be disastrous. U.S. and allied forces at times became too heavily dependent on helicopter support. The "chopper" is a versatile machine which accords great advantages of mobility, logistic support, fire support, and medical evacuation. But there is still no substitute for lean, tough troops who can march long distances on foot and can survive with minimum support. The availability of the helicopter makes it too easy to overfly trouble on the ground or to withdraw troops from difficult positions. The latter action in particular can undermine the tenacity and willingness of troops to fight to the finish that must characterize first-class infantry.

The helicopter also allows senior officials to visit their people operating on the ground more readily, but this is a double-edged sword. It can lead to oversupervision of junior officials and can make senior leaders believe they know more about the situation on the ground than they actually do.

As I indicated in a previous chapter, logistic support of American forces was generally outstanding. Americans tend to be profligate, however, and our armed forces are no exception. Amassing huge quantities of all kinds of supplies in Vietnam on the grounds that supply lines might be interrupted was an example of overly cautious logistic planning. Similarly, administrative support and base facilities were too comfortable for some American headquarters and personnel in Vietnam. This had bad psychological effects, set a poor example for our own fighting soldiers as well as those of our allies, and lent an air of unreality at times to the American military presence. A more spartan existence would have been better for all.

Overall, our troops had little, if anything, to complain about. Communications support, logistic support of all kinds, medical care which made miracles seem commonplace, and engineer support—all without exception were outstanding. Even the military police earned the respect if not affection of the "GI" in Vietnam. Nevertheless, a more efficient logistic system could have conserved precious resources without hurting overall troop performance.

The Army's most serious problems were in the manpower and personnel area. Basically they stemmed from the failure to mobilize and the decision to hold to a one-year tour in Vietnam. Without at least a partial mobilization the Army was denied the use of the trained, experienced units and personnel present in the National Guard and organized reserves. This meant that, as the Army expanded from roughly 950,000 in 1964 to about 1,550,000 in 1968 to meet the requirements of Vietnam, the additional men and women entering the service were mostly very young, untrained, and inexperienced, resulting in the dilution of overall experience in the Army, particularly in the leadership ranks, the officers and noncommissioned officers. The failure to mobilize or to declare an emergency also meant that personnel would flow in and out of the armed forces on a peacetime basis rather than being held in the service for the duration of the emergency. Thus draftees conscripted for two years could serve at the most about sixteen months overseas. This factor, coupled with a judgment that all personnel (career and noncareer) serving in Vietnam would perform better if on a known, fixed tour, led to the one-year rotation policy, a very bad mistake in my view. Finally, as its troop strength built up in Vietnam, the Army reached the point at which almost as many soldiers (about 725,000) were serving overseas as in the continental United States (about 825,000). Of those overseas, more than half were serving in Vietnam and Korea and had to be replaced every year. The number of replacements required in Vietnam steadily grew, of course, as the fighting intensified and battle losses and noncombat casualties rose. Moreover about 250,000 soldiers in the United States (almost one-third of the total on duty there) were undergoing basic training and were not available for assignment to units.

For the Army the overall simple arithmetic was that its so-called sustaining rotation base in the continental United States was not large enough to furnish the large number of trained replacements required each year for Vietnam and Korea, to maintain the forces in Europe on a three-year tour, and to give career soldiers much of a breathing spell between repetitive tours in Vietnam. The length of the tour in Europe had to be progressively shortened and in the end the proud, combat-ready Seventh Army ceased to be a field army and became a large training and replacement depot for Vietnam. For political reasons ("guns and butter" and the demands of "The Great Society"), Defense secretary McNamara would not recognize the legitimate manpower shortfalls of the Army and disapproved Army requests for increases in its authorized strength to meet worldwide demands. The principal cumulative effects of these misguided policies on the Army's posture in Vietnam are discussed below.

Although new units, with very few exceptions, arrived in Vietnam with a reasonably high level of unit proficiency, and incoming replacement personnel likewise generally possessed the required individual skills, the problem was to maintain unit efficiency and cohesion, and develop teamwork in the face of a high personnel turnover rate. Because of battle casualties, injuries, sickness, and other personnel losses, and the steady loss of soldiers returning home at the end of their one-year tour, the average rifle company, for example, became an entirely different outfit in terms of individual men every nine or ten months.

Maintaining a high standard of leadership in Vietnam was another major problem. The Army simply was unable to provide an adequate replacement flow of leaders, officers, and NCOs with experience commensurate with their responsibilities. The one-year tour, as well as the failure to mobilize, stretched the experienced leadership available from career personnel very thin throughout the Army worldwide. Moreover, many career and noncommissioned officers, after completing two or three tours in Vietnam and coming under increasing pressure from their families, decided to retire, thus further increasing the loss of experience. The end result was a slow, steady deterioration of experienced leadership in Vietnam that hurt the continuity of our effort and eroded our dedication to assigned missions.

Without mobilization, the one-year rotation policy was logical for our two-year draftees. But the tour for the career officer and NCO should have been two to three years. Proponents of the one-year tour for careerists argued that the high tempo of combat operations and the severe, constant strain on leaders dictated the shorter tour in the combat zone. They pointed out that helicopter operations could keep troops in almost constant contact with the enemy and that combat units could be shifted suddenly from the relatively safe environment of a base camp into a hot fire fight in a matter of minutes. This is a telling point, but such a problem could have been alleviated by in-country rotation between combat jobs and more secure noncombat positions.

Vietnam uncovered a major deficiency in the training of American military personnel, both officer and enlisted. This weakness lay in the area of the Geneva Conventions and their applicability to unconventional, guerrilla warfare. Our armed forces did not do an effective job—either in the United States or in Southeast Asia—of orienting their uniformed personnel, particularly ground combat troops, to what they would face in this kind of war. As a result, our troops were not prepared for this ambiguous, complex type of warfare and did not fully understand how the internationally accepted rules of warfare applied to Vietnam. One can make the case that the tragic My Lai aberration largely stemmed from inadequate orientation and training on the Geneva Conventions, further aggravated by the scarcity of mature, experienced leadership among lower ranking American officers and noncommissioned officers. As a result of My Lai, while American soldiers were still in combat in Vietnam, the Army inaugurated a massive orientation program to correct this deficiency.

Having examined the performance of American forces, U.S. intelligence, some of our tactical and logistic shortcomings, and the serious weaknesses of our manpower system, we might well ask whether any significant improvements in U.S. performance would have made any difference in the outcome. The answer is probably "no." The war was lost primarily at strategic, diplomatic, and domestic political levels, although the final defeat of South Vietnamese forces on the ground was more tactical and military in nature. Nevertheless, we American military professionals have much to learn from the tragic experience of Vietnam, because heeding those lessons could mean the difference between winning and losing in a future conflict.

9

American Strategy

The hard lessons learned, the questions raised, and the lingering issues will be part of the legacy of Vietnam. No doubt our experiences there will have a lasting impact on our foreign policy and related defense policy. The Vietnam tragedy will probably be an inhibiting factor in our external relations and domestic policies for at least a generation. On the other hand, a sudden shock like Pearl Harbor or a domestic disaster on the order of the Great Depression of the 1930s could well turn American attitudes around very quickly. In fact, in the early 1980s definite signs of a turnaround in American attitudes are apparent.

This chapter ventures an overall strategic assessment of our involvement in Vietnam, discussing the factors working against the United States, reviewing U.S. strategy, and examing Hanoi's strategy. Our failure to understand the implications of our basic decisions in dealing with Vietnam, and the consequences, are examined, and a possible alternative strategy is explored.

The term "strategy," derived from the ancient Greek, originally pertained to the art of generalship or high military command. Today the original military term is now applied to many other fields—political, economic, financial, and so on. Since the 1950s the term "national strategy," meaning the coordinated employment of the total resources of a nation to achieve its national objectives, has attained wide usage. The current definition of military strategy used by the JCS is "the art and science of employing the armed forces of a nation to secure the objectives of national policy by the application of force, or the threat of force."[1] In this book I use strategy with its original military meaning principally in mind, but never losing sight of the essential link between military means and political ends.

Let us make no bones about it—the United States failed to achieve its objectives in South Vietnam. All our efforts to build a viable nation went down to defeat when the Republic was overrun by North Vietnamese troops in April 1975. Was it all in vain? Was it worth the cost—almost 57,000 American lives, many billions of dollars, and untold material resources, not to mention the high Vietnamese casualties and physical destruction in the area of operations? Certainly the damage to our own self-esteem and self-confidence at home, as well as to our prestige abroad, has been incalculable, and only in time can the lasting effects be judged.

Nevertheless, we as a nation should not view Vietnam in too narrow a context, but should try to look at the war in a broader perspective. A strong case can be made that our efforts, viewed in an international reference, produced some positive and significant results. Had we not committed our ground combat forces in 1965, there is no doubt that South Vietnam would have collapsed and North Vietnam would have immediately taken over at that time. Those ten years, 1965–75, bought invaluable time for the other noncommunist countries in the area exposed to the same threat.

Thailand survived in good shape, while Malaysia and Singapore fared extremely well in that period. In Indochina, however, Vietnam appears determined to bring Kampuchea (Cambodia) under its direct control, as has already happened in Laos, and the remainder of the Southeast Asian mainland now feels the deadly threat from Hanoi. Ironically, Vietnam has become a surrogate of the USSR, China's number one enemy, while Hanoi's former ally, China, is now the protector of noncommunist nations in the region and went all out in February 1979 "to teach Vietnam a lesson" for invading Kampuchea.

But of even greater significance was the countercoup in 1965 which saved Indonesia from almost certain complete communist control in September of that year. The fact that the United States had committed its power in Vietnam was undoubtedly a major factor in the success of the countercoup. Decades before the Vietnam War, Indonesia was recognized as the strategic prize in Southeast Asia, and that is even truer today. Occupying the world's largest archipelago, this nation of about 150 million people, with vastly rich natural resources, has the talent and capacity to become one of the world's major power centers. Its strategic importance is enhanced by its geographic position with respect to the Strait of Malacca, one of the major international waterways of the world. Had Indonesia gone the other way, the threat to Australia, the Philippines, and New Zealand would have become very real.

Our stand in Vietnam indeed contributed to our overall position in all of the western Pacific, as our allies, especially Japan, the Republic of Korea, and Taiwan, not to mention Australia and New Zealand, prospered under our security shield during the period. If we had not fought on the side of South Vietnam, the position of these Pacific allies would have been seriously weakened.

Having shown the other side of the coin with respect to our defeat in Vietnam, let me now assess our involvement, attempting to determine where we went wrong and to identify our major missteps. At the outset, one must recognize the disadvantages facing the United States in assisting South Vietnam, which at the time seemed to be the right thing to do. Three basic disadvantages were of major proportions.

First, South Vietnam, comprising Cochin China, centered about Saigon, and Annam, centered about Hue, lacked political and social cohesion, having no history or tradition as a unified nation or as a united people. Leaders were scarce and generally came from the privileged class.

Second, the people in the southern part of Vietnam are more like the Laos and the Cambodes, peaceful people very different from the more aggressive and militant people in the Red River Delta. The Montagnard region in the Central Highlands was a distinct political and sociological handicap to Saigon. The Montagnards are a primitive, tribal people subsisting on a marginal basis, moving frequently in the wild forests of the region, and using "slash and burn" techniques to carve out new temporary home sites. The Vietnamese suspect their loyalty and do not trust them. There is no love lost between the two ethnic groups.

And third, the United States seems to share a common weakness of Western democracies, an inability to inculcate in people the kind of determination and almost religious zeal which communist countries have achieved. Whether this motivation has been accomplished through fear, terror tactics, or other methods, it is nonetheless a formidable weapon. Particularly effective is the communist indoctrination given to the chosen few among the youth who are to become the hard-core party members and future leaders. Moreover, we must remember that by the early 1960s some populated parts of South Vietnam had been under communism for over a generation.

Strategically, the United States also was at a great disadvantage vis-a-vis the Soviet Union and the People's Republic of China. Whereas these two powers suffered no casualties and expended only material resources, the United States took heavy casualties and expended an enormous amount of resources, maintaining an ever-expanding U.S. force in combat halfway around the world, supporting very large South Vietnamese forces and sizable Free World forces, and providing bounteous economic aid to the Republic of Vietnam.

To begin with, the United States put itself at a great strategic disadvantage by assuming that communism was a monolithic, immutably solid entity, with Moscow at the epicenter calling the shots. The true nature of the Sino-Soviet split and its enormous strategic implications initially were not appreciated by our government. We seemed to be unaware of the past centuries of conflict between China and the Soviet Union, and the great rivalry between them over the future orientation of Asia.

Indeed, the split placed the United States in a position to play the key role in maintaining a stable balance of power among the nations of the world.

To compound an inherently difficult military situation, the United States decided not to mobilize but to expand its active forces as the war broadened and intensified. This failure to mobilize, coupled with other internal Defense Department decisions, resulted in a steady deterioration of American forces, not only in Southeast Asia but also in other areas, especially in Europe, where a once magnificent American field army became singularly unready, incapable of fulfilling its NATO mission. The decision also brought into question the need for our National Guard and reserve forces, and severely damaged their prestige and morale. Ultimately the United States became precariously off balance strategically because of the neglect of our forces in Europe and the Atlantic.

The United States was also at a serious political and psychological disadvantage. However unfairly, it was charged that American entry into Vietnam was no different from the former French presence, and consequently the United States was tarred with the same colonial brush as any other Western power. Whereas this was a major psychological handicap for our side, it was an enormous advantage for the Viet Cong and North Vietnam. In addition, our European allies, still upset by American support of former colonies seeking independence from their European overseers, declined to support our efforts. The only allies who supported us were those in Asia and the western Pacific. As a result of our apparent colonialism, the United States was very vulnerable to hostile propaganda and lost popular support both at home and abroad. U.S. bombing of North Vietnam is a good example of this vulnerability. No matter how carefully we conducted these air attacks to avoid civilian casualties, we were always pictured as the giant bully picking on a helpless small country trying to defend itself against insuperable odds.

Furthermore, the United States badly misjudged the situation in Vietnam. The extent of subversion from local to national levels we did not fully realize. When U.S. ground combat forces were committed in 1965 we were quite aware of the outward manifestations of near collapse—a demoralized, defeated army and a staggering economy—but we did not comprehend the depth of the Viet Cong insurgency in certain areas. We could see only the tip of the iceberg. We also greatly underestimated the Viet Cong and the NVA, particularly their staying power. They had an extraordinary ability to recuperate, absorbing heavy casualties in numbers unthinkable to us, replacing people, retraining and reindoctrinating them, and then bouncing back.

We likewise underestimated the will, tenacity, and determination of the Hanoi regime. North Vietnamese leaders were playing for keeps, believing that the use of any means was justified by their ends. They thought in terms of generations; the longer the war continued, the more persistent they became. Their will to persist was inextinguishable.

Conversely, the United States was overconfident in believing that superior U.S. technology, Yankee ingenuity, industrial and military might, modern military organization, tactics, and techniques, and a tradition of crisis solving in peace and war would surely bring success in Vietnam where the French had failed. Many American military leaders, myself included, realized the serious disadvantages of limiting ourselves to the defensive and confining our ground operations to the territorial boundaries of South Vietnam, but still believed that we would somehow find a way to overcome these handicaps—the "can do" syndrome. But for most of us the realization that time would run out on us very quickly came too late.

One of our handicaps was that few Americans understood the true nature of the war—a devilishly clever mixture of conventional warfare fought somewhat unconventionally and guerrilla warfare fought in the classical manner. Hanoi never lost sight of its political objectives, and every action it took, military or nonmilitary, was designed to further those objectives. Moreover, from Hanoi's point of view it was allout, total war, while from the outlook of the United States it was quite limited.

U.S. top leaders, civilian and military, appear not to have grasped fully the implications of the decision to fight a localized war with limited objectives, seeking to deny North Vietnam success in the South by making the cost too high. Consider the consequences of that decision to fight a passive strategic defense of South Vietnam. First, it gave the initiative and the advantage of the strategic offensive to Hanoi. Allied forces in the South could only react, their only strategic offensive weapon being airpower against the North. Moreover, piecemeal, gradual application of airpower made matters worse. This allowed North Vietnam to build its air defenses to an unprecedented level and to condition its people to withstand the effects of the bombing. On the other hand, one must not understate the devastating effect of airpower. Certainly the all-out so-called "Christmas bombing" of the Hanoi area in December 1972 was instrumental in bringing about the cease-fire agreement reached in January 1973. Nor must one underestimate the critical necessity of U.S. airpower in the later years of the war to make up for the inadequate size and capabilities of South Vietnamese ground and air forces. But in the final analysis, airpower against the North without a credible and integral ground threat to Hanoi was indecisive.

In addition, the limitation of the war zone meant that there was no practical way to stop the infiltration of men and materiel into South Vietnam. Air interdiction throughout North Vietnam and in the panhandle of Laos could inflict personnel and materiel losses, but predictably could not stop the flow. South Vietnam was virtually impossible to seal off.

This difficulty was made worse by allowing Hanoi to use Laos and Cambodia as sanctuaries and base areas. Eventually the North Vietnamese built a large, effective, all-weather logistic structure in those neighboring countries.

Their limited goals also forced the allies to fight enemy forces on the enemy's terms, in areas of their choosing, and on South Vietnamese soil. The destruction in the South, disruption of all normal economic, social, and political life, and damage to nation-building efforts were inevitable.

Certain political initiatives taken by the United States had even more adverse effects. President Johnson beginning in 1965 let it be known to North Vietnamese leaders that the United States did not intend to invade North Vietnam or otherwise try to bring down the Hanoi government. Thereafter U.S. actions without exception reaffirmed that impression of U.S. intent.[2] This practically sealed South Vietnam's doom, for it allowed Hanoi complete freedom to employ all its forces in the South. One cannot quarrel with the decision not to invade North Vietnam because it was too close to China; our experience in misjudging the Chinese intervention in Korea was still fresh in our memory. But the United States should have kept its intentions ambiguous and never taken Hanoi off the hook with respect to an invasion. By maintaining a clear amphibious threat off the coast of North Vietnam we could have kept the North Vietnamese off balance and forced them to keep strong troop reserves at home. We know that the Son Tay POW camp raid near Hanoi on 20 November 1970, had a severe impact. This skillfully conducted joint operation demonstrated how vulnerable the North Vietnamese were and incurred the scorn of the Chinese, who reportedly threatened to cut off aid if they could not defend themselves any better.[3] As it was, freed of any credible threat, the North Vietnamese built up their strategic reserves and eventually sent practically all of them to the South.

The United States further weakened its hand by seeking peace negotiations prematurely. During the 1964–68 period President Johnson took over seventy peace initiatives, interspersed with sixteen bombing pauses. Our position in South Vietnam was far from strong enough to justify negotiations until 1968. Hanoi took these early American attempts as a sign of weakness and a lack of confidence on our part.

With this background, let us turn to a brief examination of U.S. strategy. It consisted of two parts, only partially related in a military sense, but closely related in political and psychological terms. The first part was the air offensive in the North coupled with diplomatic peace overtures, designed primarily to persuade Hanoi to cease and desist in its bid to take over South Vietnam. The other part, the fundamental one, was the ground war in the South. Although the air offensive was intensely debated in Washington, comparable debate with respect to the ground war came somewhat late in the game. Washington in part relinquished the initiative to General Westmoreland, who in 1965–66 made the most of a deficient overall strategy by fighting a war of attrition, confined within the borders of South Vietnam and spear-headed by American ground troops. There were many weaknesses in this strategy which in numerous interrelated ways played into the hands of the enemy.

First, we put too much faith in the effectiveness of the air offensive, hindered by a policy of gradual escalation and essentially used in isolation, to make the North Vietnamese cease and desist. Air interdiction was more effective, but again, because it was employed without ground operations, or at least the threat of such operations, it was not as effective as it might have been. The flow of enemy men and material was certainly impeded, but not decisively so. To make matters worse, the inconclusive air offensive in the North gave Hanoi an ideal propaganda weapon that they used with great effect worldwide.

Second, we were fatally handicapped by a strategy of passive defense and could not decisively erode the enemy's forces. Despite enormous casualties, the North Vietnamese actually built up their strength in the South. They had ample manpower resources and could control the tempo of the ground war and thereby their casualty rate.

The strategy of passive defense, moreover, dictated that large combat forces be deployed throughout much of South Vietnam. The unlimited mission of defending all of the country and defeating the enemy wherever he could be brought to battle had a synergistic effect in terms of the demand on U.S. manpower and material resources. The geographic configuration of South Vietnam and the nature of its road and railroad system—the main roads and the single railroad running generally parallel to the coast—added up to a major vulnerability. Enemy forces based in the remote border and mountainous areas did not have far to go to reach the populated coastal plains. Using the river and land routes available, these forces had rapid and easy access to the population centers, main roads, and railroad lines which they could readily attack in any number of vulnerable places.

Third, we tried to Americanize the war, quickly building to a large U.S. combat force of eight and one-third division equivalents and seven tactical air wings by the end of 1966, widely deployed throughout South Vietnam. Where we did not have U.S. units we had numerous advisers, 23,000 in all by the end of 1964. By 1968, the American force had expanded to roughly 11 division equivalents and nine tactical air wings. By this time, moreover, the U.S. Army adviser contingent, in terms of officers and senior NCOs, was the equivalent of another seven U.S. Army divisions, and the aviation elements of almost the entire U.S. Army had been deployed to Vietnam. This massive American effort had to be discouraging and disconcerting to our South Vietnamese allies, many of whom, however, were not averse to letting Uncle Sam do it. And we should not overlook Free World forces, which reached a level of two and two-thirds divisions by the end of 1966 and three divisions by 1967, mostly Korean, all supported and financed by the United States.

But despite the massive buildup of U.S. and allied forces, we seemed to be involved in an endless war, and for the fighting troops it was frustrating to destroy the same enemy units every few months in battles that took place in the same general locations. We had little to show for American and allied losses and it was extremely difficult to demonstrate clearly that progress was in fact being made. Press accounts published in the United States made this painfully evident.

Perhaps most serious was that, engrossed in U.S. operations, we paid insufficient attention to our number one military job, which was to develop South Vietnamese armed forces that could successfully pacify and defend their own country. This was particularly true of the U.S. Army, where there was no separate military assistance and advisory group dedicated solely to that mission. We demonstrated that our troops could defeat the best that the Viet Cong and NVA had to offer, but this was not our basic objective.

The consequences of our conscious decision to give first priority to the defeat of enemy regular forces in the field, using American forces almost exclusively, were wide-ranging with many adverse ramifications. That decision:

(1) diverted U.S. attention, priority of effort, and precious resources away from the primary task of developing South Vietnamese forces capable of defending their country from subversion or overt invasion from the North;

(2) presented Hanoi with a propaganda prize: the Americans, they could claim, were pushing the South Vietnamese aside and fighting the war for selfish U.S. imperialist goals;

(3) played into the hands of Hanoi's overall political strategy of inflicting maximum casualties on U.S. forces, raising the costs of the war beyond the limits we were willing to bear, and wearing down American will and determination to stay the course;

(4) damaged South Vietnamese forces psychologically by inferring that they were not competent or courageous enough to defeat North Vietnamese forces (in this connection, "southern" people and leaders from the South had a definite inferiority complex vis-à-vis their northern cousins);

(5) finally, it consumed time that we could not retrieve. Americans at home lost patience with the war, lost confidence in their leaders, and listened to their own fears. By the time the United States changed direction and gave South Vietnamese forces top priority, it was too late. American popular support had been frittered away.

Much of the foregoing is a review in retrospect, but it can also be argued that most of these consequences could reasonably have been anticipated.

Having briefly examined U.S. strategy, let us take a look at the North Vietnamese side. The Viet Cong and various "patriotic fronts" I include along with the North Vietnamese proper because it was always clear that Hanoi closely controlled the entire effort. The enemy's strategy is revealing. North Vietnam maintained an unwavering consistency in driving toward its basic political aim of not only reunifying and communizing all of Vietnam, North and South, but also subjugating and communizing the rest of former French Indochina, that is, Laos and Cambodia (now Kampuchea). For Hanoi, the struggle was a test of will rather than of strength, and any means were justified by that end.

Only the United States stood in the way, and so Hanoi's second objective was to eliminate American influence through humiliating defeat, by imposing unacceptable political, economic, social, and military costs on the American people. To this end, the North Vietnamese mobilized world opinion against the United States and turned public opinion at home against the war by inflicting maximum U.S. casualties. They exhausted American patience by prolonging the conflict and raising the cost in dollars and material resources. They also painted the U.S. effort as an immoral, illegitimate, and unlawful war against a weak, small country (North Vietnam) seeking to unify its people under one government.

How to use the supporting military arm of this overall strategy was apparently the subject of some debate among North Vietnamese leaders when the United States surprised them by intervening in strength on the ground in the latter part of 1965. A year earlier, in 1964, Hanoi had intervened in the South with NVA troops, and now, despite U.S. air attacks in the North, a decisive early victory in the South still looked quite possible. The question for Hanoi was whether to continue to seek a quick collapse before the Americans could turn the South Vietnamese around, or to settle down for a more protracted struggle. Hanoi's answer appears to have been to plan and prepare for a long war but at the same time to be ready to exploit any possibility of early success. At the heart of the subversion in the South was a healthy political structure, the shadow government of the Viet Cong, operating at every level. And so the primary mission of North Vietnam's supporting military arm was to protect that structure while it grew ever stronger, by defeating all South Vietnamese pacification efforts dedicated to the destruction of that apparatus, and by wearing down South Vietnamese regular, regional, and local forces.

The military strategy developed with this mission in mind was consistently pursued before, during, and after the U.S. intervention. Although at times North Vietnamese execution of its strategy was faulty, their concept was brilliant. Basically, the strategy took advantage of the long, narrow geographic configuration of South Vietnam that made the country very vulnerable to penetration from its land border flank, and that in the northern and central regions provided very little depth between the generally wild and sparsely inhabited border areas and the heavily populated coastal region. The strategy also took advantage of the geopolitical weaknesses of South Vietnam and exploited the high foot and sampan mobility of main force units of Viet Cong and NVA infantry. The strategic concept was three-pronged, directed toward Saigon, the northernmost provinces, and the Central Highlands.

A large credible threat directed at the capital city of Saigon was constantly maintained. Large, almost impregnable, war zones were developed in the lightly inhabited and heavily forested areas north of Saigon, and safe base areas were established at several places along the border just within Cambodia. Numerous high-speed avenues of approach leading from these war zones and Cambodian sanctuaries were developed by which foot troops could reach the environs of Saigon in a matter of hours. The crack 9th VC Division, the elite VC outfit in the heyday of the Viet Cong, was based in this area generally north of Saigon.

In the northern provinces of I CTZ, the enemy took advantage of the fact that the approach to the South through the DMZ was the shortest and most direct, as well as the easiest to support and supply from the North. The area was also the narrowest part of South Vietnam in terms of the distance between the inland border and the seacoast. Periodically the enemy built up great pressure in the area, threatening the integrity of the northernmost province, Quang Tri, or menacing Hue, the ancient capital of the Annamite Kingdom—a symbol of great psychological importance—in Thua Thien Province immediately south of Quang Tri.

In the Central Highlands of II CTZ, the enemy also exploited the lack of depth, periodically threatening to take over the border provinces of Kontum and Pleiku, thereby getting into position to drive along Highway 19 to the sea and split the country in two. The Central Highlands constituted an additional source of worry for South Vietnam because this is Montagnard country, never completely loyal and responsive to the central government. Because of the natural antipathy between the Montagnards and the Vietnamese, Americans in the area found themselves walking a tightrope between them. Ban Me Thuot, located in the province of Darlac, south of Pleiku Province, is the traditional Montagnard capital and therefore often a prime target of the enemy. If there was one strategic key to the military defense of South Vietnam, it was the Central Highlands, called by some the fulcrum of that defense. The loss of this area, particularly if it was precipitous, invited disaster, for it could lead to cutting the country in half, trapping all forces and people to the north, and then dismembering piecemeal what was left. Indeed, Ban Me Thuot was destined to be not only the first major battleground in the NVA's final offensive in 1975, but also the fatal one which started South Vietnam's unraveling.

By skillfully orchestrating their moves in these three major pressure point areas, North Vietnamese leaders sought to keep the Saigon high command worried continually about all three, and to compel priority attention to garrisoning and defending them. All the while the enemy tried to induce premature commitment of South Vietnamese strategic reserves, normally stationed in the Saigon area. During the period before major U.S. intervention, Hanoi succeeded in such efforts to confuse Saigon, and there were times when the strategic reserves, essentially the South Vietnamese airborne troops and marines, were exhausted as a result of frequent moves and offensive combat. There were other purposes behind this enemy strategy—weakening South Vietnam's pacification program by drawing forces away from populated areas, exposing other important areas to attack, inflicting casualties on allied forces, and expending their valuable time and resources in unnecessary and unprofitable moves. This well conceived strategy at times was reminiscent of the strategy used by Lee and Jackson in the Shenandoah Valley and in the areas west and northwest of Washington during the first years of the American Civil War.

In the final campaign, Hanoi faithfully followed the same prescription.The fall of the Central Highlands came first in mid-March 1975, followed by the ARVN collapse in the northern provinces. South Vietnam's defenses rapidly became unraveled as the coastal areas of I and II CTZs were overrun in quick succession. Then it was only a matter of time before Saigon was invested from all sides, and on 30 April 1975 it was all over.

In the early years of the U.S. commitment, could we have done things differently? Was there a more feasible alternative? One answer to both questions is "probably yes." Our strategy had fatal flaws which another strategy might have avoided. The major elements of an alternative strategy are described as follows. The concept has two principal strategic thrusts.

First, in sharp contrast to the eventual commitment of sizable American forces in each corps tactical zone, the fulcrum of the U.S. troop effort would be in the north in I CTZ, just south of the DMZ. Most of the U.S. troops and all Free World forces, which consisted mostly of Korean forces (a two-division ROK Army corps), would eventually be concentrated in the northern provinces to form an international force along the DMZ. Rather than trying to hold ground under direct observation and heavy artillery fire from enemy units in and just north of the DMZ, the most defensible positions south of the DMZ would be selected and organized for defense. This defensive line would be extended into Laos across the narrow waist of the panhandle region. Hanoi could attempt to outflank this position via Thailand, but this would greatly magnify NVA logistic problems. Moreover, it would bring the NVA into more open terrain (far easier to defend than much of South Vietnam), where U.S. air-ground operations and air interdiction would be considerably more effective.[4]

If for political reasons we were denied authority to enter Laos in force, a variation of the concept would be to refuse the inland flank, denying the enemy access to the approaches to the Ashau Valley inside South Vietnam, and to conduct major raids into Laos against the enemy's infiltration system. Coupled with air interdiction in North Vietnam and Laos, such ground operations would be quite effective. With a large allied force on their flank, in position to trap enemy troops in the South and to cut their supply line, the North Vietnamese could not afford to ignore the risk.

Second, U.S. naval power would maintain a constantly visible and credible amphibious presence off the coast of North Vietnam, threatening possible invasion from the sea of various important areas of North Vietnam. Additionally, U.S. air and naval power would be employed in a blockade of northern ports, but "strategic bombing" of North Vietnam would be avoided. Air interdiction would be conducted only in sparsely settled areas along the North Vietnam-Laotian border, in the area of the DMZ, and in the Laotian panhandle.

Weaponry used in populated areas would be limited to infantry-type direct-fire weapons. The employment of close air support (fixed wing and attack helicopter), artillery, and mortars would be permitted only in very lightly populated areas.

The focus of the overall U.S. effort would be on the development of a South Vietnamese capability to defend the nation from North Vietnam. For the U.S. military command this would mean a conscious, deliberate policy of avoiding taking over conduct of the war in the South, and instead concentrating on improving and developing effective South Vietnamese forces, in particular the ARVN. This would be the primary American mission in the South, while shielding the republic from invasion by North Vietnam.

From the beginning, U.S. operational and logistic planning would be so designed that the major operational efforts of American and other foreign forces would eventually be made in the extreme northern part of South Vietnam. The movement of major forces into this area would take place just as soon as the situation to the South was reasonably stabilized and just as rapidly as base development would support a buildup of forces in the northern region of South Vietnam. Under this concept, only minimal U.S. forces would initially be deployed in II and III CTZs, as well as in the southern parts of I CTZ. Likewise, the bulk of Free World forces would be deployed initially in the far north of South Vietnam.

U.S. ground combat forces employed on a sustained basis in South Vietnam would generally be U.S. Army divisions and separate infantry brigades. Other than the relatively small Marine force originally deployed in the Danang area, available U.S. Marine forces would be held in MACV reserve, with major elements constantly afloat in local waters and exercised frequently. Two amphibious forces would be maintained, one off the North Vietnamese coast as a constant threat to Hanoi, the other, perhaps smaller, force operating in waters off South Vietnam from which landing operations, over-the-beach or by helicopter, could be launched for operations of relatively short duration in any of the four corps tactical zones.

From the beginning the major U.S. logistic effort would be concentrated in the far north, developing ports, bases, and roads capable of supporting an international force of field army size (about seven allied division equivalents) by the end of 1966. Base development in other parts of South Vietnam would be limited to the extent needed to support the initial U.S. forces deployed to those areas. Thus enormous U.S. bases such as those at Long Binh (III CTZ) and at Cam Ranh Bay (II CTZ) would not be built. (As it was, the "big war" moved away from Cam Ranh Bay and consequently the base was underutilized.) Moreover the heavy U.S. logistic efforts expended on other base areas in I, II, and III CTZs could be substantially scaled down.

The international force on the DMZ front would be under the operational control of a U.S. field army commander, with three corps commands. For purposes of illustration these commands could be a U.S. corps of two divisions; an ROK corps of two ROK Army divisions and the ROK Marine Brigade; and a mixed corps of one U.S. and one ARVN division under a U.S. or ARVN corps commander. Other U.S. Army combat units would be held in army or corps reserve.

The drive into Laos would have to be undertaken at a later phase after the DMZ international force and a substantial part of the logistic base were in place. A U.S. corps of three divisions could undertake this task initially, later being replaced in part by ROK and ARVN troops.

Admittedly, this is a bold concept, entailing some risk of losing ground in the pacification of South Vietnam while the country's indigenous security forces found themselves. But the risk would be more than offset by the fact that the United States would now have the initiative, not Hanoi. Consider the advantages of this concept:

A profound change in our relative strategic position would be achieved because this concept puts a rather restricted strategic shoe on Hanoi's ᵗt. North Vietnam would no longer have a free ride in terms of pro-ᵪ for the ground defense of its homeland. Hanoi would be denied its three main pressure points so skillfully used against South Vietnam—the DMZ, which would be transformed into the fulcrum of the U.S. allied military efforts. Most of South Vietnam could now breathe more easily and concentrate on defeating the Viet Cong in the South and on pacifying the country.

For the United States, it would mean true economy of force in that a definite limit could be placed on the size of the American force commitment. Indeed, it is likely that fewer U.S. divisions would be needed than were actually employed. More importantly, these forces would be used decisively, for their positioning would positively deny NVA entry into South Vietnam in strength. The bulk of our forces, moreover, would be fighting on ground of their own choosing that the enemy would be forced to attack if he wanted to invade South Vietnam. In defending well-prepared positions, U.S. troops would suffer fewer casualties. The same advantages would accrue to the Free World forces committed to South Vietnam.

A much smaller U.S. logistic effort would be required since only one large port, base, and lines of communications area would need to be constructed. This would further reduce the size of the total U.S. force, the number of American casualties, and U.S. dollar expenditures. Furthermore much of the U.S. dollar and other resources poured into American military operations country-wide could now be used more gainfully to develop the ARVN and other South Vietnamese forces. The immense economic and cultural shock of the American presence would be considerably softened, and inflationary pressures on the Vietnamese economy would be reduced.

The magnitude, likelihood, and intensity of the so-called "big war," involving heavy firepower, would be lessened in South Vietnam, for this kind of war would be fought largely in very sparsely inhabited country in the north. Hanoi would be unable constantly to escalate the war in the South. Consequently, the level of "revolutionary warfare" in the South would be held to a lower intensity. And Hanoi would now be denied the immense propaganda advantage the regime used so effectively with respect to U.S. bombing in North Vietnam.

The Viet Cong, cut off from sustained outside support, would be bound to wither on the vine and gradually become easier for South Vietnam to defeat on its own. With the Viet Cong attrited, the South Vietnamese could then concentrate their very considerable talents and energies on restoring normal life, building institutions, opening schools, and developing a sound economy based on their own culture, human resources, and natural endowments rather than in the image of the United States. Most of the numerous gigantic base areas, large ports, and international-size jet airfields, as well as many smaller airfields and bases built by the United States, were of no real value to South Vietnam over the long term and in some ways were a liability.

Once the Viet Cong was whittled down and Hanoi realized that it could not infiltrate and support large NVA forces in the South, serious negotiations might be possible sooner. More importantly, negotiations with more viable prospects than the cease-fire of January 1973 might be achieved. The international force south of the DMZ, already established and operational, would be a diplomatic plus, for it could help keep the peace and support any political settlement reached.

The foregoing discussion of a possible alternative strategy raises the question of whether the United States might have been more successful had we gone all out from the beginning in support of the U.S. strategy actually pursued. This implies a U.S. declaration of war and mobilization; a sustained, allout U.S. bombing offensive against the North with no "pauses" or "halts"; and an American ground force presence in the South of perhaps one million men—an estimate supported by some knowledgeable U.S. officials in high positions at the time. We will never know the answer to such a question, of course, but in my own mind I have serious reservations about achieving success if the war were protracted indefinitely, principally because of the question of will; that is, the will of the opposing governmental leaderships with the support, willing or otherwise, of their respective peoples. The record clearly indicates that Hanoi possessed the requisite will and was playing for keeps, while Washington did not and was not. Whether changed circumstances and indications of possible success would have turned things around in the United States and transformed world opinion in our favor as time dragged on seems to be problematic.

Nevertheless, even assuming successful negotiations and a cease-fire, as well as the associated disengagement of U.S. and Free World forces, the ultimate viability of South Vietnam against renewed aggression from the North would still depend on the U.S. commitment. With a declared and demonstrated U.S. willingness to support South Vietnam, including military actions and the provision of necessary U.S. military and economic aid, South Vietnam would have an excellent chance for survival and even prosperity, as has been the case in South Korea since the armistice that ended the Korean War in July 1953. But history records that the United States was unwilling to make such a long-term commitment in the case of Vietnam.

One could also speculate as to whether the United States might have attained a less disadvantageous cease-fire agreement, one which would have given Saigon a better chance to survive, had an experienced senior negotiator been designated to talk secretly with the Vietnamese, rather than relying almost exclusively on the peripatetic Henry Kissinger. Many other significant international events took place during this period of extended negotiations: SALT I (November 1967–May 1972), the Four Power agreement on Berlin (1971), the treaty between the two Germanys (1972), the "Autumn of Crises" (Chile, August 1970; Cienfuegos, Cuba, August 1970; Jordan and the Middle East, September 1970), opening contact with China (July 1971), the Indian-Pakistan war (November–December 1971), secret talks with Sadat of Egypt (begun in April 1972), Sadat's expulsion of the Soviets from Egypt (July 1972), and negotiations with Omar Torrijos on a new Panama Canal Treaty (serious negotiations begun in 1972).[5]

All of these significant matters not only required Kissinger's personal attention but often resulted in extensive overseas trips and talks on his part. The question naturally arises as to whether in fact he could give his undivided attention, skills, and energy to negotiating the best possible cease-fire in Vietnam. The answer is obviously no. But it remains an irrelevant one in light of Watergate and its devastating effect on the American presidency. After Watergate, there was little, if any, possibility that the United States would ever again use its military power to save South Vietnam. President Ford, unelected and unsure of himself as the commander-in-chief, realized that the American people could see no visible end to the war and the great loss of blood and treasure. Moreover he was very much aware of repetitive Congressional efforts to restrict presidential war powers and of the negative mood in the Congress toward Vietnam. The inevitable result was that the United States turned away from any long-term commitment of support to the Republic of Vietnam, even a limited one that would stop short of direct U.S. military involvement.

In summary this review of American strategy in Vietnam has revealed its many grave weaknesses and the fatal consequences that flowed from its lack of a decisive thrust. An alternative strategy has also been described, one that in my opinion promised far better chances of success. The time to have taken this different direction was in 1966 while the U.S. troop buildup was underway. As already described, the great bulk of U.S. and other non-Vietnamese troops would be deployed in the north along the DMZ and extending into Laos with the mission of physically blocking any enemy entry of forces from North Vietnam to South Vietnam. This international blocking force would provide not only a legitimacy for the true nature of the contest (North versus South rather than a purely internal civil war in the South) but also a better foundation for negotiations undertaken to end the war. Similar proposals were made during the war but they were not truly alternative strategies. The JCS concept of operations articulated in August 1965 included land actions in the Laotian corridor and in the DMZ area, but only as an element of a U.S. basic strategy that visualized the employment of U.S. forces, along with Vietnamese and third country forces, to defeat the enemy inside South Vietnam and to extend governmental control over all the country—in short, an open-ended commitment of U.S. forces. The Army chief of staff, General H.K.

Johnson; the commander of U.S. Army Pacific, General John K. Waters; the MACV commander, General Westmoreland; and NSC adviser W.W. Rostow also proposed similar ideas. None, however, were truly alternative strategies, but were encompassed within an Americanized war of attrition conducted throughout South Vietnam. This meant, among other things, that the proposals would require even more U.S. troops and American logistic effort, whereas the alternative described in this chapter was not only feasible in my view, but also doable, well within the U.S. force levels that were actually approved and deployed. The U.S. resources were there—what was missing was a bold decision, admittedly involving some risk, and an imaginative concept that would have allowed the United States and its allies to turn the strategic tables on Hanoi. Abrams understood this when he undertook the South Vietnamese attack in force into the Laotian corridor in February 1971, LAMSON 719, unfortunately five years too late. Hanoi also understood the audacity of that move and could not breathe easily until the South Vietnamese broke off the action and withdrew to South Vietnam.

The next and final chapter will go beyond the strategic aspects of the U.S. involvement and will discuss the larger lessons of the war, including those that have particular application to possible future conflicts that, unlike Vietnam, might involve vital U.S. interests, or perhaps even the survival of the United States.

10

The Larger Lessons

Let us now turn to what we as American citizens and military professionals should have learned from Vietnam. We are probably too close to this long, difficult period to grasp fully all its implications and ramifications. Many years will go by before the American people will begin to understand the war, and even more years before history makes a judgment. Nonetheless, we can examine what appear at this time to be the larger lessons, particularly those that in potential future conflicts could have far more serious consequences for the United States than was the case with Vietnam. This chapter will also address lessons that are pertinent to adequate U.S. preparations for war.

One larger lesson concerns the national interest. From the beginning our leaders realized that South Vietnam was not vital to U.S. interests. Yet for other reasons the nation became committed to the war. As hostilities dragged on interminably, with no clearly discernible end in sight, more and more questions were raised—some people even questioning the morality of the war, harking back to the theological thesis of the Middle Ages which conceived a "moral" or "just" war as one in which the good done outweighs the evil. Finally, legitimate questions were raised as to whether our goals in Southeast Asia were worth the high costs. Was the war in our national interest?

Coupled with this growing questioning of the war and our deepening commitment was a heightened public feeling that the executive branch of the government was not dealing honestly with the American people. For some this feeling of frustration became resentment, even outrage, with many believing that they were being deceived deliberately by their leaders. Right or wrong, the perception of deception existed.

So one obvious lesson is that public acceptance and support of a war require a consensus of understanding among our people that the effort is in our best interests. To achieve such a consensus the American people must perceive a clear threat, or need, to cause the United States to go to war. The fighting in Vietnam, a country unfamiliar to our people and halfway around the world, was difficult to view credibly in this light. Such a perception of threat or need is greatly enhanced if it can be clearly shown that the conflict area is vital to important U.S. interests. Vietnam was of only secondary importance to the United States, but its geopolitical position was important in that our actions, or lack thereof, in Southeast Asia would be watched carefully by our allies in the Western Pacific, especially by Japan and South Korea in Northeast Asia, an area that *is* considered vital to U.S. interests.

Whether Vietnam was vital or not, however, the fact remains that the president committed the nation to war without involving the Congress and the people in that crucial process. It seems rather obvious that a nation cannot fight a war in cold blood, sending its men and women to distant fields of battle without arousing the emotions of the people. I know of no way to accomplish that result short of a declaration of war by the Congress and national mobilization. But such public and congressional support is not attainable unless our governmental leaders, particularly those in the executive branch, themselves fully understand the enormous consequences of taking the nation to war and agree that such a step is necessary.

Our Vietnam experience convincingly demonstrated the criticality of the time element, that is the duration of hostilities. Time is somewhat less important if the American people are aroused, involved, and supportive of the war effort. But our government failed to mobilize public support, and time ran out. When critical interests are not in jeopardy but the United States decides nevertheless to commit its power, to include ground combat forces in a limited way and for limited objectives, the approximate size and likely nature of the American commitment should be thoroughly debated in the councils of government in advance. With respect to Vietnam, our leaders should have known that the American people would not stand still for a protracted war of an indeterminate nature with no foreseeable end to the U.S. commitment.

The U.S./OAS intervention in the Dominican Republic of 1965–66 provides a good example of how to use the time element to maximum advantage. We exploited the great political, military, and psychological advantages of intervening quickly in strength, and we withdrew our intervention forces as soon as conditions permitted and in any event before they wore out their welcome. The United States intervened in late April 1965 in a rapid, decisive way with a large force, peaking in early May at about 28,000 men. By June the troop contingents of five other OAS nations had arrived and the Inter-American Peace Force had been created. By early summer 1965 the IAPF had been reduced to an American brigade and a Latin American brigade, totaling about 5,000 personnel. In the secure environment guaranteed by the IAPF, an interim political solution was negotiated and a caretaker government was inaugurated in September 1965. On 1 June 1966 elections were held under peaceful conditions and the elected president was inaugurated on July 1. On 21 September the last foreign troops were withdrawn from the Dominican Republic. The intervention had lasted approximately seventeen months, an impressively brief period in light of the significant accomplishments of the IAPF. Admittedly, the Dominican affair is in no way comparable to the Vietnam problem, but the fact remains that the United States intervened with its military power in Vietnam in a graduated, piecemeal manner, overwhelmed its South Vietnamese ally with its large, pervasive military presence, and kept its forces there too long.

The approval and support of major allies in the case of hostilities are also of great value. I mean by this self-sufficient allies capable of fielding and supporting substantial forces on their own and willing to commit forces side by side with American troops. The political and psychological benefits of such allied presence can be even greater than its military worth. Other than South Vietnam itself, our only allies who committed forces were Pacific ones, and the United States bore the bulk of the cost of fielding and maintaining these so-called Free World forces. Japan did allow us to use bases on her soil in support of the war, but not a single European ally would help us. The absence of such allies badly damaged the legitimacy of our war effort. Indeed, a strong case can be made that the lack of European allies was overriding and that the United States should not have gone to war without at least one European ally. In the spring of 1954 during the siege of Dien Bien Phu, when the French requested U.S. air and naval support, President Eisenhower's decision hinged in great measure on whether the British would join the effort. When they declined, Eisenhower decided against any direct U.S. intervention with combat forces—a wise decision.

Ironically, the United States misjudged the cohesion of the communist alliance opposing it—the Soviet Union, China, and North Vietnam. We were slow to recognize the depth of the Sino-Soviet split, overestimated the threat of Chinese communist expansion, and misunderstood Chinese equities in the Vietnam War. China and the Soviet Union did deter a U.S. invasion of North Vietnam, and the United States did avoid war with those two superpowers. But in a strategic sense, both China and the United States "lost," while the Soviet Union "won." China would have preferred a relatively weak buffer state on its Southeast Asian border, but now has a "reunified" Vietnam, whose army is the third largest and one of the best in the world, and is allied with China's worst enemy, the Soviet Union. The latter, moreover, has gained another foothold in the Third World and enjoys air and naval bases in Vietnam. The Soviets have also gained a strengthened communist ally that shares their hostility toward China and can hold its own vis-a-vis the noncommunist nations in Southeast Asia.

This failure to understand the nature of Sino-Soviet relations cannot be charged to any particular person or group. Rather, it is a reflection of unsophisticated and uninformed American views at the time. Today, although Americans like to see themselves as more worldly and better educated, the root cause of such misjudgments—ignorance—may still be present. What do we know, for example, about Chinese-Indian relations as they have evolved over the centuries? Do we have enough political scientists, economists, and military experts who are at the same time Soviet, Chinese, or Indian scholars? Or for that matter, Middle Eastern, Latin-American, African, or Pacific Basin scholars? More to the point, however, what is the United States doing to develop generalists, as opposed to specialists, who can interrelate domestic and international aspects of issues, and integrate political, economic, and military considerations in an overall strategic or geopolitical context?

Like other so-called "sciences," the employment of military force—in peace, cold war, or actual conflict—is an art, not an exact science. It is supremely important that our national leaders, civilian and military, have a fundamental understanding of the capabilities and limitations of military power. Vietnam demonstrated how the lack of such understanding can lead to disastrous failure.

Given the essentially unusable nature of nuclear warfare (strategic intercontinental, or tactical/theater), conventional—that is, nonnuclear—is the more likely kind of warfare that might involve the United States. This is not to say that nuclear weapons are less important; to the contrary, they are of prime importance. But nuclear warfare is a vastly different matter and the world has had no human experience with it since Hiroshima and Nagasaki. Indeed, the effects of nuclear warfare, in my opinion, are impossible for the human mind to comprehend. At any rate, I have limited my discussion of military force to conventional terms, albeit with the ever present possibility of nuclear warfare in the background.

Limited war—that is, war fought with limited objectives, or within limited territorial boundaries, or with the commitment of only limited resources—is in many ways more difficult to conduct than an allout effort. Willingness to fight a limited war implies that vital interests, such as survival, are not at stake, and that although important interests nevertheless are involved, they do not warrant the employment of all available military force. Limited war entails the development of a wide range of rules of engagement concerning weaponry, territorial limitations/sanctuaries, limitations on nations considered to be belligerents, and the like. The complications of limited warfare, including the constant calculations of escalation or widening of the conflict, are obvious. And, as I have already noted in the context of Vietnam, "success" or "victory" is extremely difficult to define in a limited war.

At the risk of being pedantic, I would like to suggest that our civilian and military leaders involved in national security should be well grounded in the major principles involved in the use of military force. These principles are clearly applicable to conventional conflict as well as to unconventional warfare, and at least in part are relevant to nuclear warfare. The time-honored principles of war remain highly pertinent and valid even today. The first principle, *the objective,* focuses on our military aims. What is to be accomplished? Goals must be clearly defined, decisive, and attainable. The second principle, *the offensive,* states in broad terms how the objective will be attained. It stresses the fact that offensive action is necessary to achieve decisive results, to seize the initiative, and to maintain freedom of action. In Vietnam, we violated both principles. We lacked a clear objective and an attainable strategy of a decisive nature, and we relinquished the advantages of the strategic offensive to Hanoi. The best of initiatives, resources, exemplary conduct, and fighting spirit cannot make up for these deficiencies.

Other principles of war include *mass* (concentrating superior power at the critical time and place for a decisive purpose); *economy of force* (skillful and prudent use of combat power); and *maneuver* (the disposition of force to maximize combat power). All three principles support the second principle concerning how to conduct operations. In Vietnam we could not apply these principles effectively. Our flawed strategy precluded the concentration of force, the principle of *mass,* in a decisive way. Likewise, the deployment of U.S. forces in numerous areas all over Vietnam tended to create an open-ended commitment and prevented the effective application of the principles of *economy of force* and *maneuver.*[1] The graduated, piecemeal employment of airpower against North Vietnam violated many principles of war, in particular *mass.*

In contrast to the actual U.S. strategy pursued, the alternative strategy discussed in the previous chapter embodies all of the above principles— the objective, the offensive, mass, economy of force, and maneuver.

The final major principle I will mention is *unity of command* (vesting a single commander with the requisite authority to obtain unity of effort toward a common goal). It did not exist with respect to U.S. efforts in Southeast Asia. CINCPAC—the unified commander in the Pacific with headquarters in Hawaii far removed from the war zone—had overall control and direction of the air war against North Vietnam, while COMUS-MACV ran operations in South Vietnam. The U.S. ambassador in Saigon had a large if not predominant voice in South Vietnam but no control over our ambassadors in Thailand, Laos, and Cambodia. For optimum overall supervision, the ambassador and the military commander, both located in Saigon and working in close harmony, should have exercised political and military control over all U.S. operations and activities in Southeast Asia.

In South Vietnam, HQ MACV tried to be both the U.S. theater headquarters, with critically important politico-military responsibilities, and the operational headquarters that directed U.S. operations in great detail, two very different but equally demanding roles. A more effective arrangement would have separated the two tasks by establishing a separate American field headquarters to conduct U.S., or at least predominantly U.S., military operations. Such a separate field commander could have stayed in close contact with important engagements, free of the continuing necessity to return to Saigon, and devoted his entire attention to operational and planning matters.

MACV also directly handled the advisory effort in support of the armed forces of the Republic of Vietnam, a third major area deserving the undivided attention of its commander. The results were less than optimal. There should have been a separate senior Army military advisory group commander of four-star rank with clout second only to COMUSMACV himself and dedicated solely to the training and development of the South Vietnamese Army with the objective of improving its operational capabilities. This was admittedly difficult in a situation where ARVN was fighting for its survival, but it was paramount that every U.S. adviser keep this objective constantly in mind.

Our allied command arrangements, too, left much to be desired. We should have developed a better system than the separate, parallel lash-up we used with the South Vietnamese and should have given the senior commander operational control of all forces involved in situations requiring close coordination between American and South Vietnamese troops. Unity of effort would have been enhanced even further had we exercised more leverage on the South Vietnamese government and its top leadership with respect to the selection of key commanders, province chiefs, and district chiefs, and had we insisted on high standards of both operational performance and personal conduct. We had nothing to lose by applying more direct and greater leverage with respect to key personnel and I am convinced that our relationships with our South Vietnamese friends would not have suffered unduly.

Third country forces in Vietnam, so-called Free World forces, numbering about 60,000 troops, were valuable military, political, and psychological assets for the United States and its principal ally in the war, the Republic of Vietnam. As I have pointed out, however, command and control, planning, and conduct of operations were essentially decentralized to the American, South Vietnamese, South Korean, and other Free World commanders operating in South Vietnam. Although a combined campaign plan was developed annually, it was essentially a U.S. plan dominated by American concepts. There was no combined command with a combined planning, operations, and logistic staff. Instead, the various national commanders mostly developed their own plans and ran their own shows according to their assigned missions and geographical areas of responsibility.

The ultimate result was unfortunate because after American and other allied troops withdrew, the South Vietnamese were left with no survival strategy of their own, only the flawed strategy inherited from the United States. Nor had the Americans adequately prepared them for this basic national security task. Overly reliant on American leadership and support, the South Vietnamese did not develop the self-reliance and initiative needed for survival, particularly when U.S. military and economic aid was severely reduced.

The Vietnam experience pointedly brought out the woeful unpreparedness of the United States to establish an adequate intelligence organization in a "new" overseas theater of operations, that is, one where there are no U.S. commands or forces in being in the area, as for example in Europe or in Korea. It was years before a competent MACV J-2 organization became operational—an inexcusable performance. In peacetime the art of intelligence and requisite intelligence resources for field operations must not be allowed to atrophy, but must be maintained at all times. My comment applies in particular to intelligence on ground military organizations and operations.

In Vietnam, moreover, unity of the U.S. intelligence effort was lacking. As the senior U.S. commander, the MACV commander should have exercised overall direction of intelligence collection and analysis (as distinguished from covert activities) in the area, including the CIA's, while still authorizing the CIA station chief in Saigon to submit his own views to the U.S. ambassador and CIA headquarters in Washington. To avoid the confusion that resulted from allowing both the CIA and MACV to work with South Vietnamese intelligence organizations, MACV should have been given coordinating authority for these activities.

Since good, timely national intelligence is critical to the nation's performance in wartime and equally important to the nation's prospects of achieving its overall policy objectives beyond and after the war, it goes without saying that the intelligence views of the Pentagon should not have undue influence with the president and his national security adviser at the expense of other legitimate views within the intelligence community. Rather it is imperative that the president have the full benefit of divergent intelligence judgments on the larger, more strategic issues critically affecting the outcome of the war. Our Vietnam experience should tell us that when the views of the Central Intelligence Agency—the preeminent national intelligence organization—are not given adequate consideration in the policy councils of government, flawed policy judgments are more likely to result and the chances of policy failure are raised accordingly. In time of national emergency or war, the director of Central Intelligence should continue to serve the president directly and to maintain his central intelligence role. But he should act in such a way as not to hamper the Department of Defense in carrying out its responsibilities. Current statutes and executive orders are not entirely clear in this respect. They should be reviewed and modified to underscore the importance of the central intelligence role in time of war or a national emergency.

The nation's organization for defense is a key element of our ability to prosecute a war successfully. By statute, the chain of command runs from the president, as commander-in-chief of all U.S. armed forces, to the secretary of defense and then to the unified commanders. By custom, not statute, the secretary of defense normally exercises command through the JCS. The JCS, however, do not exercise command but assist the secretary of defense in directing the unified commanders, orders from the JCS being issued under the authority and in the name of the secretary of defense. By law, all operational forces of the Army, Navy, Marine Corps, and Air Force must be assigned to one of the unified commands.

Subject to the approval of the president and secretary of defense, the JCS establish unified commands responsible for contingency planning in various areas of the world and assign to each command appropriate forces from the several services. Currently these commands with geographic areas of responsibility are the European Command, Pacific Command, Atlantic Command, Central Command (Egypt, the Arabian Peninsula, Iraq, Iran, and the Horn of Africa), and Southern Command (generally Latin America). In addition, there is the Readiness Command, with no designated geographical area of responsibility, to which are assigned the Army's operational units in the United States (Forces Command), and the tactical air units of the Air Force in the United States (Tactical Air Command). At present, no unified command exists for Africa South of the Sahara. The European Command, in addition to its responsibilities with respect to NATO Europe, is also responsible for contingency planning for the Israel-Lebanon-Syria confrontational area.

The unified commanders do not directly command their assigned forces but direct them through their component commanders, who command the forces provided by their respective services—Army, Navy, Air Force, and Marines. Each component commander looks to his parent service for the administrative and logistic support as well as the maintenance (personnel and materiel) of his assigned forces. Thus the unified commanders, although responsible for the readiness and operations of their forces, have no direct authority or responsibility for (and usually little voice in) providing the people, things, and money needed to maintain readiness. These resources must come from the separate services.

This anomaly stems from the basic fact that the services by law are organized, administered, and supported as separate, autonomous entities. This cannot be fundamentally altered unless the law of the land is drastically changed and the services are unified. Although I am opposed for many cogent reasons to complete unification of the services, I will not address the question, which is beyond the scope of this book.

Because of the way in which the Department of Defense is organized, the five equal JCS—the chairman and the Army, Navy, Marine, and Air Force chiefs—must function on a cooperative basis, a committee system, if you will. This is one principal reason why the JCS are constantly criticized (in large measure unfairly) for not being able to agree on major issues or to articulate clear, incisive recommendations to the secretary of defense. So long as there are separate services, each with statutory responsibilities of fundamental importance, there will be fundamental differences of opinion among the service chiefs and hence the JCS. This is both a weakness and a strength, but there is no way to change it except by a drastic reorganization of the Department of Defense that would actually unify the services.

This problem extends very naturally to the staffs involved. The JCS are assisted in carrying out their statutory joint duties by the Joint Staff, composed of staff officers from each service. But the service chiefs (i.e., all of the JCS except the chairman) also have service staffs to assist them. Again there is no way to eliminate friction and disagreement within the Joint Staff or between it and the service staffs, short of unifying the services. Moreover, only the service staffs have the depth of technical knowledge needed to handle matters unique to each service; the Joint Staff could not possibly duplicate the reservoir of service know-how found in the several service staffs. This statement also applies to the joint staff of a unified command, as distinguished from the service staffs of the component commanders.

Periodically proposals surface to reform the JCS system, but it must be recognized that, given the present organization of the Department of Defense, drastic reform is simply not possible. There is nonetheless room for much improvement within the present system. To several recent proposals for such "reform," my reactions are as follows:

Proposal 1: Create a four-star deputy chairman of the JCS. This is neither necessary nor desirable. Only one individual, the chairman, should exercise the authority and assume the responsibilities that go with that position. Moreover, the service chiefs should not be relegated to a position of influence below that of a deputy chairman. The present arrangement presented no particular problem during the Vietnam War. The senior service chief present (determined by the date he became a member of the JCS) acted as chairman during the latter's absence. Planned trips were coordinated in advance among the chiefs, and the secretary of defense was kept informed. It worked well. A better alternative than creating a deputy chairman would be to rotate the duty among the service chiefs for periods of three or four months at a time, and require their presence during those assigned periods.

Proposal 2: Strengthen the roles of the JCS chairman and the unified commanders. These are desirable goals provided the service chiefs and staffs at the national level and the component commanders and staffs at unified command level are not excluded from the joint process. The JCS chairman should play the predominant role in the JCS, but to deny the service chiefs a role in the joint process would be a grave mistake involving great risks. In this connection, the president should regularly see *all* the chiefs, not just the chairman. The unified commanders should be brought into the staffing processes of the services, the JCS, and the Office of the Secretary of Defense, processes that determine the level of resources to be provided to component commands under the unified commanders. But this change would in no way affect the basic service responsibilities prescribed by law. Determining this resource level is difficult in peacetime when the unified commanders are competing for the relatively limited resources available. Once hostilities break out, however, priorities between theaters are usually set clearly and quickly. During the Vietnam War, Southeast Asia received first priority, and CINCPAC and the MACV commander played key roles in determining the resource levels established for that theater of operations.

Proposal 3: Strengthen the joint educational system and improve the quality of personnel assigned to the Joint Staff. These are sound, attainable goals, but in my opinion they would require a major change in the concept of what constitutes a full military career. The current limits of thirty years of service for colonels and thirty-five years for almost all general and flag officers do not allow them enough time to become thoroughly grounded in their parent service *and* to gain the experience required for the Joint Staff. The thirty-five-year limit also inhibits the development of capable chiefs of staff. Forty years, including a four-year tour as service chief, should be the *minimum* total length of service for a chief of service. (The Joint Staff, incidentally, during the Vietnam years was of outstanding quality. Most of the staff had previous joint experience and many had served with major joint headquarters in the Pacific area.)

Proposal 4: Create a Council of Advisers. Proposals to this effect would eliminate the JCS as presently known, taking the service chiefs out of the joint arena and substituting a council of senior military advisers for the JCS. This is unsound and unworkable. The "clout" of the JCS stems from the dual role of the service chiefs as members of the JCS. No one will pay any attention to a senior military officer with only advisory responsibilities. The president and the secretary of defense are going to turn to a service chief for advice; to the chief of Naval Operations for naval advice, for example, *not* to a naval officer with no operational responsibilities. Moreover, the proposed advisers, divorced from their service of origin and the real world, would tend toward an "ivory tower" outlook.

Proposal 5: Forward dissenting views within the JCS to the secretary of defense. This is a highly desirable policy. It is dangerous to submerge divergent views on important issues, and a disservice to civilian authority to infer JCS agreement when, in fact, the chiefs disagree. This occurred during the Vietnam War, a matter which I underscored in chapter one dealing with the JCS and Vietnam in the 1963–67 period.

There are other areas in which the JCS could do a better job than they have done in the past. They should be able to sort out issues arising out of role and mission conflicts, especially when brought on by advancing technology. Technological change is inevitable and no service or its chief can prevent it. Examples of the issues involved are the roles and mission implications of missiles versus aircraft, coordinating air defense and air operations, and coordinating electronic warfare operations. A good example occurred during the Vietnam War. In chapter one I described how the secretary of defense had to decide on an interservice controversy over the helicopter, a controversy that extended from Washington to Vietnam. The JCS should have settled this role and mission issue among themselves.

The JCS also should take more initiative in proposing strategic policy guidance and related fiscal policy guidance for issuance by the secretary of defense. And they should be able to find a way of involving the unified commanders in resource determinations concerning their commands without derogating basic service responsibilities. These matters are central to effective strategic planning and adequate preparations for war—in peacetime, the most important contributions the JCS can make.

Those who frequently blame the JCS for much of what seems to be wrong in the Department of Defense should bear in mind that the chiefs can only advise their civilian superiors on the strategic implications of the international scene and make recommendations as to the kind of defense establishment needed to protect U.S. interests. Decisions pertaining to the U.S. role in the world, U.S. foreign policy, the role worldwide of the Department of Defense in support of U.S. policy, U.S. strategy in time of war, the size, structure, and composition of U.S. armed forces, and defense budget levels—all lie clearly in the civilian domain, far beyond the authority of the military. Thus, strategic and political guidance, as well as fiscal guidance, must of necessity emanate from the civilian leadership, that is, the secretary of defense and the president, although they should be approved only after the views of the JCS have been fully taken into account.

This brings me to the adage that having the right people in the right jobs is in many ways far more significant than organization. Reorganization cannot compensate for the lack of capable, experienced people in key positions, nor can organizational changes accomplish much when key personnel do not remain in a job very long.

The secretary of defense, in particular, should be a person with broad background in international affairs and national security matters. He should have the same kind of background and experience that we seek in a secretary of state. Unfortunately businessmen, scientists, lawyers, systems analysts, or budget analysts do not necessarily make good secretaries of defense. These more technical and administrative capabilities are very much needed, however, in the positions of the deputy and assistant secretaries of defense. (Qualifications similar to those desired for the secretary of defense are also highly desirable for individuals selected to be service secretaries.)

Of the fifteen secretaries of defense appointed to the office to date, only five—George C. Marshall, Robert A. Lovett, Melvin R. Laird, Donald H. Rumsfeld, and James R. Schlesinger—possessed this kind of education and experience, a background that in my opinion would be extremely valuable in the conceptualization of defense strategy and the formulation of defense policies. The other ten secretaries had to learn on the job, some, such as Elliot L. Richardson, learning rather quickly, while others never got very far up on the learning curve.

The tenure of our defense secretaries has been markedly different. Not counting the present incumbent, the average tenure has been only about two and one-third years, scarcely long enough to accomplish much in a field as complex and ill-defined as defense. McNamara holds the record, slightly more than seven years, while three others served out a full term of four years. Admittedly it has always been difficult to entice good people to serve in the government as political appointees, and unfortunately it is getting even more difficult as a result of overly restrictive and essentially impractical conflict-of-interest legislation and a federal pay cap imposed in recent years.

To be sure, the problem of attracting high calibre men and women to serve as political appointees in our government is not confined to the Pentagon. The same situation exists with respect to the Department of State and other departments, the CIA, and the NSC staff in the White House. On the one hand our country does not seem to be producing Stimsons, Marshalls, Lovetts, and Achesons any more; and on the other our government continues to make it even less attractive, if not impossible, to serve. I have no answers to this dilemma, but I have the uncomfortable feeling that while the situation is worsening, no one appears to be particularly concerned.

Civil-military relations in the United States, especially at the highest levels where political and strategic issues become entwined, have not always been close and harmonious. In fact, the history of those relations contains several stormy chapters. There has been a tendency to blame solely the civilian political leaders of the United States for what went wrong in Vietnam, to point out that they had the ultimate authority and power of decision. One body of opinion believes that things would have turned out differently had the military not "had their hands tied." I have much difficulty with this thesis because I feel that our top-level military leaders must share the onus of failure. And this leads to another larger lesson concerning the civil-military relations within the executive branch at the seat of government.

In the great emergencies bound to arise in the future, it is imperative that our highest civilian and military heads be in close, even if not cordial, contact with each other, maintaining a continuous and candid discussion of the purpose of the undertaking, the risks involved, and the probable costs, human and material. Differing views must be surfaced to the highest level—the president—in order that no false sense of security is engendered through what appears to be unanimity. In fact, it would be beneficial for the president to seek diversity in terms of background, experience, and known military views when selecting his military chiefs. In any event, a hostile relationship between our civilian heads and the Joint Chiefs of Staff invites disaster. Indeed, to attain essential interaction, the civilian and military heads have no choice but to trust each other, freely exchange their views, and share their thoughts.

In our system of government, the president, with his dual role as civilian chief executive and commander-in-chief of the armed forces, is the indispensable key to national security. For the president to control the nation's armed forces, he must command them; he cannot delegate this to his secretary of defense or to the military chiefs. He must have direct access to the Joint Chiefs of Staff, collectively and individually, and must regularly see them. If he shunts them off or allows his secretary of defense to isolate the chiefs, he does so at the nation's peril. The president *is* the commander-in-chief and there is no substitute for his forceful and visible leadership in discharging this supreme command function over the Department of Defense and the armed forces. The military chiefs, in turn, must understand and be willing to accept the reality that their commander-in-chief will no doubt reject JCS recommendations which do not suit the political purposes or goals that the president seeks.

But in Vietnam there was ample evidence of poor civil-military relations at the highest levels in Washington. Senior U.S. military leaders recognized the weaknesses of the U.S. strategy being pursued, but unfortunately seemed unable to articulate their misgivings and communicate them effectively to their civilian superiors. Military views and judgments varied in many respects and often reflected fundamentally different viewpoints held by each service. The central point, however, is that our military leaders failed to get across the message that the U.S. strategy was not working and over time would probably fail to achieve stated U.S. objectives. Indeed, the JCS apparently did not clearly and unequivocally tell the president and secretary of defense that the strategy was fatally flawed and that U.S. objectives were not achievable unless the strategy was changed. Ironically, Defense Secretary McNamara in November 1967, apparently without consulting the JCS, did advise President Johnson that U.S. strategy was not proving to be effective. McNamara discussed two alternative courses of action—(1) reducing the level of U.S. military operations in the South and of U.S. air operations in the North, ending all bombing of North Vietnam by the end of 1967; or (2) widening the war—and then recommended the first option because he considered the second too risky. Late in 1967 Johnson and his principal advisers, after carefully considering McNamara's proposal, rejected it as a thinly disguised proposal for U.S. disengagement. Subsequently in March 1968 Johnson replaced his defense secretary.[2]

The present national security statutes which place the secretary of defense in the operational chain of command between the president and the unified commanders in the field are a recipe for disaster in wartime. This command arrangement has very serious flaws. Our experience in the Vietnam War convinces me that in time of crisis, emergency, or war, the operational chain of command should run from the president/commander-in-chief directly to the JCS and thence to the unified commanders. The secretary of defense should not be in a position to veto or second-guess the president on an operational decision involving instructions to the combatant forces. There can be only one commander-in-chief and he should be able to make final decisions with the advice of his cabinet, the JCS, and the NSC staff, then transmit his instructions directly to the JCS and the commanders in the field. Moreover, present statutes should be revised so that the JCS are formally placed in the chain rather than continued in their present off-line advisory position.

Under the present law, the JCS can be subjected to conflicting orders and guidance. This happened both to General Wheeler while he was CJCS, and to his successor, Admiral Moorer. Both men, Wheeler in 1970 and Moorer in 1972, received orders personally from President Nixon with instructions that Secretary of Defense Laird was not to be informed. Military men obviously must not be placed in such an untenable position. Under the circumstances these incidents did not matter very much because the Vietnam War did not put our survival at risk, nor was Vietnam vital to U.S. interests. In future situations in which national survival might indeed be at stake, I do not believe the nation can accept this state of affairs. Admittedly much, if not all, will depend on the courage and wit of our president, as well as on the valor and skill of our armed forces, but I do not believe that we can afford to take a chance on having crucial orders issued by the commander-in-chief at a critical time delayed, amended, or otherwise thwarted.

Likewise, to reinforce the direct relationships that the CJCS, the JCS, and each service chief should have with the commander-in-chief, I strongly support changes in current legislation. The JCS chairman should be made a statutory member of the National Security Council, not just an adviser. All too often he is excluded from the high councils of the government, some of which, although more informal and smaller than the normal NSC meetings, carry much weight. When military advice is deliberately excluded from such councils, the nation is not well served. Similarly, the law should be made more specific about the relationships between the military chiefs and their commander-in-chief. These military men cannot carry out their role as intended by the Congress if they are inhibited from direct contact with the president.

Having briefly examined our national organization for defense, and civil-military relations at the seat of government, let me turn to a look at how America has fought its past wars and how Vietnam fits into that perspective. Such a historical examination brings out some cogent, if not striking, facts.[3]

American armies at war have been at various times small, professional volunteer forces; large, mass, conscripted armies composed mainly of citizen soldiers; or a mixture of both. By the time of the Mexican War the regular Army had been professionalized. During that war both the volunteer professionals and volunteer citizen soldiers with relatively little training performed very well.

In the Civil War, and again in World Wars I and II, the United States raised and sustained very large armies. Only partly volunteer, these forces had to rely on conscription to carry on the war, generally drafting men for the duration. These were total wars involving the whole nation in a political, economic, and industrial sense, and employing mass armies of citizen soldiers in a grinding, relentless warfare of attrition. Out of this experience grew the Army's conviction that victory in such allout warfare lies in directly confronting and methodically destroying the enemy's armed forces.

After the Civil War, the American Army reverted to a small, professional volunteer service, and for the rest of the nineteenth century fought our Indian wars as a frontier army. Partly constabulary in nature, it conducted a mobile war with the objective of destroying the warriors of the American Indian tribes in the West. The Spanish-American War did not last long enough to put the frontier Army to a severe test, but it did give the Army a taste of the frustrations of countering guerrilla warfare during the Philippine insurrection until it was officially declared over in 1902.

After World War II, the Korean War gave the United States its first experience with the problems of fighting a major limited war of significant duration. The conflict was sustained by the draft, which allowed the United States to mobilize a large Army and send a substantial force overseas. But destruction of the enemy's armed forces was no longer the military objective; instead, the war was fought for limited objectives, on a limited territorial scale, and with limited means. The consequent political strains at home hurt the morale of the fighting men and shook the Army's high command and its relations with civilian authority.

Vietnam was, of course, another limited war, invoking a broader, more liberal interpretation of the U.S. policy of containment, and in a sense was an extension of the Korean War. But Vietnam shook the morale of our fighting men to a far greater degree than did Korea. It left our military leaders confounded, dismayed, and discouraged, and it caused deep divisions in our society that have yet to heal.

Analyzing how well the United States has done with respect to mobilizing its manpower in wartime and sustaining the strength of its forces in the field is also revealing. Indeed, the U.S. Army in its long history has yet to devise a wholly satisfactory way of maintaining the strength and integrity of combat units long exposed to the unremitting hardships and dangers of prolonged combat. Up through the Civil War the Army did not have a replacement system. Regiments fought in campaign after campaign until they were no longer effective. In World Wars I and II the Army organized an individual replacement system which continues today in peacetime. But in wartime, combat units usually remained in the line, exhausted or not, for the duration of the war, rarely getting any respite by assignment to lighter, rear-area duties.[4]

Nevertheless, our World War II replacement system was vastly superior to the systems used in the Korean and Vietnam wars. The main difference was that in World War II (until after V-E Day in Europe, when a rotation system was established in the Pacific), troops served for the duration, while in Korea a point rotation system was inaugurated in 1951 that established thirty-six points as the criterion for return to the United States for discharge from the service. Four points were awarded per month in the battle line, three for duty within the designated combat zone, and two for service elsewhere in Korea. Thus, a combat infantryman went home after nine months, while a soldier outside the combat zone had to serve eighteen months in Korea.

This system hurt unit cohesion in Korea as men counted the days to rotation and lost any sense of identity with their unit. Unit pride and esprit suffered as well as teamwork within units. According to one study made after the Korean War, the enemy did not rate American soldiers very high, noting that they lacked aggressiveness and stamina under pressure.[5] When a similar point system went into effect in the Pacific in May 1945 during World War II, it had a disastrous effect on the division I was serving in, still in active combat against the Japanese in northern Luzon. Rifle companies suddenly lost all their most experienced men, with only green replacements available to bring units up to strength. In my opinion the program resulted in unnecessary casualties among new arrivals because of the dearth of combat-experienced leaders. There was a grimly humorous side to it, however, as soldiers compared the depth of a "120-point" foxhole dug by a veteran just before rotation with the shallowness of the zero-point foxhole of a new rifleman.

In Vietnam the one-year tour policy had the same effect as a rotation system and badly damaged unit cohesion. It also greatly compounded the Army's problem of maintaining strength in combat units, especially rifle companies. In both Korea and Vietnam rifle companies were rarely if ever at full authorized strength and operated routinely at strengths as low as 60 percent of authorized. In Korea rifle companies sometimes fought with musters as low as 25 percent authorized strength, the overall manpower problem being aggravated (as was the case in Vietnam) by overly elaborate construction in base areas and a standard of living that was inappropriate for an active theater of operations.[6]

Although generalizations often lead to serious misconceptions, it is widely recognized that American armies, particularly in the twentieth century, have relied heavily on the technological superiority of their arms and equipment, as well as on the industrial capacity of the nation, once geared to wartime production of vast amounts of materiel. And so the allegation is frequently made that the U.S. Army pins its hopes for battle success on heavy, massed firepower rather than on the professional skill and tenacity of its infantry, who in the final analysis must close with the enemy and finish him off. This explains why the Army tends to put its more highly educated and qualified personnel into artillery and armor units rather than infantry, and traditionally has looked upon the artillery as the elite combat arm. In my parochial view, such attitudes are seriously flawed. The training of truly professional infantry is more complex and difficult than many military men realize, and all too often it is relatively neglected. In fact, good, solid, realistic training is the only way that the American Army can overcome its tendency to rely on the weight of firepower to compensate for any lack of professional skill in the art of maneuver.[7]

A recent critique of the Army's martial skills concerns the European theater during World War II and covers the campaigns from the Normandy landings to the end of the war. It is quite harsh in its judgment of many senior U.S. Army commanders and flatly asserts that the German army was qualitatively superior throughout World War II. The author argues that the preponderance of American materiel weight, not professional skill, brought success, and that our victory was more costly (in lives, time, and materiel) than it should have been.[8]

As I have already pointed out, the U.S. Army and its South Vietnamese allies in Vietnam at times demonstrated a tendency to rely on superior firepower and technology rather than on professional skill and soldierly qualities. Moreover, during Vietnam there were U.S. officials who constantly sought to develop some magical scientific breakthrough—something akin to the Manhattan Project of World War II that developed the first atomic bomb—that was to produce dramatic results and bring the war to a quick close. But it was a will-o'-the-wisp, an unattainable, somewhat foolish wish.

Vietnam generally was a war involving small unit operations as opposed to large ground, air, or naval formations or large joint task forces. Major joint airborne or amphibious operations were not conducted in Southeast Asia. Nevertheless, the need for effective interservice coordination and training was reaffirmed in Vietnam because there are very important joint operational interfaces that must be permanently organized and capable of handling sustained operations, whether large units are involved or not. One such joint endeavor concerns the close air support of ground forces; another coordinates the actions of ground air defenses and tactical air operations. These joint organizational arrangements are essential for successful air-ground operations during any major land campaign. In Vietnam they functioned well.

The Army/Air Force land-based team and the Navy/Marine Corps sea-based combination usually operate reasonably well, each team in its own environment. As our Vietnam experience bore out, Marine and Army ground elements can operate very effectively together on land, and with some practice Army and Marine combat ground troops can work out good close air support relationships with the aviation elements of any service. But it is much more difficult for land-based aviation to work closely with sea-based aviation. Aircraft characteristics, operational doctrine, tactics, techniques, communications systems, weapons systems, munitions, and sometimes even the fuel used are different for each service and not always compatible. This fact of life underlay the prudent decision in Southeast Asia to keep U.S. Air Force land-based operations and U.S. Navy carrier operations more or less geographically separate.

Joint air/surface operations are inherently easier to coordinate for the Navy and the Marines. Their shore installations and bases are usually located near each other, and they go to sea and operate together habitually. The land-based services, on the other hand, are completely separate, autonomous, and self-supporting administratively and logistically. Joint training which exercises the necessary operational interfaces between the Army and the Air Force does not just happen but must be deliberately planned, scheduled, and conducted. Left to their own devices, the Army and Air Force will not conduct such joint training on a regular basis.

Joint training is one of the basic peacetime tasks of the unified commanders overseas, who conduct periodic joint field exercises involving the forces assigned to their operational control from the various services. In the United States the unified command known as the U.S. Readiness Command performs this training function with respect to its assigned tactical air units (Air Force) and ground combat units (Army). Many experienced military leaders attribute the outstanding Army-Air Force cooperation in Vietnam at least in part to the demanding joint field exercises and other joint training undertaken before the war by the U.S. Readiness Command and its predecessor, the U.S. Strike Command.

In addition to such conventional joint operations, there are other joint operations of a less conventional nature—so-called special operations—which concern extraordinary missions and require not only special skills, training, and equipment, but above all a special kind of people. By nature this work entails high-risk missions which demand meticulous planning, repeated rehearsals, perfect timing and coordination, daring leadership, and men with uncommon valor and tenacity. Once committed, such operations must press on under their tactical field commander to the end, regardless of obstacles. Operational decisions are decentralized; senior military and civilian officials at higher headquarters must resist interfering or risk inviting failure. Success in such ventures comes only to the bold, and the bold must be left to their own intuition, judgments, and decisions.

Simplicity becomes even more crucial in such operations; involving forces and headquarters from too many services in one operation is especially inadvisable. The Son Tay POW camp raid during the Vietnam War, described in an earlier chapter, is a classic example of a well conceived, thoroughly planned and rehearsed, and boldly executed special operation.

But what about future conflicts involving the United States? Some sobering facts are in order: The United States no longer enjoys clearcut technological superiority over its most dangerous potential adversary, the Soviet Union. The United States is no longer the arsenal of democracy; the Soviets far outproduce the United States in every category of weapons systems. Less powerful potential adversaries are no longer primitively armed. They have sophisticated weapons in quantity and have access to highly professional military advice and training.

I conclude that America must change its traditional way of fighting a war. We cannot afford to follow the unwise, unsound, and wasteful manpower and logistic policies we have pursued in past wars, particularly in Korea and Vietnam. We cannot count on possessing greatly superior weapons and equipment in unlimited amounts. Rather, we must, as a matter of previously announced policy, plan to mobilize the necessary men and women to meet a major emergency with the intention of their serving for the duration. We must continue to develop quality weapons and equipment that can compete with those of anticipated adversaries, but at the same time stress affordability, reliability, simplicity of maintenance, and producibility as clearly equal priorities. In other words, we must produce good, serviceable weapons that we can afford to buy in the numbers needed. We must also continue to stress professionalism in our armed services, but give realistic, professional training the priority it demands as the number one peacetime mission of every service.

In trying to reach any final conclusions about our Vietnam experience, questions arise for which I have no sufficient answers. One of the most intriguing questions and perhaps one involving a critically important lesson concerns the seeming "David and Goliath" image evoked by the war. Can a great power and a democracy wage war successfully against a small power and a totalitarian state, especially if that great power has a national conscience and is influenced and inhibited by "world opinion"? Putting it in a different way, can a great power fight a limited war against a small power which is waging total war, especially if that country is being supported by large outside powers? Was it really practicable for the United States to fight a limited war against North Vietnam, whose war-making capabilities, other than manpower, were provided almost entirely by the Soviet Union and China? It seems to me that the answer lies closer to "no" than to "yes."

Vietnam raised hard personal questions for many Americans to face—reconciling their sense of loyalty to our country, for example, with their personal views about the war, views that ranged from very pro to very con. The young man facing the draft had little choice—either to serve his country if and when called, or to flee to a haven like Canada—but the risks and costs either way were high. The high school teachers and college professors who urged our young men to avoid the draft, on the other hand, had nothing to lose except possibly their self-respect. And neither did the "draft counselors" who made money out of the plight of our young people. To their great credit, the large majority of our young men served when they were called. Congressmen and Senators spoke out against the war but continued to vote appropriations to fight the war. Were their actions in support of the war despite their personal views commendable, or were they the height of hypocrisy?

For the American soldier already drafted and the serving career military professional, there was likewise little choice but to serve. Desertion was not a suitable way out for an individual who was opposed to the war. Having taken an oath to uphold the Constitution and to obey the orders of appointed leaders, refusing to obey orders or inciting a mutiny were not attractive options, either.

Then there is the matter of public support in wartime. How is it defined? How is it measured? Who makes such assessments? Who influences and mostly determines the extent of public support—the leaders or the followers? Or the news media and well known commentators? Can partisan politics ever be eliminated in a democracy like the United States? Is bipartisan or nonpartisan support a thing of the past? What is a popular war? Has there ever been such a war? I cannot cite one from our American experience. The rebels who fought for and the people who supported our revolutionary cause during the War for Independence were in the minority. Yet had it not been for the Continental Army and General George Washington, there would have been no United States. Our Civil War was not particularly popular in the North—bloody riots against the draft broke

out in Chicago, and draft-age men could easily buy their way out of fighting for their country. Still, were it not for the Union Army and President
Abraham Lincoln, there would be no United States as we know it today.
The Indian wars were a key to the opening and settling of the West, but
the great mass of our people hardly knew that the wars were going on.
World War I and World War II were relatively popular, but by no means
overwhelmingly so. Where do Korea and Vietnam fit in? Are we a better
people, a greater nation as a consequence of having fought those limited
wars? I might venture a response. We are probably wiser, but certainly
not stronger.

Some years ago when I visited the British Army Museum in London,
I was impressed by the way in which the history of the British Army was
presented. Basically the display briefly and succinctly gave for each war
involving the British Army the immediate and more remote causes of the
war, British casualties, and the outcome, politically, territorially, eco-
nomically, and the like. As I went through the display covering centuries
of English history in a few minutes, I was struck by what perhaps should
have been obvious from the outset. The history of the British Army also
chronicles the history of Great Britain. And so it is in our own case—
the history of the U.S. Army is inseparable from the history of the United
States. We who have been or are privileged now to serve in the American
Army should keep that fact in mind.

Although each of our armed services is unique and different, the U.S.
Army holds a special position of significance and trust. Its ranks come
from the people, the country's roots, and it is closest to the people. In
foreign confrontations the United States is not committed until its land
forces—its Army—is committed. And in the event of hostilities, the Army
historically has borne the brunt of war, the human cost, taking the great
bulk of the casualties. The Army as an institution knows this and has
been traditionally reluctant to go to war, its leaders seeking to insure that
war is truly necessary and that our civilian leaders exploit all other avenues before taking that final step.

The Vietnam War is behind us but not entirely forgotten. Like our
Civil War, Vietnam holds a fascination for many Americans, and I suspect that this will grow rather than diminish as research continues and
new works are published about the war. For the older military professionals who served during the Vietnam War and for the still older career
military men who were perplexed by it, my advice is to look at Vietnam
in a broader historical perspective. For the young military professional
who did not serve in Vietnam, my advice is to learn all you can about
the war and try to understand it. Finally for those military men now serving at the top military positions, as well as those who will rise to those
positions later, my advice is to do all you can to improve the civilian-
military interface in the highest councils of our government. This is the

best way I know to better the chances that our civilian leaders truly understand the risks, costs, and probable outcomes of military actions before they take the nation to war.

The United States cannot afford to put itself again at such enormous strategic disadvantage as we found ourselves in in Vietnam. How deep Vietnam has stamped its imprint on American history has yet to be determined. In any event, I am optimistic enough to believe that we Americans can and will learn and profit from our experience.

Notes

Prologue

1. *U.S. Policy in Southeast Asia*, Reports of Student Committees #13-17 (Carlisle Barracks, Pa: U.S. Army War College, 1951).

2. George W. Allen, "The Indochina Wars, 1950-1975" (unpublished manuscript, March 1983), pp. 18-21. (A lifelong student of Indochina, George Allen, now retired, was a veteran intelligence officer with long service successively with the U.S. Army, the Defense Intelligence Agency, and the Central Intelligence Agency.)

3. James Lawton Collins, Jr., *Development and Training of the South Vietnamese Army, 1950-1972*, Vietnamese Studies (Washington, D.C.: U.S. Department of the Army, 1975), pp. 2-4.

4. Allen, "Indochina Wars," pp. 87-99; J. Lawton Collins, *Lightning Joe: An Autobiography* (Baton Rouge, La: Louisiana State Univ. Press, 1979), pp. 394-98.

5. Allen, "Indochina Wars," pp. 29-33, 101-12, 122-26, 149-52; Collins, *Development and Training*, pp. 8-9, 152.

6. Collins, *Development and Training*, pp. 8-16, 127, 151.

7. Allen, "Indochina Wars," pp. 103-6, 145-46.

8. William E. Colby, *Honorable Men: My Life in the CIA* (New York: Simon and Schuster, 1978), pp. 191-92.

9. Other Army officers who served in MAAG, Vietnam, during the late 1950s and were virtually ignored upon their return from Vietnam included Major General Samuel L. Meyers (senior training adviser), Brigadier General Donald D. Blackburn (special forces and ranger adviser), and Colonels James B. Lampert (logistics adviser) and Ernest P. Lasché (adviser to the Minister of Defense and Chairman of the Joint General Staff).

10. Maxwell D. Taylor, *Swords and Plowshares* (New York: W.W. Norton, 1972), pp. 222-26, 245-47.

11. W.W. Rostow, *The Diffusion of Power* (New York: Macmillan, 1972), pp. 264-65.

12. Taylor, *Swords and Plowshares*, pp. 227-51.

13. Colby, *Honorable Men*, pp. 193-200.

14. Taylor, *Swords and Plowshares*, pp. 288-95; Roger Hilsman, *To Move a Nation* (New York: Dell, 1964; revised 1967), pp. 455-93; Colby, *Honorable Men*, pp. 206-12.

15. Taylor, *Swords and Plowshares*, pp. 296-301; Hilsman, *To Move a Nation*, pp. 494-521.

16. Charles J. Timmes, "The Naive Years" (Washington, D.C.: *Army* magazine,

May 1977), pp. 36-40. (Major General Timmes, U.S. Army, was chief of the U.S. Military Assistance and Advisory Group in Vietnam from July 1962 to May 1964 when the MAAG was absorbed by the U.S. Military Assistance Command in Vietnam. See also Ronald H. Spector, *Advice and Support: The Early Years, 1941-1960* (Washington, D.C.: Center of Military History, U.S. Army, 1983), pp. 375-79.

1. 1963–1967: The JCS and Vietnam

1. New York: Harper and Brothers, 1959.
2. Hilsman, *To Move a Nation*, pp. 440-67.
3. Taylor, *Swords and Plowshares*, pp. 296-301; Hilsman, *To Move a Nation*, pp. 494-521.
4. Taylor, *Swords and Plowshares*, pp. 29-95.
5. Ibid., pp. 301-2.
6. Hilsman, *To Move a Nation*, pp. 522-23.
7. Ibid., pp. 524-37.
8. The complexity of control and coordinating arrangements for air operations in Southeast Asia, including the operations of B-52s under the separate authority of the commanding general, Strategic Air Command, are discussed in detail in *Airpower in Three Wars* (Washington, D.C.: HQ U.S. Air Force, 1978), by General William W. Momyer, U.S. Air Force-Retired.
9. John K. Galbraith, *A Life in Our Times* (Boston: Houghton Mifflin, 1981), pp. 196-99, 226-27, 231.
10. The debate about committing U.S. airpower was not confined, of course, to the JCS and the military. Senior U.S. civilian officials seriously questioned the wisdom of bombing North Vietnam and interdicting Hanoi's lines of communications through Laos, pointing out the adverse political (both domestic and international), psychological, and military implications involved. Some of the most articulate discussions on the subject can be found in Roger Hilsman's *To Move a Nation*, pp. 526-34.
11. Momyer, *Airpower in Three Wars*, pp. 77, 84-88.
12. Ibid., pp. 99-107.
13. William C. Westmoreland, *A Soldier Reports* (Garden City, N.Y.: Doubleday, 1976), pp. 104-5; Hilsman, *To Move a Nation*, pp. 529-33.
14. Taylor, *Swords and Plowshares*, pp. 238-44; Westmoreland, *A Soldier Reports*, p. 123.
15. Herbert Y. Schandler, *The Unmaking of a President: Lyndon Johnson and Vietnam* (Princeton: Princeton Univ. Press, 1977), p. 20.
16. Westmoreland, *A Soldier Reports*, p. 129.
17. Ibid., pp. 228, 234.
18. Schandler, *Unmaking of a President*, pp. 30-32.
19. *The Pentagon Papers* (New York: New York Times Co., 1971), pp. 409-12.
20. Schandler, *Unmaking of a President*, pp. 33-35.
21. Westmoreland, *A Soldier Reports*, pp. 145-53.
22. These statements are based on my examination of approximately 250 national intelligence documents, most of which were produced by the CIA, covering the 1965-75 period.
23. Schandler, *Unmaking of a President*, pp. 41-55; Westmoreland, *A Soldier Reports*, pp. 160, 193.
24. Taylor, *Swords and Plowshares*, pp. 363, 375, 389.
25. Westmoreland, *A Soldier Reports*, pp. 227-28, 230.

26. This ommission on the part of the JCS was first pointed out to me by General H.K. Johnson, Army chief of staff and a member of the JCS for four years (1964-68), but he too could offer no logical rationale for this apparent lapse.

2. 1967: Corps Command, Vietnam

1. In late April 1965 a revolution that had started within the Dominican military spread through most of Santo Domingo and threatened to engulf the whole country. President Johnson intervened early in the crisis with U.S. forces, initially to protect U.S. and other foreign nationals, and later to restore law and order. I was ordered to Santo Domingo on 30 April to take command of all U.S. forces in the Dominican Republic, my implicit mission being to prevent "a second Cuba" and to avoid another Vietnam-type situation. I was to work closely with our ambassador, the able and courageous W. Tapley Bennett. The Organization of America States also responded and established a multinational force which became known as the Inter-American Peace Force. The IAPF kept the peace in the country, while an OAS commission, chaired by Ellsworth Bunker, the U.S. ambassador to the OAS, negotiated a political settlement that installed an interim president in September 1965 to govern until elections were held in June 1966. The new president was inaugurated on 1 July and by 21 September 1966 all U.S. and other foreign troops had departed the Republic. For a detailed account of the Dominican affair, 28 April 1965-21 September 1966, see "Commander's Summary of the Report of Stability Operations, Dominican Republic," U.S. Forces Dominican Republic, APO NY 09478, in four parts, dated 31 August 1965, 16 January 1966, 1 October 1966, and 14 October 1966, on file at the U.S. Army War College, Carlisle Barracks, Pennsylvania.

2. Private discussion with Ambassador Bunker in June 1981, McLean, Virginia.

3. Westmoreland, *A Soldier Reports*, p. 214.

4. Private discussion with Ambassador Bunker, June 1981, McLean, Virginia.

5. Lawrence J. Korb, *The Joint Chiefs of Staff* (Bloomington: Indiana University Press, 1976), pp. 165-66; Schandler, *Unmaking of a President*, pp. 167-76, 256-65; Lyndon B. Johnson, *The Vantage Point* (New York: Holt, Rinehart, and Winston, 1971), pp. 394-401, 409, 416-18, 422; Westmoreland, *A Soldier Reports*, pp. 358-62.

6. General Cao Van Vien, Chairman, JGS, 1965-1975, stresses the lack of unity of command and the adverse consequences in South Vietnam, in his book *The Final Collapse* (Washington, D.C.: Center of Military History, U.S. Army, 1983), p. 162.

3. 1967–1968: Army HQ, Vietnam

1. Westmoreland, *A Soldier Reports*, pp. 233, 354, 357; Korb, *Joint Chiefs of Staff*, pp. 165-66; Schandler, *Unmaking of a President*, pp. 54-59.

2. Westmoreland, *A Soldier Reports*, p. 222.

3. Ibid., pp. 230-35.

4. In May 1970 during the Cambodian invasion, the capture of numerous important enemy documents roughly confirmed the validity of the generally higher enemy strength estimates held by the CIA in November 1967.

5. Johnson, *Vantage Point*, pp. 493-507.

6. Ibid., pp. 394-401; Schandler, *Unmaking of a President*, pp. 167-76.

7. Johnson, *Vantage Point*, pp. 416-18; Schandler, *Unmaking of a President*, pp. 156-65.

4. 1968–1969: The Transition Years

1. New York: Warner Books, 1981.

2. Martin Binkin and Mark J. Eitelberg, *Blacks in the Military* (Washington, D.C.: Brookings Institution, 1982) pp. 32-33.

3. Data source: Department of Defense, Desertion Rates, U.S. Army, World War II, Korea, and Vietnam, compiled in August 1978.

4. New York: Oxford Univ. Press, 1978.

5. New York: Norton, 1979.

6. P. 527.

5. 1969–1971: Vietnamization

1. Henry A. Kissinger, *The White House Years* (Boston: Little, Brown, 1979), pp. 241-43.

2. Ibid., pp. 484-87; Westmoreland, *A Soldier Reports*, p. 389.

3. Kissinger, *White House Years*, pp. 980-81.

4. Ibid., pp. 984-87.

5. For the most eloquent and detailed documentation of Kissinger's unique political-military role during the Vietnam War, see his monumental book (over 1,500 pages) *The White House Years*, covering the period from after the November 1968 elections through January 1973.

6. Kissinger, *White House Years*, pp. 988-89.

7. John J. Tolson, *Air Mobility, 1961-1971*, part of the Vietnamese Studies series (Washington, D.C.: Department of the Army, 1973), pp. 138-240; Dave R. Palmer, *Summons of the Trumpet* (San Rafael, Calif.: Presidio Press, 1978), pp. 238-43.

8. Tolson, *Air Mobility*, pp. 240-41.

9. Ibid., pp. 242-43.

10. Ibid., pp. 251-52.

6. 1972–1973: Cease-Fire Achieved

1. Westmoreland, *A Soldier Reports*, pp. 391-92.

2. Kissinger, *White House Years*, pp. 258-59.

3. Ibid., pp. 242, 278-82, 439, 1341-45.

4. Ibid., pp. 305, 685, 1087.

5. Ibid., pp. 1341-45.

6. Elmo R. Zumwalt, Jr., *On Watch* (New York: New York Times Company, 1976), pp. 384-89.

7. Kissinger, *White House Years*, pp. 1468-70.

8. Momyer, *Air Power in Three Wars*, pp. 30, 195, 217.

9. Kissinger, *White House Years*, pp. 1241-42.

10. See also Henry A. Kissinger, *Years of Upheaval* (Boston: Little, Brown, 1982), pp. 44-71, for a detailed discussion of Chinese objectives and strategy in Southeast Asia.

7. 1973–1975: The Final War Years

1. William E. Le Gro, *Vietnam from Cease-Fire to Capitulation* (Washington, D.C.: U.S. Army Center of Military History, 1981), pp. 2-3. Le Gro served in Vietnam in 1966-67 as the G-2 (intelligence officer) of the U.S. Army 1st Infantry Division, and from December 1972 to 29 April 1975 as a senior staff officer (colonel) in HQ MACV and its successor headquarters, the Defense Attache Office, Saigon. His principal sources are MACV official histories; documents preserved by the Intelligence Branch of DAO, Saigon; enemy (NVN) documents captured by ARVN and POW interrogations made by ARVN; Foreign Broadcast Information Service unclassified quotations from Hanoi press and radio; docu-

ments from DIA; Joint General Staff (SVN) documents; documents from ARVN Corps/ MR Headquarters; documents from the U.S. embassy, Saigon; reports from various U.S. consul general officers in Vietnam; articles by the North Vietnamese commanding general of the final offensive, General Van Tien Dung; and innumerable personal interviews with senior South Vietnamese commanders and staff officers.

2. Le Gro, *Vietnam from Cease-Fire*, pp. 5-15, 27-31; Kissinger, *Years of Upheaval*, pp. 16, 36-43, 332.

3. Le Gro, *Vietnam from Cease-Fire*, pp. 3-5, 33, 36-40; Kissinger, *Years of Upheaval*, pp. 16, 38-40, 302-03, 323-24; Alan Dawson, *55 Days: The Fall of Saigon* (Englewood Cliffs, N.J.: Prentice-Hall, 1977), p. 99.

4. Le Gro, *Vietnam from Cease-Fire*, pp. 96-131.

5. Ibid., pp. 80-87.

6. Ibid., p. 145; Kissinger, *Years of Upheaval*, pp. 302, 324-28.

7. Le Gro, *Vietnam from Cease-Fire*, pp. 132-37.

8. Ibid., pp. 148-54; Dawson, *55 Days*, pp. 37-38.

9. Le Gro, *Vietnam from Cease-Fire*, pp. 156-58; Dawson, *55 Days*, pp. 210-11.

10. Le Gro, *Vietnam from Cease-Fire*, pp. 159-60.

11. Ibid., pp. 160-61.

12. Ibid., pp. 165-68.

13. Dawson, *55 Days*, p. 176.

14. Le Gro, *Vietnam from Cease-Fire*, pp. 170-75.

15. Ibid., pp. 173-77; Vien, *Final Collapse*, pp. 150-53.

16. Frank W. Snepp III, *Decent Interval* (New York: Random House, 1977), pp. 195-96.

17. Ibid., p. 198.

8. American Operational Performance

1. Westmoreland, *A Soldier Reports*, pp. 342-45.

2. See Benjamin F. Schemmer, *The Raid* (New York: Harper and Row, 1976). It is the most comprehensive unclassified account of the Son Tay POW camp raid published to date.

3. The judgments in this book about the CIA's performance during the war reflect my personal opinion. They are largely based on a personal examination in the fall of 1979 of several hundred intelligence documents produced or contributed to by the CIA during the 1965-75 period. It should be noted that CIA-controlled operations in the region during the period are beyond the scope of this book.

4. Helm's role under president Nixon is well documented in Kissinger's book *The White House Years*. See, for example, pp. 36-38, 319-20, 491-97, 995-1001.

9. American Strategy

1. *Dictionary of Military and Associated Terms*, JCS Publication 1 (Washington, D.C.: JCS, 1979).

2. Taylor, *Swords and Plowshares*, pp. 348-408.

3. Schemmer, *The Raid*, pp. 253-54, 259-61, 267.

4. In anticipation of such a possibility, the United States in the early 1960s built a substantial modern complex of logistic bases in Thailand capable of supporting the operations of a large U.S. force in the northeast part of the country. American forces, of course, were never so committed.

5. For a detailed account of Kissinger's intensive activities during the 1968-72 period, see his *The White House Years*.

10. The Larger Lessons

1. For a detailed analysis of the principles of war in the context of the Vietnam War, see Harry G. Summers, Jr. (Colonel, U.S. Army), *On Strategy: The Vietnam War in Context* (Carlisle Barracks, Penn.: Strategic Studies Institute, U.S. Army War College, 1981). This thoughtful book provides an excellent analysis of the Vietnam War. At times its judgments about U.S. senior military leadership (specifically U.S. Army) are harsh and in my view not entirely fair, but on balance the book is well worth study, particularly by military professionals.

2. Johnson, *Vantage Point*, pp. 372-78.

3. See Russell F. Weigley, *History of the United States Army* (New York: Macmillan, 1967); William A. Ganoe, *History of the United States Army* (New York: Appleton-Century, 1936); Emory Upton, *The Military Policy of the United States* (Washington, D.C.: U.S. Government Printing Office, 1904); Walter Millis, *The Martial Spirit* (Boston: Houghton Mifflin, 1931); John McAuley Palmer, *America in Arms* (New Haven: Yale University Press, 1941); and Robert M. Utley, *The Contribution of the Frontier to American Military Tradition*, Proceedings of the Seventh Military History Symposium, U.S. Air Force Academy, 30 September-1 October 1976 (Washington, D.C.: Office Air Force History, 1978).

4. Russell F. Weigley, *Eisenhower's Lieutenants* (Bloomington: Indiana University Press, 1981), pp. 370-75.

5. T. R. Ferenbach, *This Kind of War: A Study in Unpreparedness* (New York: Macmillan, 1963), pp. 503-04, 514.

6. James G. Wadsworth, *Combat Support in Korea* (Washington, D.C.: Combat Forces Press, 1955), p. 190.

7. Arthur S. Collins, Jr., *Common Sense Training* (San Rafael, Calif.: Presidio Press, 1978), pp. 214-17.

8. Weigley, *Eisenhower's Lieutenants*, pp. 727-30.

Glossary of Acronyms

ABM: antiballistic missile

AID: Agency for International Development (U.S.)

ARVN [pronounced "arvin"]: Army of the Republic of Vietnam [South Vietnamese Army]

CG: commanding general

CIA: Central Intelligency Agency (U.S.)

CIDG: Civilian Irregular Defense Group [South Vietnamese nationals recruited in remote areas to operate with U.S. Army Special Forces]

CINCFE: commander-in-chief, Far Eastern Command [a former U.S. unified commander whose area of responsibility was Northeast Asia, including Japan and Korea; disestablished after the Korean War]

CINCPAC: commander-in-chief, Pacific [U.S. unified commander of all American forces in the Pacific, including Southeast Asia]

CJCS: chairman, Joint Chiefs of Staff (U.S.)

COMUSMACV: commander, U.S. Military Assistance Command, Vietnam

CORDS: Civil Operations and Revolutionary Development Support [a U.S. organization created within the U.S. Military Assistance Command, Vietnam, in 1967 to direct the American pacification effort]

COSVN [pronounced "cosvin"]: Central Office for South Vietnam [the senior headquarters used by the North Vietnamese communist party for political and military control of its organization in South Vietnam]

CTZ: corps tactical zone in South Vietnam [numbered I to IV from north to south (see Map 2)]

DAO: Defense Attache Office (U.S.) [established in Saigon after the January 1973 cease-fire to replace MACV]

DCSOPS: deputy chief of staff for operations (U.S.) [the service operations staff officer of a service at the Washington level (a statutory position)]

DIA: Defense Intelligence Agency

DMZ: demilitarized zone [created by the Geneva Accords of 1954 along the 17th parallel dividing South and North Vietnam]

HQ: headquarters

JCS: Joint Chiefs of Staff (U.S.)

JGS: Joint General Staff of the Armed Forces of the Republic of Vietnam [South Vietnam]

KMAG: Military Advisory Group, Korea (U.S.)

MAAG-V: Military Assistance and Advisory Group, Vietnam (U.S.)

MACV: Military Assistance Command, Vietnam (U.S.)

MAF: Marine Amphibious Force

MR: military region in South Vietnam [numbered I to IV from north to south (see Map 2)]

NSC: National Security Council

NVA: North Vietnamese Army

NVN: North Vietnam [Democratic Republic of Vietnam]

PF: popular forces [local South Vietnamese militia]

REDCOM: U.S. Readiness Command [a unified command with operational control of the tactical U.S. Army and U.S. Air Force units in the United States]

RF: regional forces [South Vietnamese troops under the command of the province chief]

ROK [pronounced "rock"]: Republic of Korea [South Korea]

RVN: Republic of Vietnam [South Vietnam]

SAC: Strategic Air Command (U.S.)

SAM: surface-to-air missile

SVN: South Vietnam [Republic of Vietnam]

USAF: U.S. Air Force

USARV: U.S. Army, Vietnam

USSAG: U.S. Support Activities Group [headquarters established in Thailand after the January 1973 cease-fire to control any U.S. air or naval actions in Southeast Asia; the commander was double-hatted as CG, 7th Air Force]

VC: Viet Cong [Vietnamese communists]

Selected Bibliography

This bibliography does not include all the books, articles, documents, and other material that I have read on the Vietnam War, nor is the list intended to be exhaustive. It is rather a selection of unclassified written material that I found to be especially useful or thought-provoking. Generally excluded from the list is the steady stream of worthwhile articles appearing in periodicals of various persuasions devoted to international affairs and national security matters. I have also had the benefit of my own notes and papers, and have discussed many different aspects with numerous responsible civilian and military personalities of the time.

Allen, George W. "The Indochina Wars, 1950–1975." 1983. Unpublished.

Baestrup, Peter. *Big Story.* Boulder, Colorado: Westview Press, 1977.

Blufarb, Douglas. *The Counter-Insurgency Era.* New York: Free Press, 1977.

Brandon, Henry. *Anatomy of Error.* Boston: Gambit, 1969.

Bryan, C.D. *Friendly Fire.* New York: G. P. Putnam's Sons, 1976.

Bundy, McGeorge. "Reflections from Southeast Asia." [Three lectures given at the Council of Foreign Relations, New York, in the spring of 1971, concerning the 1965–71 period of American engagement in Vietnam.] Unpublished.

Caputo, Philip. *A Rumor of War.* Toronto: Holt, Rinehart and Winston, 1977.

Colby, William E. *Honorable Men.* New York: Simon and Schuster: 1978.

Collins, Arthur S., Jr. *Common Sense Training.* San Rafael, Calif.: Presidio Press, 1978.

Collins, J. Lawton. *Lightning Joe: An Autobiography.* Baton Rouge: Louisiana State University Press, 1979.

Collins, James L., Jr. *Development and Training of the South Vietnamese Army, 1950–1972.* Vietnam Studies. Washington, D.C.: U.S. Department of the Army, 1975.

Collins, John M. *Grand Strategy.* Annapolis: U.S. Naval Institute Press, 1973.

Cooper, Chester L. *The Lost Crusade.* New York: Dodd, Mead, 1970.

Dawson, Alan. *55 Days: The Fall of Saigon.* Englewood Cliffs, New Jersey: Prentice-Hall, 1977.

Don, Tran Van. *Our Endless War.* San Rafael, Calif.: Presidio Press, 1978.

Draper, Theodore. *Abuse of Power*. New York: Viking Press, 1967.

Dung, Van Tien. *Our Great Spring Victory: An Account of the Liberation of South Vietnam*. New York: Monthly Review Press, 1977.

Eckhardt, George S. *Command and Control, 1950–1969*. Vietnam Studies. Washington, D.C.: U.S. Department of the Army, 1974.

Fall, Bernard. *Street without Joy*. Harrisburg, Penn.: Stackpole Books, 1963.

———. *Hell Is a Very Small Place*. Philadelphia: J.B. Lippincott, 1966.

The Fall of South Vietnam: Statements by Vietnamese Military and Civilian Leaders. Santa Monica, Calif.: Rand Corporation, 1978.

Ferenbach, T.R. *This Kind of War: A Study in Unpreparedness*. New York: Macmillan, 1963.

Fitzgerald, Frances. *Fire in the Lake*. Boston: Little, Brown, 1972.

Fleming, Thomas. *The Officers' Wives*. New York: Warner Books, 1981.

Galbraith, John K. *A Life in Our Times*. Boston: Houghton Mifflin, 1981.

Gelb, Leslie, with Richard Betts. *The Irony of Vietnam*. Washington, D.C.: Brookings Institution, 1979.

Giap, Vo Nguyen. *People's War, People's Army*. New York: Praeger, 1962.

Goodman, Allan E. *The Lost Peace*. Stanford, Calif.: Hoover Institute for War, Revolution, and Peace, 1978.

Halberstam, David. *One Very Hot Day*. Boston: Houghton Mifflin, 1967.

———. *The Best and the Brightest*. New York: Random House, 1969.

———. "Letter to My Daughter." *Parade*, 2 May 1982.

Hannah, Norman B. "Vietnam Now We Know." In *All Quiet on the Eastern Front*, ed. Anthony T. Bouscaren. New York: Devin-Adair, 1977.

Heiser, Joseph M., Jr. *Logistic Support*. Vietnam Studies. Washington, D.C.: U.S. Department of the Army, 1974.

Herr, Michael. *Dispatches*. New York: Avon Books/Alfred A. Knopf, 1978.

Hersh, Seymour. *My Lai 4*. New York: Random House, 1970.

Hilsman, Roger. *To Move a Nation*. New York: Dell, 1963; revised in 1967.

Hoopes, Townsend. *The Limits of Intervention*. New York: David McKay, 1969.

Johnson, Lyndon B. *The Vantage Point*. New York: Holt, Rinehart and Winston, 1971.

Just Ward. *Military Men*. New York: Alfred A. Knopf, 1970.

Kattenburg, Paul M. *The Vietnam Trauma, 1945–75*. London: Transition Books, 1980.

Kinnard, Douglas. *The War Managers*. Hanover, N.H.: University Press of New England, 1977.

———. *The Secretary of Defense*. Lexington: University Press of Kentucky, 1980.

Kissinger, Henry A. *The White House Years*. Boston: Little, Brown, 1979.

———. *Years of Upheaval*. Boston: Little, Brown, 1982.

Komer, Robert W. *Bureaucracy Does Its Thing: Institutional Constraints on U.S.-GVN Performance in Vietnam*. Santa Monica, Calif.: Rand Corporation, 1972.

Korb, Lawrence J. *The Joint Chiefs of Staff*. Bloomington: Indiana University Press, 1976.

Lake, Anthony, ed. *The Legacy of Vietnam*. New York: New York University Press, 1976.

Lansdale, Edward G. *In the Midst of Wars: An American's Mission to Southeast Asia.* New York: Harper and Row, 1972.

Le Gro, William E. *Vietnam from Ceasefire to Capitulation.* Washington, D.C.: U.S. Army Center of Military History, 1981.

Lewy, Guenter. *America in Vietnam.* New York: Oxford University Press, 1978.

Manchester, William. *American Caesar: Douglas MacArthur, 1880–1964.* Boston: Little, Brown, 1978.

Marshall, S.L.A. *The Fields of Bamboo.* New York: Dial Press, 1971.

Momyer, William W. *Airpower in Three Wars.* Washington, D.C.: HQ U.S. Air Force, 1978.

Oberdorfer, Don. *Tet!* New York: Doubleday, 1971.

Ott, David E. *Field Artillery, 1954–1973.* Vietnam Studies. Washington, D.C.: U.S. Department of the Army, 1975.

Palmer, D.R. *Summons of the Trumpet.* San Rafael, Calif.: Presidio Press, 1978.

Peers, W.R. *The My Lai Inquiry.* New York: W. W. Norton, 1979.

The Pentagon Papers. Senator Gravel Edition. Boston: Beacon Press, 1971.

The Pentagon Papers. New York: New York Times Company, 1971.

Pike, Douglas. *The Viet Cong.* Cambridge: Massachusetts Institute of Technology Press, 1966.

———. *The Viet Cong Strategy of Terror.* Saigon: U.S. Mission, 1970.

———. *History of the Vietnamese Communist Party.* Stanford, Calif.: Hoover Institute for War, Revolution, and Peace, 1978.

Podhoretz, Norman. *Why We Were in Vietnam.* New York: Simon and Schuster, 1982.

Race, Jeoffrey. *War Comes to Long An.* Berkeley: University of California Press, 1971.

Ridgway, Matthew B. *The Korean War.* Garden City, New York: Doubleday, 1967.

Rodman, Peter W. "Sideswipe: Kissinger, Shawcross and the Responsibility for Cambodia." *American Spectator* 14, no. 3, March 1981.

Rostow, W.W. *The Diffusion of Power, 1957–72.* New York: Macmillan, 1972.

Rowe, James N. *Five Years to Freedom.* Boston: Little, Brown, 1971.

Schandler, Herbert Y. *The Unmaking of a President: Lyndon Johnson and Vietnam.* Princeton: Princeton University Press, 1977.

Schell, Jonathan. *The Military Half.* New York: Alfred A. Knopf, 1967.

———. *The Village of Ben Suc.* New York: Alfred A. Knopf, 1967.

Schemmer, Benjamin F. *The Raid.* New York: Harper and Row, 1976.

Schlesinger, Arthur M., Jr. *The Imperial Presidency.* Boston: Houghton Mifflin, 1973.

Sharp, U.S.G., and Westmoreland, William C. *Report on the War in Vietnam.* Washington, D.C.: U.S. Government Printing Office, 1969.

Shawcross, William. *Sideshow: Kissinger, Nixon and the Destruction of Cambodia.* New York: Simon and Schuster, 1979.

Snepp, Frank W., III. *Decent Interval.* New York: Random House, 1977.

Spector, Ronald H. *Advice and Support: The Early Years, 1941–1960.* U.S. Army in Vietnam Series. Washington, D.C.: Center of Military History, U.S. Army, 1983.

Summers, Harry G., Jr. *On Strategy: The Vietnam War in Context.* Carlisle Barracks, Penn.: Strategic Studies Institute, U.S. Army War College, 1981.

Taylor, Maxwell D. *The Uncertain Trumpet.* New York: Harper and Brothers, 1959.

———. *Swords and Plowshares.* New York: W.W. Norton, 1972.

Thompson, W. Scott and Frizzell, Donaldson D., eds. *The Lessons of Vietnam.* New York: Crane, Russak, 1977.

Timmes, Charles J. "Military Operations after the Cease Fire Agreement, Part II (1974–75)." Military Review, September 1976.

Tolson, John J. *Air Mobility, 1961–1971.* Vietnam Studies. Washington, D.C.: U.S. Department of the Army, 1973.

U.S. Policy toward Southeast Asia. Reports of Student Committees #13–17. Carlisle Barracks, Penn.: U.S. Army War College, 1951.

Vien, Cao Van. *Reflections on the Vietnam War.* Washington, D.C.: U.S. Army Center of Military History, 1980.

———. *The Final Collapse.* Indochina Monographs. Washington, D.C.: Center of Military History, U.S. Army, 1983.

Vietnam Settlement: Why 1973, Not 1969? Rational Debate Series. Washington, D.C.: American Enterprise Institute for Public Policy Research, 1973.

Wadsworth, James G. *Combat Support in Korea.* Washington, D.C.: Combat Forces Press, 1955.

Walt, Lewis, W. *Strange War, Strange Strategy.* New York: Funk and Wagnalls, 1970.

Webb, James. *Fields of Fire.* Englewood Cliffs, New Jersey: Prentice-Hall, 1975.

Weigley, Russell F. *History of the U.S. Army.* New York: Macmillan, 1967.

———. *The American Way of War.* New York: Macmillan, 1973.

———. *Eisenhower's Lieutenants.* Bloomington: Indiana University Press, 1981.

Westmoreland, William C. *A Soldier Reports.* Garden City, New York: Doubleday, 1976.

White, Theodore H. *The Making of the President, 1968.* New York: Simon and Schuster, 1968.

Zumwalt, Elmo R., Jr. *On Watch.* New York: New York Times Book Company, 1976.

Index